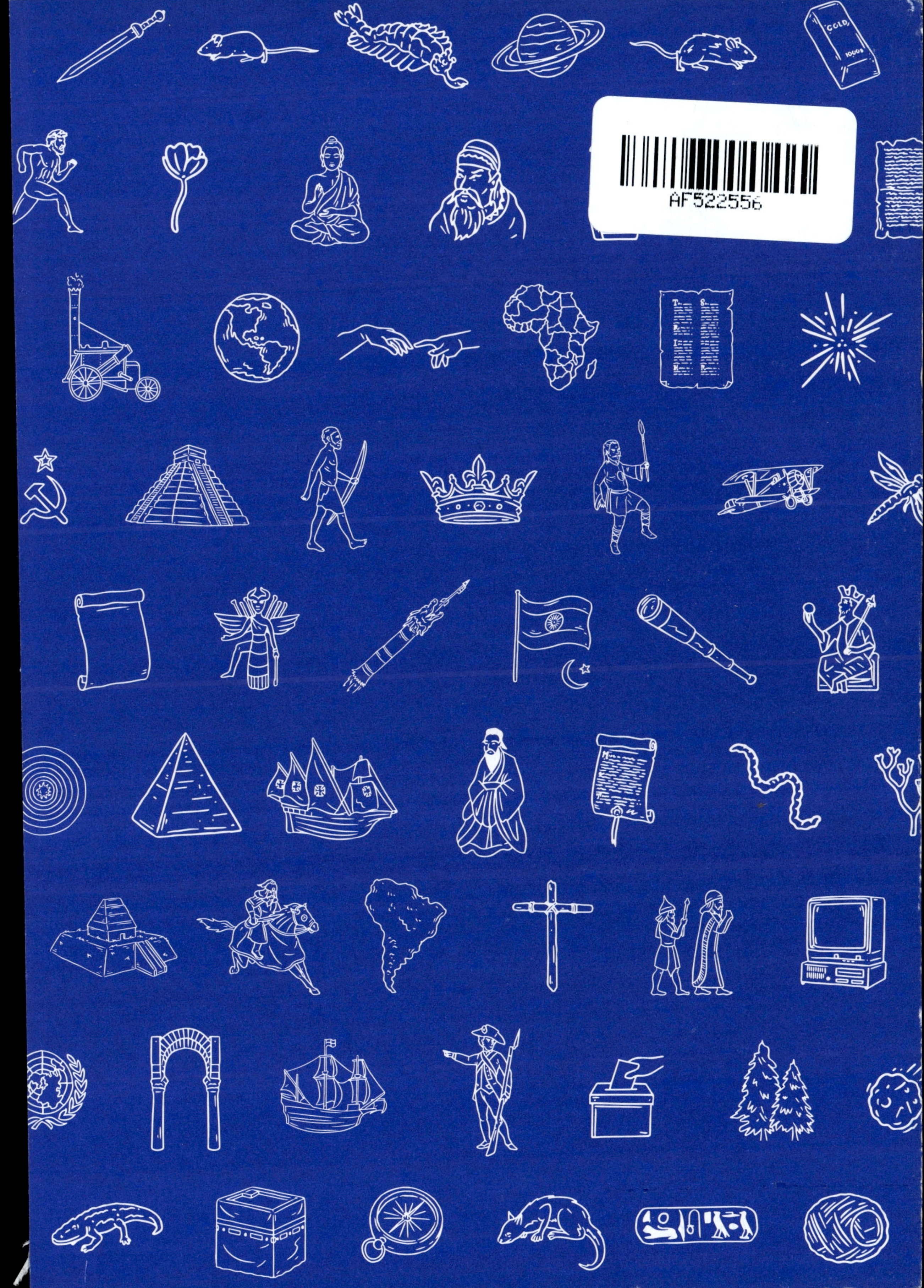
GOLD
1000g

REVISED & EXPANDED
ABSOLUTELY
EVERYTHING!

What on Earth! is an imprint of What on Earth Publishing
The Black Barn, Wickhurst Farm, Leigh, Tonbridge, Kent, UK, TN11 8PS
30 Ridge Road Unit B, Greenbelt, Maryland, 20770, United States

First published in the United States in 2018
This edition published in the United States in 2023

Written by Christopher Lloyd
Illustrated by Andy Forshaw
Cover by Andy Smith

Special thanks to Satu Fox for fact-checking and research

Staff for this book: Nancy Feresten, Publisher; Katy Lennon, Senior Editor; Andy Forshaw, Art Director; Nell Wood, Senior Designer; Lauren Fulbright, Production Manager.

Library of Congress Cataloging-in-Publication Data available upon request

ISBN: 978-93-5954-612-4

Published and Distributed in India by
Scholastic India Pvt. Ltd.

This Reprint Edition: September, 2024

Printed in India : VK Global Digital Private Limited

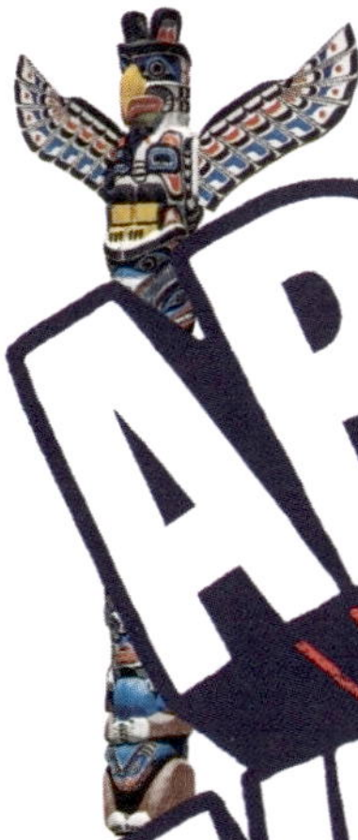

REVISED & EXPANDED

ABSOLUTELY EVERYTHING!

A HISTORY OF EARTH, DINOSAURS, RULERS, ROBOTS and OTHER THINGS too NUMEROUS to MENTION

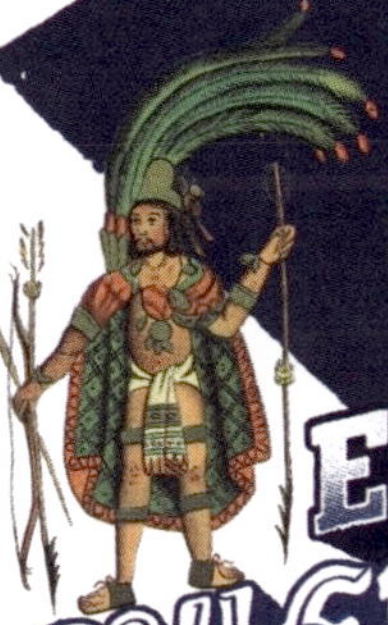

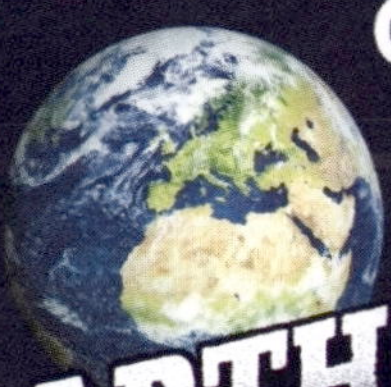

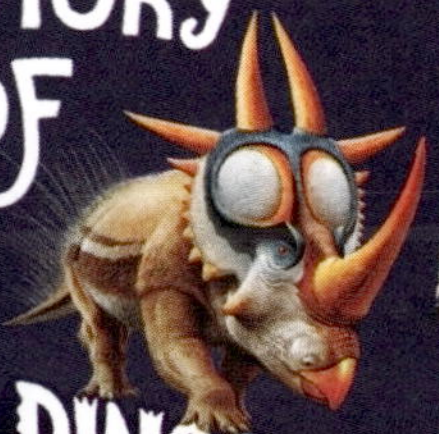

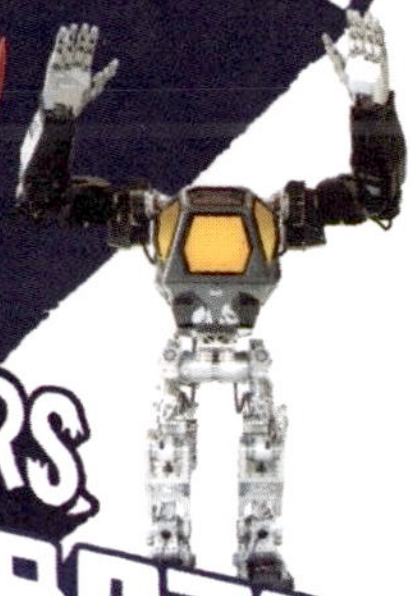

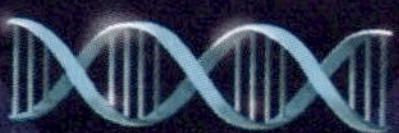

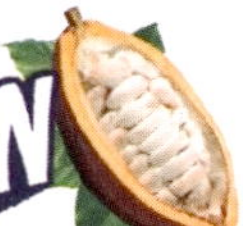

CHRISTOPHER LLOYD

Contents

Foreword

Have you ever been on a camping trip? Camping is one of the best things my family and I have ever done—we had a huge amount of fun!

If you have ever camped, you'll know there are quite a few jobs that need to be done when you visit a campsite. As well as a few other chores, it was always my job to wash the dirty dishes.

It was OK. Actually, I started to enjoy doing the dishes. As soon as I checked in at the dishwashing station, I could ask people what the place was like, where we should visit, or, just as importantly, where we should not visit. So whenever I washed dishes, my mind was always bursting with questions.

And then one day, just after we had arrived at a new campground, I went to wash the dishes and, although there were loads of cars, tents, and RVs, there was absolutely no one else there doing dishes. It was just me. All on my own.

I was gutted.

"Honestly," I thought. "How on earth am I supposed to do my research when there is no one here to talk to?"

And then I heard a tweeting noise coming from somewhere behind me. It was a beautiful day and, as with all the best campgrounds, the dishwashing station was out in the open.

About 150 feet (about 50 m) behind me, I saw a bird high up in a tree. And then a thought struck me that I will never forget.

"If only I could speak Bird!"

That creature, with its amazing wings, must have such a wonderful view of all that is worth seeing in the area. The only thing stopping me from finding out everything I want to know is a communication barrier. How frustrating to think that, despite us sharing the same air, the same sunshine, and time of day, that bird and I could never talk to each other.

Another thought then wriggled its way into my brain. Not only can I not speak Bird, but I have no idea what kind of bird this is, twittering high up in that untouchable world of leafy green.

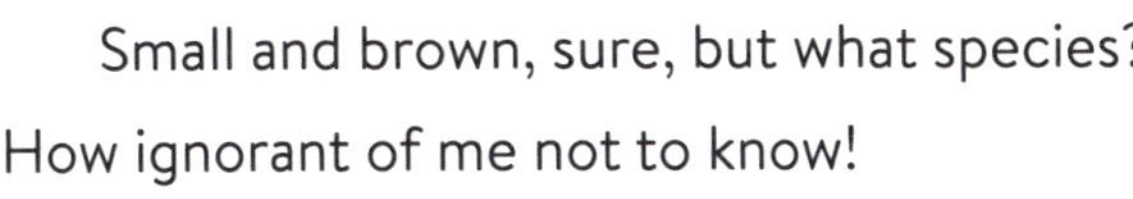

Small and brown, sure, but what species? How ignorant of me not to know!

Things got worse.

I looked at the tree. I had no idea what kind of tree it was.

I looked down at the ground.

I realized I didn't even have a clue how old Earth was.

I was shocked and ashamed!

There I stood, a newspaper writer with a college degree in History, yet I didn't seem to know the answers to questions about the everyday things I was looking at! How much more information was missing from my mind? How could I find out what other things I didn't know?

Now my head was spinning. I needed a book, something simple enough to understand but sweeping enough to connect the dots of the past. My brain felt like it was a pane of shattered glass. I knew lots of bits of information, but if I were to take a step back, there was no big picture to make sense of it all.

After the camping trip, I searched many bookstores trying to find that simple guide to the history of everything.

The bookstore managers I quizzed said they had all the information, but it was spread out among many different books.

"But I want it all in just one book that connects it together."

"Sorry, sir, I can't help you there."

So that was it. I decided then and there to write this book. It was first published in 2018, and lots of kids loved it.

But there have been so many changes in our world since then. New things have happened, of course. But also experts (historians, archaeologists, paleontologists, and others) have discovered new things about the past. That means, five years after my book was published, there is so much more to share.

Absolutely Everything! A History of Earth, Dinosaurs, Rulers, Robots, and Other Things Too Numerous to Mention, The Revised and Expanded Edition, will take you on an epic journey from the beginning of the universe, about 13.8 billion years ago, all the way to the modern world we live in today. It's got 64 more pages than the 2018 edition and loads more photos and new information. Plus, I reorganized it so it tells the story in a way that I hope will help you see how vast the world is and how important all cultures and peoples are to history. I've been very keen to ensure that people often overlooked in history are given a voice, because their stories are just as important and inspiring as those frequently written about.

I hope the book will answer all kinds of questions you have.

Some things you will already know, and other things you won't. That's how it was for me when I did all the research and writing.

How old is the universe? What happened to the dinosaurs? When did humans first discover how to make fire? How does climate change affect us all?

Of course, this book doesn't really include absolutely everything everyone knows. That would be impossible. Instead, it is a gateway to all the knowledge in the world. For every question it answers, it sparks more questions, which I hope will lead you into a lifelong love of questioning and finding answers.

So, if you're the kind of person who loves to ask questions as much as you like to find answers, this story is the one for you. Hold on tight because there is one other fascinating thing I found out along the way—the real world is far more amazing than anything you can make up!

Christopher Lloyd

Oh, and by the way, since I came back from that camping trip, I always wash the dishes at home, too, because, well, I have learned that you never really know what's going to happen next.

This spectacular image taken by the James Webb Space Telescope shows a part of the Carina Nebula, one of the places new stars are born.

1

NOTHING *to* SOMETHING

13.8 billion – 540 million years ago

The beginning of the universe, life, and everything

13.8 BILLION YEARS AGO
The Big Bang.

13.6 BILLION YEARS AGO
The Milky Way forms.

4.6 BILLION YEARS AGO
The solar system forms.

4.5 BILLION YEARS AGO
Earth and Theia collide, forming the Moon.

3.8 BILLION YEARS AGO
Early microscopic life appears in the seas.

3.6 BILLION YEARS AGO
Plate tectonics begin shuffling continents around the planet.

2.9 BILLION YEARS AGO
Cyanobacteria make oxygen, which changes Earth's atmosphere.

540 MILLION YEARS AGO
The Cambrian Explosion.

Take a good look around. Imagine putting everything you can see inside a super-powerful crushing machine. Plants, animals, buildings, your entire house, your hometown, even the country where you live. Put the rest of the world in there, too. Add the other planets in our solar system, and the Sun.

Now put in our galaxy, the Milky Way, which includes about 300 billion other suns. Finally, add in all the other galaxies in the universe. Turn on the machine and see all this stuff squeezed together to the size of a tennis ball. See it crushed even smaller than the dot on top of this letter i, until you can't see it at all. Imagine all those stars, moons, and planets in a speck of nothing.

That's how experts think the universe began—as a dot too small to see. This dot was so hot and under such pressure from all the energy trapped inside, that something big was bound to happen. About 13.8 billion years ago, it did. It burst.

You've probably heard of the Big Bang—the theory that tries to explain the beginning of the universe. But hang on a minute—the beginning? That's what's so hard to

An artist's impression of the whole history of the universe, from the Big Bang on the far left to the present on the right. Over time, the universe has expanded and the stuff it is made of (called matter) has clumped together to form stars, planets, and other objects in space. The blue arrows show that the universe is expanding. The brown arrows represent gravity, which holds the universe together but is not strong enough to stop it from getting bigger and bigger.

understand. If the universe had a beginning, what happened before the beginning? No one really knows. As you'll see, there are plenty of mysteries that even modern science hasn't solved yet.

An unimaginably big blast of energy was released when the Big Bang happened. Next came the basic forces of the universe. Gravity is one of those forces. It is what makes all the stuff in the universe pull together. Next came countless too-tiny-to-see subatomic particles. Think of them as miniature toy bricks ready to build a whole wide universe. It's amazing to think that everything in the world is made out of billions of these subatomic particles created by the Big Bang. And that includes the furniture in your home and the hair on your head.

> "DURING THIS TIME [THE DARK AGES], THE UNIVERSE QUIETLY WAITED FOR CLOUDS OF HYDROGEN TO OBEY THE INFLUENCE OF GRAVITY AND COLLAPSE INTO THE VERY FIRST STARS AND GALAXIES."
>
> Aaron Parsons, astrophysicist

About 380,000 years after the Big Bang, the universe had cooled down enough that the subatomic particles stuck together to make larger (but still too-tiny-to-see) structures that we call atoms. First, there were only two kinds of atoms—mostly hydrogen and a bit of helium—which were gathered into giant clouds of very hot dust. Then, after a long pause known as the Dark Ages, the hydrogen atoms crushed together and lit up as the first stars. That's what stars are. They are fiery balls full of atoms and energy left over from the Big Bang.

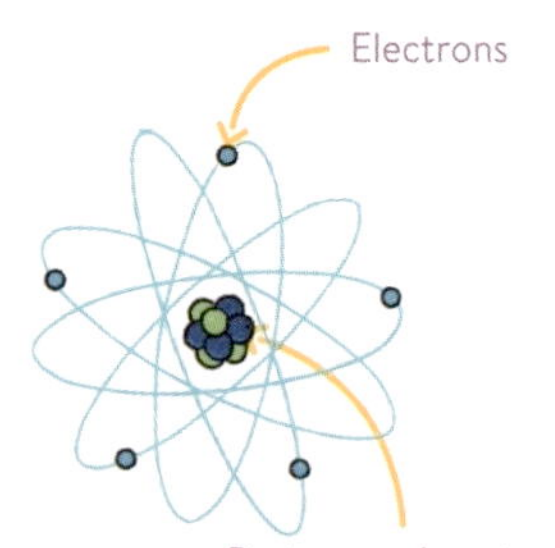

An atom is made up of subatomic particles called electrons, protons, and neutrons. The protons and neutrons make up the center (or nucleus) of the atom, and the electrons zip around it.

Stars gathered together into galaxies of many shapes and sizes. Stars were born and stars died. More stars were born. More stars died. Then, about 4.6 billion years ago, about two-thirds of the way through the history of the universe, the leftover gas and dust cloud from an old burned-out star crushed together and lit up to form a new star. We care about this one the most. It's the one closest to our home: the Sun. And our planet, along with several others, was formed at about the same time as the Sun, from a mixture of leftover dust and rock. The word "solar" means sun, so we call the combination of our Sun and everything around it the solar system.

Our solar system is part of a great assembly of stars called the Milky Way galaxy. We are in one of the Milky Way's arms, spinning around the center of the galaxy at about 500,000 miles per hour (800,000 kph). You can't feel how fast you're going because our whole solar system is traveling with us at the same speed.

The young Earth was nothing like Earth today. You couldn't have survived there for a minute. A thick, melty crust of boiling hot, sticky lava oozed across its surface, and there was no solid ground. The early Earth spun so fast on its axis that each day was only about four hours long. Plus a rain of deadly particles like invisible razor-sharp daggers

Our sun, like all the other stars in the universe, is a ball of extremely hot gases held tightly together by gravity. It makes and gives off enormous amounts of energy, which warms and lights our world but can also be dangerous.

poured out of the Sun and onto Earth.

What happened next was a total fluke. Experts believe that two young planets were on the same orbit around the Sun but moving at different speeds. One was Earth. The other was a smaller planet known as Theia. You can guess what happened next. About 4.5 billion years ago, some 100 million years after Earth was formed, these two newborn planets smashed into each other.

Just think of the force of two planets crashing together. Theia's outer layers instantly broke up into billions of tiny particles. They covered Earth with a thick blanket of hot dust and rock. Volcanoes erupted, creating a vast magma ocean. Countless tons of gas that had been trapped inside Earth's core blew out into the sky, making our planet's early atmosphere.

Earth and Theia colliding

Actually, it's just as well for life on Earth that this great collision happened. The Sun's storm of deadly particles has never stopped. Even today, about 22 billion tons (20 billion tonnes) of the stuff spews out of the Sun each day. It's known as the solar wind. It can even pierce the toughest space suits and hardest helmets worn by astronauts.

But the solar wind doesn't hurt us on Earth. When Theia and Earth collided, the huge shock wave fused most of the two planets' cores into a hot metallic ball in the middle of Earth. Ever since, this core has produced a magnetic field that keeps the lethal solar wind away from our planet's surface. It also keeps the world from losing its precious supplies of water, which otherwise would blow into space. No liquid, no life. It's as simple as that.

Today there is no visible trace on Earth's surface of this dramatic collision, but there is evidence that we can see in the night sky. The force of the impact made lots of material vaporize into space as dust. That dust wrapped itself around Earth in a cloud, which eventually pulled together thanks to gravity.

Deep inside Earth, next to its core, are two continent-sized blobs of rock (red on the diagram below) that are different from the stuff around them. Some scientists think they are leftover parts of Theia.

Can you guess what this enormous cloud of dust turned into? Of course! It became our beautiful luminous companion—the Moon. The Moon's metallic core is too small for it to have a magnetic shield, so there's no liquid there. It also has no atmosphere, which means no sound can be heard on the Moon and the sky is always black and speckled with stars.

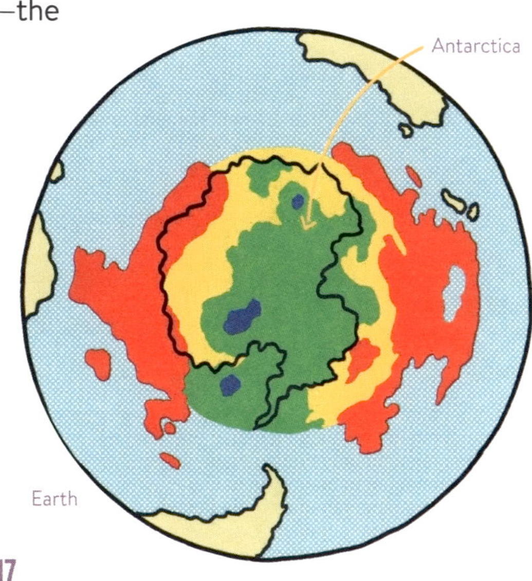

Scientists are still unsure about lots of things to do with the early history of our planet Earth. That's because Earth has changed so much that there's not a lot left from that early time for us to study. But they can look at how the planet works today and come up with some good guesses.

Of all the planets in our solar system, Earth is the only one with a large amount of liquid water (as opposed to ice or water vapor). Why does our world contain so much water? Where did it all come from? Without water, life as we know it could not have developed, so these questions are important.

Scientists who study asteroids have found that they have lots of ice on them. So one theory is that about half of the world's water may have arrived on a giant storm of asteroids about 20 million years after Earth formed.

Just imagine thousands of giant objects, some more than 100 miles (160 km) wide, smashing into early Earth. As they ripped through the atmosphere, their ice melted, producing vast amounts of water. All that water still exists. It's mostly in our global ocean. That's something to think about next time you take a bath. More than half the water in your tub possibly came from outer space.

These structures in Shark Bay, Australia, are stromatolites. They are made up of cyanobacteria, the earliest form of life to give off oxygen. Recent fossil finds show stromatolites have been growing in this area for at least 3.5 billion years.

But what about the other half of the water? That story isn't quite as violent. Remember the solar wind (that scary stuff our magnetic field protects us from)? Well, it is mostly made up of the element hydrogen. Space dust is rich in oxygen. When fast-moving hydrogen meets oxygen, they can combine, becoming water. So one way water could have come to Earth is as wet dust raining onto the planet's surface when the solar system was young.

How and where did life begin? We don't know for sure. Some scientists think that it started near underwater volcanoes in the deep sea. Others think its building blocks arrived on meteorites from outer space. However it happened, back at the beginning of life on Earth, each of these life forms was just one teeny-tiny bundle of material called a cell that could eat, grow, and—most importantly—split to become two teeny-tiny living things. That's one thing that makes life special: the ability to reproduce.

As time passed, some single-celled life forms called cyanobacteria found a way to survive near the ocean's surface. They grouped together in shallow waters to make rocky formations called stromatolites. They also used photosynthesis. This is the

Cyanobacteria enlarged

same process plants use today, to turn sunshine, nutrients, and water into the food they need to survive. And like all living things, cyanobacteria gave off waste. But the waste product from photosynthesis—oxygen—is very special. Cyanobacteria filled the air and the seas with this precious gas, completely changing the story of life on Earth. The name scientists give to how living things develop and change in response to their environments is evolution, and we're about to see a lot of it.

All this world-changing took a long time. Let's leap forward to about 2.3 billion years ago. A new type of life form called a eukaryote is now emerging. Eukaryotes take in oxygen to use as an ingredient to make energy. This marks another big change in the story of life on Earth. All plants, fungi, and animals are eukaryotes. Including us!

Usually, eukaryotic cells have a nucleus containing genetic information called DNA. They also contain organelles responsible for different functions such as producing energy (mitochondria), producing proteins (ribosomes and endoplasmic reticulum) and transporting proteins (Golgi apparatus).

Imagine Earth's history on a 24-hour clock. Earth formed right at midnight. The first signs of life emerged at about 3:00 in the morning. But already we have traveled to just past 1:00 in the afternoon. Amazingly, all the life on Earth that existed until this point lived in the seas and was too small to see. That leaves only 11 hours (less than half the day) for all the rest of life as we know it to emerge.

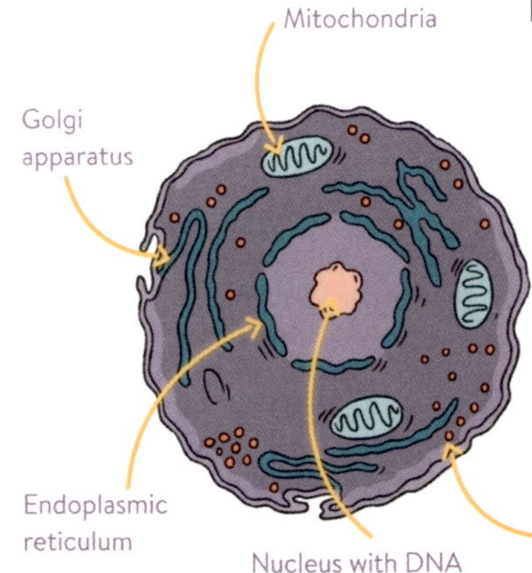

Remember how the whole solar system zips around the Milky Way unbelievably fast, far faster than any racing car? Well, we are moving in other ways, too. Earth is traveling around the Sun at about 60,000 miles per hour (100,000 kph), and it is spinning on its axis at about 1,000 miles per hour (1,600 kph). Feeling dizzy? Well, there's yet another kind of movement. You are sitting on a crust of rock that is *very slowly* drifting, like a giant raft, on a sea of boiling-hot magma, the same stuff that is called lava when it comes out onto Earth's surface. With all this traveling and spinning and floating, nobody ever really sits still!

Earth's surface is divided into moving pieces. The pieces are constantly drifting apart or bashing into one another, like slow-motion bumper cars at a carnival. It's a process called plate tectonics, and the pieces are called tectonic plates. When

As you read this, you are sitting on a tectonic plate that is very slowing moving. Here is how Earth's tectonic plates are arranged today.

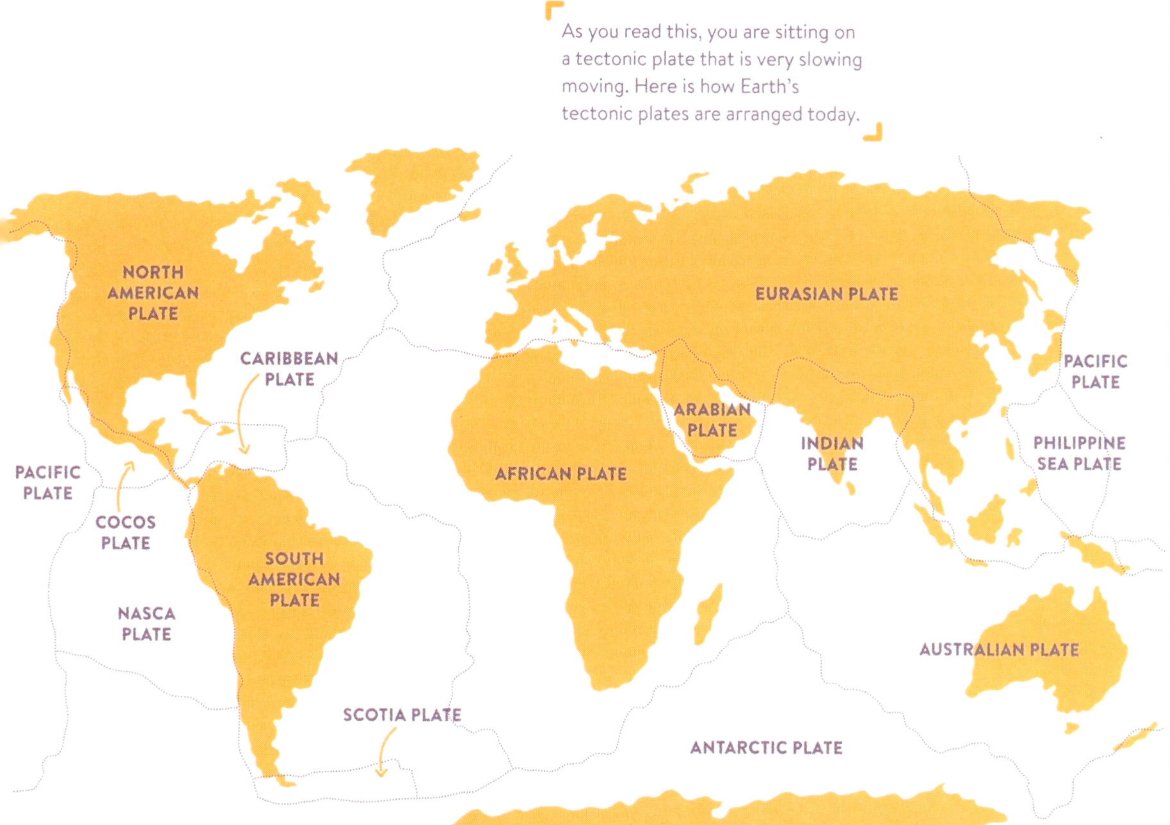

continents riding on these plates collide, they form mountain ranges soaring high up into the sky. When they drift apart, they form huge oceans or deep valleys. This gradual movement of Earth's plates is so powerful that it creates earthquakes and volcanoes, geysers and tsunamis.

These moving plates also change the climate. About 700 million years ago, Earth plunged into a super-cold ice age that lasted roughly 60 million years. Some scientists think this condition—known as Snowball Earth—was caused by moving tectonic plates. Others have found evidence that changes in the amount of sunlight reaching Earth could have been the cause. Either way, ice gripped the globe almost all the way from pole to pole.

The average global temperature during the Snowball Earth period was about -17°F (-27°C).

When the weather eventually warmed up again and the ice retreated, the story of life took a new turn. There were still plenty of oxygen-loving life forms in the sea. They had survived being trapped under ice because slightly warmer periods melted the glaciers enough to let oxygen-rich surface water flow under the ice. And now, with plenty of sunlight and lots more oxygen, larger creatures made of many cells evolved in the seas.

This leads us to one of the most amazing moments in our story. It is 540 million years ago. A quick check on our 24-hour clock shows it's now just after 9:00 p.m. There are still no plants, no flowers, no birds or animals or humans. But finally, finally, familiar-looking life forms are starting to appear.

Fossils are the preserved remains of long-lost creatures or the impressions they left behind. When creatures die, usually their bodies rot or dissolve. Sometimes, though, minerals in the ground replace once-living cells, creating a fossil. The same thing can happen to shells or teeth or footprints. Fossils are wonderful for helping scientists understand what kinds of creatures once lived on Earth. Expert fossil hunters are called paleontologists.

Charles Doolittle Walcott loved finding fossils. He was born in New York Mills, New York, in 1850. As a young boy he found school quite boring. It wasn't that he had no interest in things, just the opposite. He was so curious that he wanted to get outside and

When ammonite fossils were first found, many people thought they were fossilized snakes. Now we know they are the shells of octopus relatives. You can see what they looked like alive on page 31.

Anomalocaris

explore the world for himself—in particular, he liked to look for minerals, rocks, birds' eggs, and fossils. When he grew up he became the head of the Smithsonian Institution, a part of the U.S. government that studies the world and teaches people about it.

> "NATURE HAS A HABIT OF PLACING SOME OF HER MOST ATTRACTIVE TREASURES IN PLACES WHERE IT IS DIFFICULT TO LOCATE AND OBTAIN THEM."
>
> Charles Doolittle Walcott, paleontologist

One day in 1909, Walcott was exploring high up in a remote part of the Canadian Rockies. According to legend, his horse slipped and lost a shoe. Then, as the creature stumbled, its foot turned over a glistening rock. Walcott picked it up and saw a row of remarkable silvery fossils. These showed the perfectly preserved shapes of creatures dating back to a time known as the Cambrian Period.

Remember how the land is always moving and changing? Well, it turned out that the mountainside Walcott was standing on had been on the sea floor 508 million years before. Way back then, something—maybe a mudslide—killed these creatures and preserved them like a time capsule. Walcott's fossils are some of the oldest ever found. The place where he found them is known as the Burgess Shale, named after nearby Mount Burgess. Walcott returned to the site many times and eventually wrote a whole shelf of books about his finds.

And what a bizarre range of creatures they were! There was the strange-looking *Anomalocaris*. Possibly the biggest hunter of its day,

Opabinia

it could grow up to 3 feet (1 m) long. It used a pair of grasping arms to capture prey.

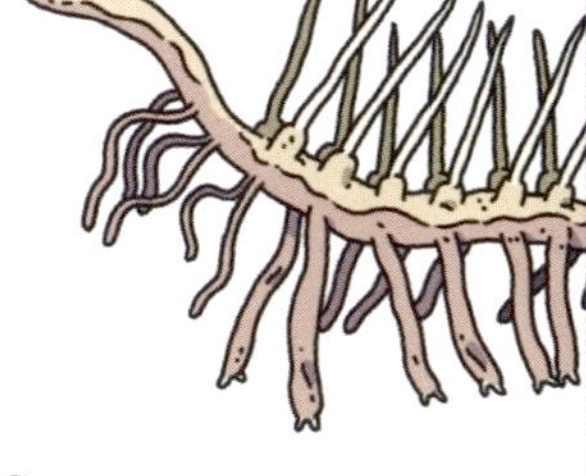
Hallucigenia

Another was *Hallucigenia*. This little beast walked on tentacle-like legs. It used the spines on its back to protect itself from being eaten by predators.

But nothing can prepare you for *Opabinia*. This oceanic oddball had five eyes, a fan-like tail for swimming, and a long nose with a mouth on the end. There's nothing remotely like it alive today.

One of the Cambrian Period's most common forms of animal life was a group of sea creatures called trilobites. Their fossils range from the size of your thumb to 2.5 feet (0.75 m) long and have been found all over the world. One very important thing about them is that they were possibly the first creatures ever to have fully developed eyes.

Some experts think that trilobite eyes triggered a new race for survival in the ancient seas. They could choose what they wanted for dinner by looking around. Of course, creatures that were easy to see were the ones most likely to be dinner. Hiding underground or being the same colors as the sea floor would have been good ways to survive

Trilobite

Timeline of Earth's history

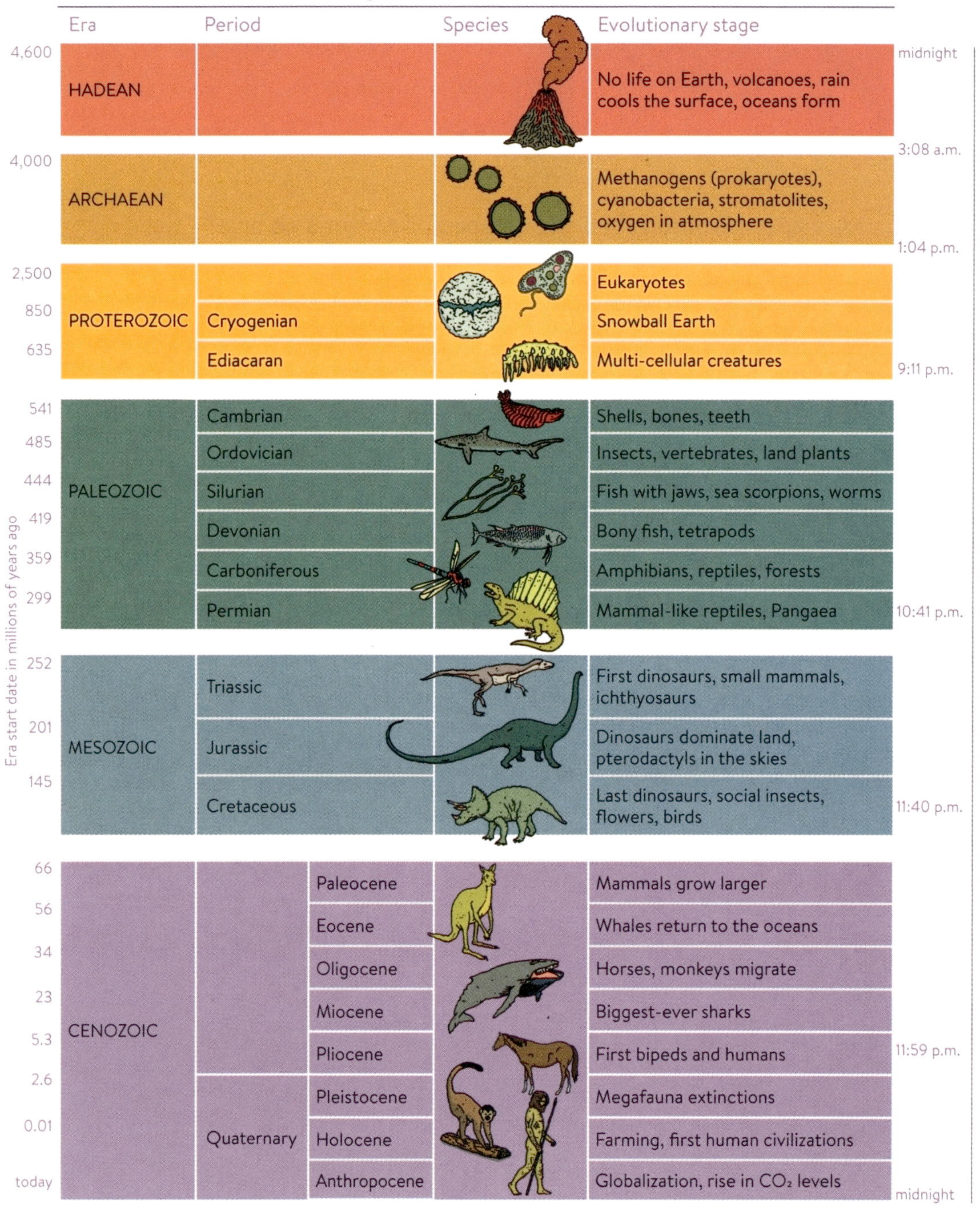

Era start date in millions of years ago	Era	Period		Species	Evolutionary stage	24-hour clock
4,600	HADEAN				No life on Earth, volcanoes, rain cools the surface, oceans form	midnight
4,000	ARCHAEAN				Methanogens (prokaryotes), cyanobacteria, stromatolites, oxygen in atmosphere	3:08 a.m.
2,500	PROTEROZOIC				Eukaryotes	1:04 p.m.
850		Cryogenian			Snowball Earth	
635		Ediacaran			Multi-cellular creatures	9:11 p.m.
541	PALEOZOIC	Cambrian			Shells, bones, teeth	
485		Ordovician			Insects, vertebrates, land plants	
444		Silurian			Fish with jaws, sea scorpions, worms	
419		Devonian			Bony fish, tetrapods	
359		Carboniferous			Amphibians, reptiles, forests	
299		Permian			Mammal-like reptiles, Pangaea	10:41 p.m.
252	MESOZOIC	Triassic			First dinosaurs, small mammals, ichthyosaurs	
201		Jurassic			Dinosaurs dominate land, pterodactyls in the skies	
145		Cretaceous			Last dinosaurs, social insects, flowers, birds	11:40 p.m.
66	CENOZOIC		Paleocene		Mammals grow larger	
56			Eocene		Whales return to the oceans	
34			Oligocene		Horses, monkeys migrate	
23			Miocene		Biggest-ever sharks	
5.3			Pliocene		First bipeds and humans	11:59 p.m.
2.6		Quaternary	Pleistocene		Megafauna extinctions	
0.01			Holocene		Farming, first human civilizations	
today			Anthropocene		Globalization, rise in CO_2 levels	midnight

Over time, many living things developed and later died out. Looking at fossils and the rocks they're embedded in helps scientists figure out when each one lived. Here's a chart showing time from the formation of Earth to the present day.

in this brave new world. This is a great example of how evolution works, how new, better-adapted creatures replace earlier ones over time.

The Burgess Shale creatures give us a glimpse into the very beginning of a time called the Paleozoic Era. Let's go on an imaginary ocean dive to check out some creatures that lived in the first part of this era, during periods called Cambrian, Ordovician, Silurian, and Devonian. Before we start, another quick check on our 24-hour clock of Earth history shows that this time lasted from 9:11 p.m. to 10:08 p.m.

Sponges were among the simplest of all animals living in the ancient Cambrian seas. They are still alive today. About 8,500 different species of sponge have been discovered. For a long time people thought sponges were plants, but actually sponges are animals. In fact, you and I are much more closely related to a sponge than to, say, a daffodil.

Coral reefs were around back then, too. These immense structures are built over hundreds of thousands of years by tiny sea creatures. The corals grow on top of the skeletons of their dead ancestors to form a reef. With their bodies, they create a rich habitat for other creatures. Today, well over 5,000 different species of living things camp out in Earth's biggest coral reef—the Great Barrier Reef off the coast of Australia.

The Great Barrier Reef is made up of almost 3,000 individual reefs and stretches for 1,429 miles (2,300 km). The ancestors of today's corals first appeared in the Cambrian Period.

Coral reefs, which first emerged in the Cambrian Period, are still around today. In November 2021, divers from the United Nations Educational, Scientific and Cultural Organization (UNESCO) discovered this gigantic reef made of rose coral deep in the southern Pacific ocean near the island of Tahiti. Though many reefs around the world have been damaged by climate change, this one is healthy. Studying it may help us understand how to help endangered reefs elsewhere.

> IT WAS MAGICAL TO WITNESS GIANT, BEAUTIFUL ROSE CORALS, WHICH STRETCH FOR AS FAR AS THE EYE CAN SEE. IT WAS LIKE A WORK OF ART.

Alexis Rosenfeld,
underwater photographer

Jellyfish like this one, a sea nettle (*Chrysaora fuscescens*), have been in the ocean for more than 500 million years. If a jellyfish is cut in two, it can regenerate and turn into two new jellyfish.

Jellyfish are related to corals but are nowhere near as friendly. Jellyfish swim by pumping their bell-like heads. They have a very simple nervous system and only one opening—a combined mouth and bottom. Some jellies pack a nasty punch. They sting using an array of poison-tipped harpoons hidden in cells along their tentacles. Jellyfish were very common in the Cambrian seas.

The ancestors of ammonites appeared during the Devonian Period. Ammonites went extinct 65 million years ago, at the same time as most dinosaurs. They looked like giant snails, but their closest living cousins are octopus and squid. Ammonites had spiral shells to protect them. Their fossils have been found all over the world with teeth marks and scars.

Ammonite

At first glance, sea squirts seem similar to sponges. But sea squirts have babies that swim around like tadpoles. They push themselves through the water with a special tail containing an early kind of backbone called a notochord. These creatures are still around today, but they first appeared in the Cambrian Period. Sea squirts are thought to be distant ancestors of vertebrates—animals with backbones. Vertebrates include fish, amphibians, reptiles, birds, and mammals. Since humans are mammals, baby sea squirts are super important. Some experts think they should go down in prehistory as our great-great-great ... grandparents!

Among the most fearsome creatures of the Silurian and

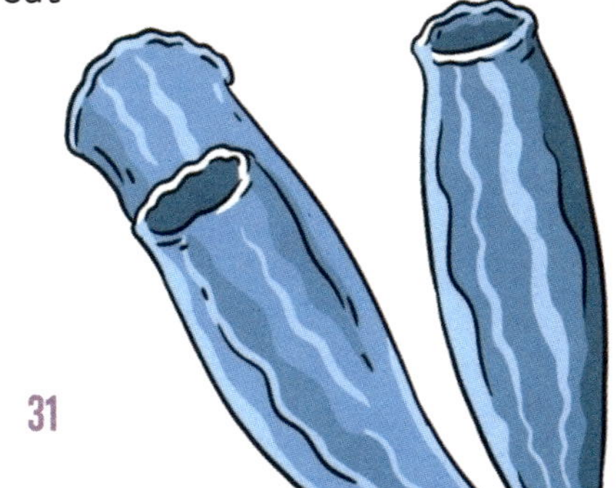

Sea squirts

Devonian seas was the now-extinct placoderm. It was a giant fish that had jaws and teeth. Heavy armor plating covered its head and throat. Its body had thick scales, and some placoderms had fins covered in armor-plated tubes. These were nature's first war machines, built like tanks. A placoderm could grow up to 30 feet (10 m) long and weigh over 4 tons (4 tonnes). If it were alive today, it could easily snap a shark in two with a single bite.

You wouldn't want to bump into a sea scorpion, either. It had a long, spiked tail that may have been equipped with a deadly venomous sting. This creature could grow to 8 feet (2.5 m) long.

Sea scorpions appeared during the Ordovician Period and died out along with many other species in what's called the Permian Mass Extinction, 252 million years ago.

Earth was formed 4.5 billion years ago. Life first appeared about 4 billion years ago. By 470 million years ago, the ocean was a busy place, home to our swimming and swaying, hunting and hiding ancestors. The land, not so much. Mostly it was raining.

LAND AHOY!

480 million – 252 million years ago

Creatures wriggle out of the seas and forests cover the land

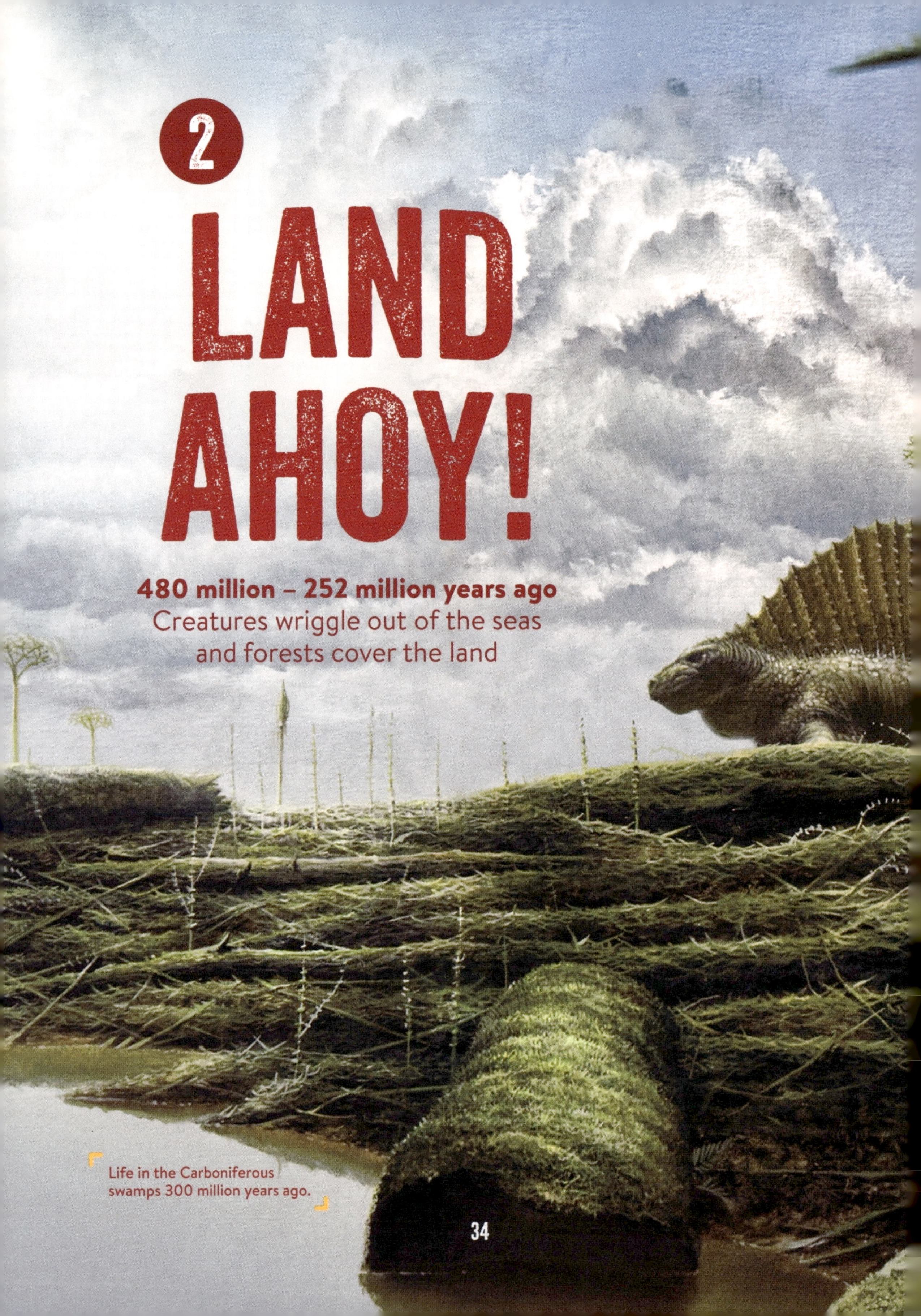

Life in the Carboniferous swamps 300 million years ago.

480 MILLION YEARS AGO

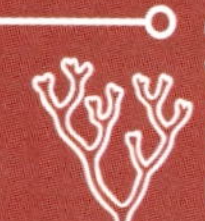

Primitive plants live on land by the water's edge.

420 MILLION YEARS AGO

Millipede-like creatures wriggle out of the seas.

400 MILLION YEARS AGO

Fungi help plants live further away from water; oxygen levels rise as some insects take to the skies.

385 MILLION YEARS AGO

Earth's land is covered with trees.

375 MILLION YEARS AGO

Vertebrates adapt to life on land.

360 MILLION YEARS AGO

Plants develop seeds.

312 MILLION YEARS AGO

Reptiles develop eggs with waterproof shells.

280 MILLION YEARS AGO

Some animals are able to control their body temperature.

252 MILLION YEARS AGO

Life suffers its worst ever brush with death.

It was raining. It had rained the day before, and the day before that, and the day before that one, too. For millions of years, life swarmed in the ocean and rain hammered the land. There was nothing to see but lifeless rock and mud.

Then, about 480 million years ago, a little bit of green appeared. The first land plants were growing near the water's edge. These were squidgy liverworts and mosses. They had evolved from green algae, a water plant still around today. Like their ancestors, these plants used photosynthesis to make the energy they needed.

Next came a new type of plant that could grow much taller. These plants had a system of tubes to carry food and water from the ground to the tops of their bodies, the way we transport blood around our body in our blood vessels. We call them vascular plants.

The first vascular plants were just a few centimetres high, with thick stems. We know about them from an accidental discovery made in 1912 by William Mackie, a Scottish doctor, when he was out and about near the village of Rhynie, in Scotland. Quite by chance he spotted some curious-looking fossils in an old stone wall. You see, it turns out that about 400 million years ago Rhynie was a steaming cauldron. There were boiling-hot pools of bubbling mud. Every so often a giant geyser would spout out a huge fountain of scorching water onto nearby plants. When the water landed on the plants, minerals in it cooled and turned them into stone. When this happens it is called petrification. That's where the word petrified comes from.

The fossils of Rhynie are so well preserved that scientists can see exactly what these

An artist's impression of early vascular plants (*Rhynia*) and giant fungi (*Prototaxites*) growing around 420–395 million years ago. The *Rhynia* plants were up to twenty centimetres tall, and the *Prototaxites*' trunks rose as high as eight metres.

2. LAND AHOY!

480 million – 252 million years ago

Vascular tissue helps plants grow big and strong. This picture, taken under a microscope, shows what it looks like inside a plant's stem. A structure called xylem transports water and nutrients from the roots to the leaves and a structure called phloem transports sugar made by photosynthesis around the plant.

ancient plants were made of and how they worked. It is clear that they contained a substance called lignin. Lignin toughens the walls of plant cells. It makes the walls waterproof so the tubes inside the plant can carry water up to the top of a high tree. It's like having plastic tubing instead of tubing made from tissue paper.

Lignin makes trees woody and keeps them standing upright. But it took at least 40 million years for these small vascular plants to evolve into proper trees. They never could have made it to these heights were it not for another group of living things, called fungi.

Do you like mushrooms? I have to say they don't score very high on my list of tasty snacks. But researching and writing this book has turned me into a big mushroom fan. That's because without fungi (the giant group, or kingdom, of living things to which mushrooms belong) the world would be a disgusting and very smelly place.

We don't know much about the origin of fungi. We don't even know if they started life in the sea or on land. That's because their soft bodies don't leave many fossils behind. But we are pretty sure that fungi were already living on land when plants got there. Since then, fungi have developed into a huge variety of life forms, from some of the smallest to the largest living things on Earth.

Small fungi are just one cell. The yeast that makes bread rise is one of those. Large fungi can be truly enormous. One fungus in Oregon, United States, is known as the Humongous Fungus. It stretches out underground across nearly ten square kilometres – the size of more than 1,300 football pitches!

Fungi feed off other organisms just as animals do. Most fungi are made up of an underground network of root-like threads called a mycelium. The mushroom is just the part of the fungus that pops up above ground. The mushroom's job is to spread spores. These tiny reproductive cells get blown by the wind then settle themselves and grow into new fungi.

Fungi are vital for all life on Earth because they eat dead things. Without them the world would be drowning under piles of the dead bodies of plants and animals – not a happy thought. They also

Mushrooms of *Armillaria ostoyae*, the humongous fungus.

make chemicals that help plants grow.

Sometimes nature has a real fondness for teamwork. Big networks of underground fungi pass nutrients and water to the roots of trees. In return, trees supply fungi with food. Fungi also pass nutrients and chemical messages from one tree to another, allowing the trees to communicate and share food. This whole network of fungi and trees is called the 'wood wide web'. Thanks to this ancient support network, primitive plant life was able to move further inland, enriching the land by turning the ground into soil as it went.

Soil is made up of sand, minerals and the decayed remains of once-living things. Plants, tiny animals including worms, and fungi all help keep this precious life force working. They turn fallen leaves and rotting trees into nutrients to help new plants grow. They have been digging up the soil for the last 400 million years. And all that digging mixes the soil, renewing and regenerating it. This is called the soil cycle.

> "THE WOOD WIDE WEB HAS BEEN MAPPED, TRACED, MONITORED, AND COAXED TO REVEAL THE BEAUTIFUL STRUCTURES AND FINELY ADAPTED LANGUAGES OF THE FOREST NETWORK."
>
> Suzanne Simard, forest ecologist and discoverer of the wood wide web

In fact, without living things, there would be no soil. Earth would be nothing more than dust and rock, like the surface of the Moon, Mars or Venus.

Fungi and plants were not the only organisms to move onto land. A few small crawly creatures emerged about 440–420 million years ago. The first-ever land animal was probably an arthropod. This group includes millipedes, insects, spiders, crabs, lobsters and a whole lot of other creatures with jointed legs and hard outer body parts called exoskeletons.

It took about 50 million years before another kind of animal made the move onto land. If you were a fish living in the seas back then, life could be over fairly quickly. Stinging jellyfish, sea scorpions with deadly tail spikes and giant placoderms were just a few of the dangers swimming around. If you were able to get out of the water, you might have had a better chance of surviving. After all, the shores were now full of plants and juicy worms to eat.

Fish aren't built to live on land, though. One problem is breathing oxygen from air instead of water. Another is working out how to move around. Imagine walking on fins instead of legs – it wouldn't be a simple stroll in the park.

Fungi and trees live closely entwined and depend on one another to live. The fungi supply water and minerals to a tree and help it communicate with other trees. The tree feeds the fungi with sugar it makes using photosynthesis.

Tiktaalik found a way around this. It used its fins to wade through shallow bogs and to heave its body out of water onto the land. Which means *Tiktaalik* is the first creature ever known to have been able to do a press-up!

Tiktaalik had wrist bones for lifting its body off the sea floor, lungs for breathing air, and a strong ribcage and neck.

Tiktaalik lived about 375 million years ago, when primitive plants were growing near the shores. Its fossils show how fish-like fins were now being used as the first real arms, shoulders, elbows and wrists.

It's bizarre to think that the reason you and I have wrists and ankles goes all the way back to creatures like *Tiktaalik*. That's because they needed hinged joints to heave their bodies up off the ground. Do a press-up yourself and you'll see just how important these hinges are!

Tiktaalik is one of the first of a group of animals known as amphibians. Amphi in ancient Greek means 'both' and bios means 'life'. They live both in the water and on the land. Not only could the first amphibians walk on land, they could also breathe through primitive lungs rather than using gills like fish. Equipped with these new features, some amphibians, such as the two-metre-long *Eryops*, became the most dominant creatures on land.

Can you see what looks like a pair of little lips in the magnifying glass? That's a stoma, which lets water and oxygen out of the leaf. As water evaporates out of the leaves in a big forest, it can form into clouds and then rain. That's why some forests are called rainforests.

They had staying power. Their descendants include today's frogs, newts and toads.

While amphibians were growing into giants, so were plants. As we saw earlier, some plants had developed woody stems to stay upright. And thanks to fungi, they could gather food in their roots even if they weren't living near the water's edge. But in order to move the water and food up their tubes against the pull of gravity, they needed a pumping system.

A plant's key to growing tall lies in millions of tiny holes that cover the surfaces of its leaves. Depending on the weather conditions, plants open or close these little holes, which are called stomata (one of them is called a stoma). When it is hot, the heat pulls the water out through the stomata to evaporate on the leaf

surface. This process is like sucking a drink through a straw. The water leaving the straw at the top pulls more up through the tube.

Early land plants, including trees, created spores just the way fungi do. They released the spores into the air and let the wind spread them. But spores need warm and wet conditions to grow. That's fine in damp marshes or bogs, but hopeless in dry areas. By about 360 million years ago, some plants had developed a new way to reproduce – seeds.

Seeds are stronger than spores. They have a hard, water-resistant coating called a testa. This protective coat prevents seeds from getting damaged in the air, on the water, or even inside an animal's guts. Inside the coating, there is an embryo, the part of the seed that will grow into a new plant. And with its own private stash of food in the form of sugars, proteins and fats, the seed has plenty of nutrients to grow even in a tough environment.

"THE SEED IS A BRILLIANT DEVICE INVOLVING A WHOLE SERIES OF INNOVATIONS."

Colin Tudge, biologist

Some of the early seed-bearing trees were cycads. They look like small palms (although they are not related) and can been traced back to about 320 million years ago. About 300 species of cycads are still

Many of the cycad species around today can be found in the warm climates of Central America, Australia and Africa.

living today. Like eyesight in trilobites, seeds changed the world entirely. For millions of years they have made plants the dominant form of life on land.

Can you imagine a millipede the size of a person? Or a sea scorpion bigger than your outstretched arms? If, like me, you are not so sure that this is a world for you, then be grateful you were not alive 300 million years ago. Welcome to the Carboniferous Period.

How insects learned to fly is still a mystery. Experts think it probably had something to do with the arrival of tall plants and trees. Wouldn't it make sense for an insect to develop little wing flaps to jump or glide from one tree to another? That way they wouldn't have to climb all the way down and then up again. Gradually the wing flaps would have grown larger. Finally, insects could glide, dive and flap their wings.

Griffinflies – seagull-sized relatives of today's dragonflies – were some of the most spectacular insects that ever lived. They had complete command of the skies. They could feed

Griffinflies had a wingspan of around 75 cm. They're now extinct, which is probably a good thing for us!

“THE DRAGONFLY IS AN EXCEPTIONALLY BEAUTIFUL INSECT AND A FIERCE CARNIVORE ... [IT] CAN PUT ON A BURST OF SPEED, ... HOVER, FLY BACKWARD, AND SWITCH DIRECTION IN A FLASH.”

Richard Preston, science writer

Like flies, ladybirds are able to switch very quickly between walking and flying, thanks to the mechanism in their wings, which easily folds in and out.

off smaller creatures as and when they liked. There were no birds back then to challenge them. They might even have had nearly all-round vision the way their relatives do today.

In a world of fierce giants, other creatures simply had to adapt or die. And adapt they did. Smaller insects evolved folding wings, just like those we see in houseflies today. This new kind of wing meant that small insects could crawl into narrow spaces. Larger, fixed-winged griffinflies and other predators couldn't reach them there. Flying insects with folding wings are by far the largest group of insects alive today. It goes to show that the folding wing probably counts as another of nature's most successful adaptations ever.

Just about this time, when griffinflies ruled the skies, the world's land masses had started colliding together into one giant continent. Scientists call it Pangaea (meaning 'all Earth'). While this was happening, the climate was becoming warmer and drier. So the ponds and puddles where amphibians laid their

The eggs of amphibians, like this frog egg, let water flow in and out. That's fine for laying eggs in the wet, but they're no good on dry land.

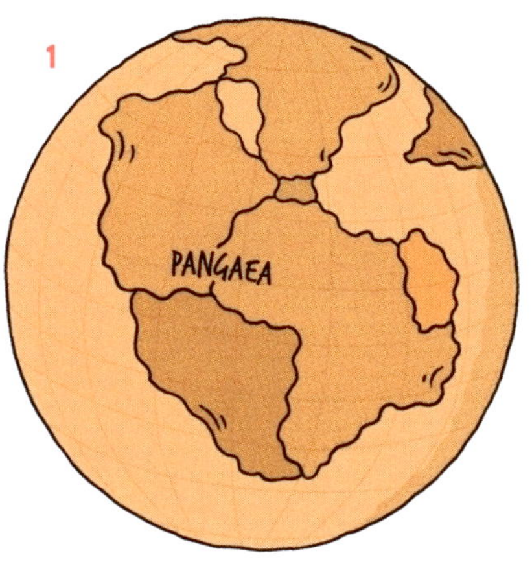

1. By about 250 million years ago, Earth's land masses had collided, resulting in a giant supercontinent, Pangaea.

2. By about 150 million years ago, Pangaea had split into two huge land masses, Gondwana in the south and Laurasia in the north, with ocean separating them.

3. By about 95 million years ago, Earth's land masses had begun to resemble the layout of the continents as they are today.

eggs probably started to dry up and disappear. More animals had to compete for less water.

Amphibian eggs are squishy, with a covering that lets water in and out. That's great if you lay your eggs in the wet. But as the land dried out, some creatures began to lay a new kind of egg, one a little like a plant seed, with all the water and nutrients a baby creature needs contained inside a leathery, soft or hard shell. Armed with their new waterproof eggs, these animals could press-up their way inland as far as they liked. They could lay their eggs on dry land and after a few weeks, hey presto! Out hatched a little creature. We call this group of animals reptiles.

So a waterproof egg is actually a portable pond or puddle.

> THE SHELL AND EGG MEMBRANES ALLOW GAS EXCHANGE TO AND FROM THE DEVELOPING EMBRYO, LETTING OXYGEN IN AND CARBON DIOXIDE OUT BUT RETAINING WATER.
>
> P. Martin Sander, paldeontologist

These little marvels of nature changed the story of animals by allowing them to give birth away from water. You may find that eggs now make for some quite interesting breakfast talk.

The earliest known reptile is called *Hylonomus*. This twenty-centimetre-long, lizard-like creature lived from about 312 million years ago in the Carboniferous Period. It ate millipedes and small insects. And large amphibians and giant griffinflies ate it.

Fast forward a few million years and reptiles ruled the land. One very cool example is *Dimetrodon*. Growing more than three metres long, this lumbering giant walked on four legs and had a long swaggering tail. *Dimetrodon* was the largest meat-eater of its time. It had a peculiar sail on its back. Some scientists think it may have been used to heat up its body and blood in the early-morning sunlight and to release heat and cool *Dimetrodon* in the warmth of the day.

Creatures like *Dimetrodon* roamed the land for about 60 million years. But their time came to a sudden end when life suffered its worst ever brush with death – the Permian Mass Extinction.

That single supercontinent, Pangaea, was now fully formed. When continents collide, one thing is certain. You can expect more and bigger volcanoes to erupt. What's the biggest volcano you can imagine? How about one that spreads lava over an area the size of Western Europe and then goes on erupting for another one million years? That's what experts think happened 252 million years ago, forming the Siberian Traps, a huge area of volcanic rock in what is now northern Russia.

But that's not all. Volcanoes throw lots of carbon dioxide into the air. Carbon dioxide is one of the gases responsible for global warming. Experts think that at the end of the Permian Period, Earth's climate became too hot for most life forms to survive. Nine out of ten species of plants and animals went extinct.

It was as if life on Earth had been struck down by a killer fever. But this was no ordinary illness because it lasted something like 60,000 years!

Dimetrodon lived around 280 million years ago. Its sail-like back may have helped it control its temperature.

Epidexipteryx lived in Asia during the Jurassic Period. It is the earliest known example of a dinosaur with feathers that can be fanned out for display.

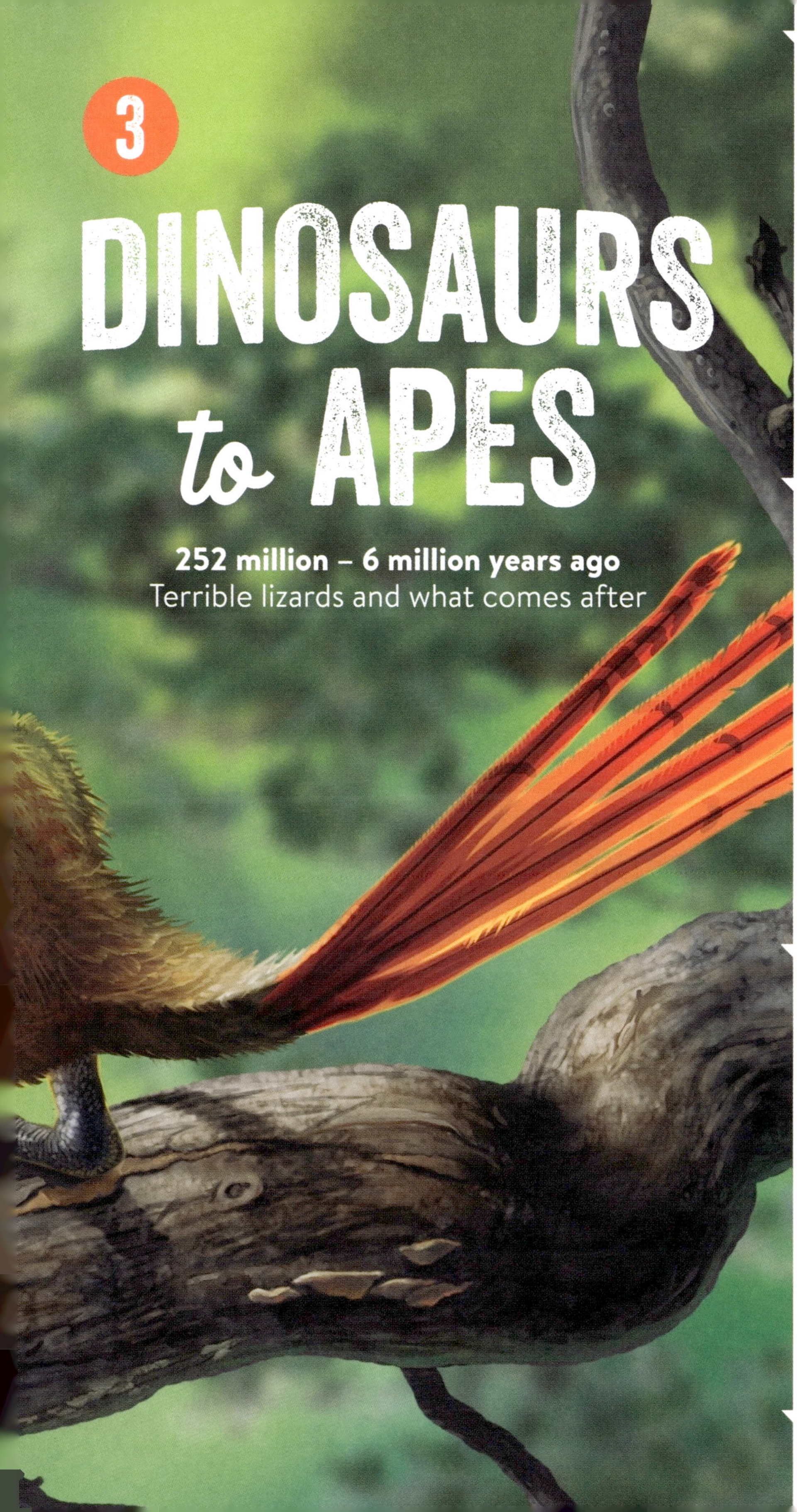

3

DINOSAURS to APES

252 million – 6 million years ago

Terrible lizards and what comes after

245 MILLION YEARS AGO
The age of dinosaurs begins.

150 MILLION YEARS AGO
Termites become the first insects to live in giant nests; some feathered dinosaurs take to the skies, becoming birds.

140 MILLION YEARS AGO
Plants reproduce using flowers and fruit.

66 MILLION YEARS AGO
A massive meteorite wipes out all dinosaurs except birds.

56 MILLION YEARS AGO
Mammals and birds dominate the land and sky.

30 MILLION YEARS AGO
Monkeys appear.

25 MILLION YEARS AGO
Apes appear.

Very few reptiles survived the terrible Permian Mass Extinction. But one of these survivors is very important to us. *Lystrosaurus* is a link between reptiles and mammals. If it hadn't survived, some experts think mammals may never have evolved at all. Humans are mammals. So we must be thankful that this possible distant ancestor of ours made it, even if it did look like a cross between a lizard and a pig. Then came a completely new generation of reptiles. These were the most fearsome creatures ever to walk on Earth. Welcome to the age of dinosaurs!

Fossils of about 1,000 types of dinosaur have been found so far, although nearly 2,000 are thought to have existed altogether. Some walked on two feet, some on four. Some ate plants, some ate animals, some ate both.

Among the first known dinosaurs were the prosauropods. These were plant eaters that could grow up to ten metres long, with small heads and long necks. They usually walked on all fours, but sometimes climbed onto two legs when reaching to nibble at the top of a tree.

At the beginning of the Triassic Period, *Lystrosaurus* was the most common animal on land. But by the middle of the period, dinosaurs had burst on to the scene. This picture shows *Lystrosaurus* and some Triassic dinosaurs along with the dates when they lived and where their fossils were found. Because they lived at different times and in different places, they would never have appeared together like this.

Mary Ann and Gideon Mantell were amateur fossil hunters who lived in Lewes, England. In 1822, Mary Ann spotted several very large fossilised teeth in a forest near their home. They worked out that these teeth belonged to an animal about eighteen metres long. That's nearly as long as two double-decker buses!

After years of argument, scientists concluded that the Mantells' teeth (well, not theirs, but the ones they found) belonged to a new type of creature that had never been known before. They called it the *Iguanodon* because they thought it would have looked something like a much larger version of a modern iguana. Fossils that were found later showed it didn't look quite like that and was only about half as big as they thought, too.

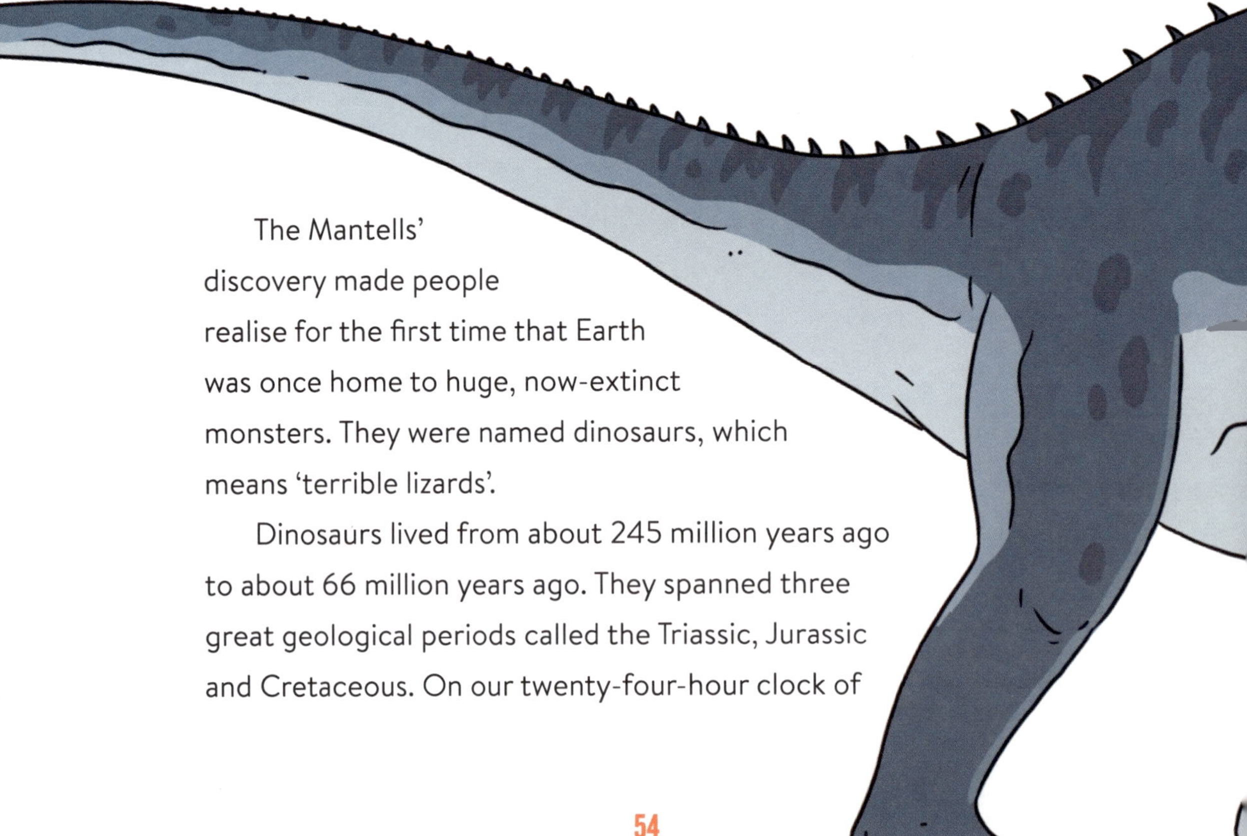

The Mantells' discovery made people realise for the first time that Earth was once home to huge, now-extinct monsters. They were named dinosaurs, which means 'terrible lizards'.

Dinosaurs lived from about 245 million years ago to about 66 million years ago. They spanned three great geological periods called the Triassic, Jurassic and Cretaceous. On our twenty-four-hour clock of

Earth's history, they lived between 10:43pm and 11:39pm.

Some of the biggest dinosaurs were the sauropods, and one of the biggest of them was *Argentinosaurus*. This huge, heavy beast walked on four legs. It could grow up to thirty-five metres long. And it may have weighed up to seventy tonnes, probably making it the heaviest animal ever on Earth. Its survival strategy was simple. It grew so large that few other creatures were big enough or strong enough to kill it.

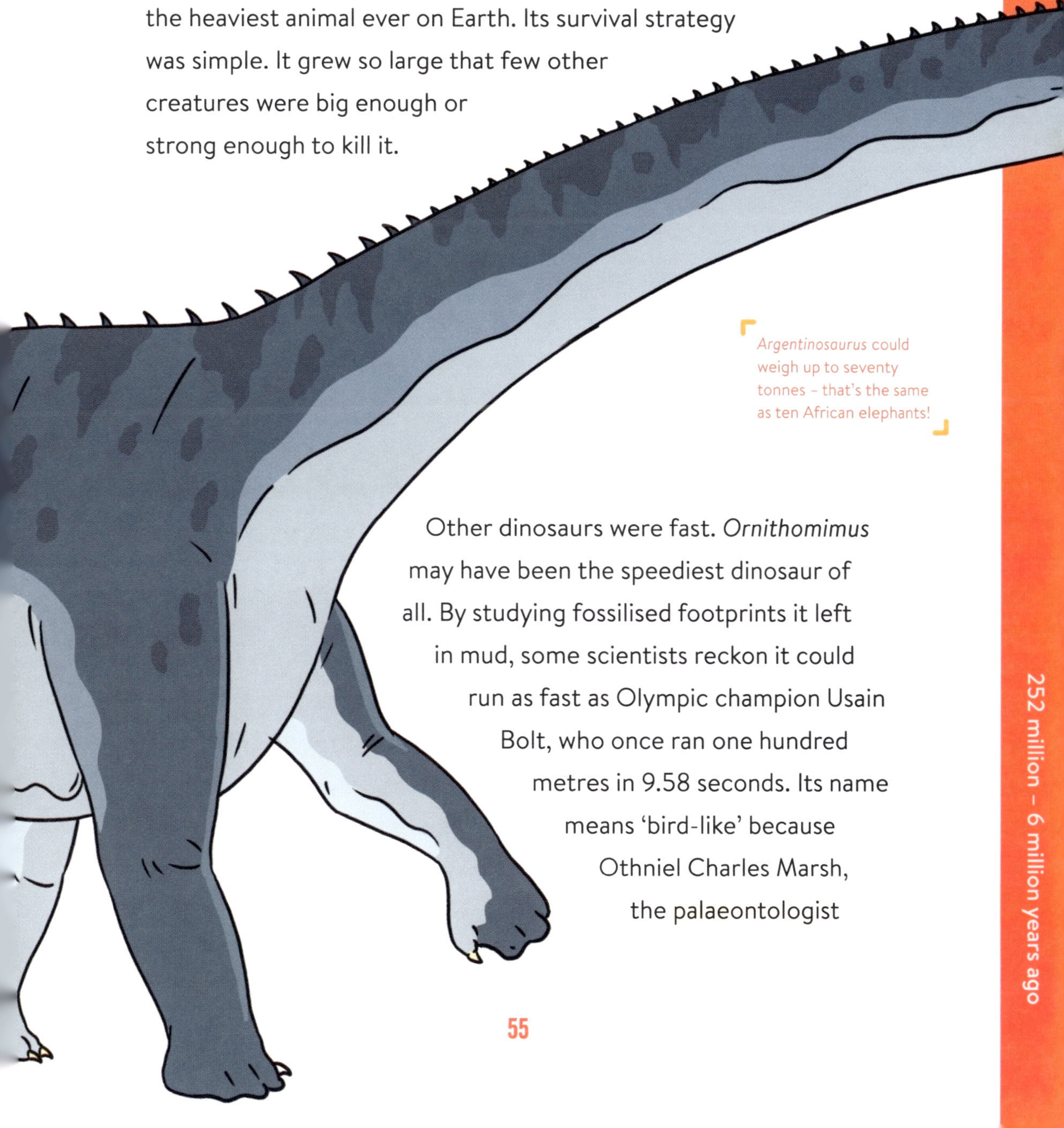

Argentinosaurus could weigh up to seventy tonnes – that's the same as ten African elephants!

Other dinosaurs were fast. *Ornithomimus* may have been the speediest dinosaur of all. By studying fossilised footprints it left in mud, some scientists reckon it could run as fast as Olympic champion Usain Bolt, who once ran one hundred metres in 9.58 seconds. Its name means 'bird-like' because Othniel Charles Marsh, the palaeontologist who named it, noticed how much its claws looked like a bird's. And that was in 1890. He didn't have any idea that over one hundred years later other palaeontologists would find fossils that showed *Ornithomimus* also had feathers.

Still other dinosaurs had unusual built-in tools. *Iguanodon* was one of those. Its thumb was shaped like a dagger. Perhaps it used its thumb to defend itself, standing upright on its hind legs to fend off attackers. But some scientists think *Iguanodon* would just have run from predators and used its thumb spike for spearing food.

The most famous dinosaur of all is the one with the strongest bite – *Tyrannosaurus rex*, or *T. rex* for short. It lived in what is now western North America. *T. rex* walked on two legs and had a massive skull, balanced by a long, heavy tail. Each of its hands had just two fingers, and its upper arms were quite short compared with its massive legs and tail. At around twelve metres long and weighing more than a modern elephant, this was one big carnivore. It dined on dead carcasses or live prey – possibly both. The most complete *T. rex* skeleton was found by fossil hunter Sue Hendrickson in August 1990. This famous fossil was named Sue after its discoverer.

Not all dinosaurs were big or fast or strong. One of the smallest, *Microraptor*, was a four-winged dinosaur the size of a crow. It couldn't fly but probably glided from tree to tree looking for food.

In 1861, Christian Erich Hermann von Meyer, a German fossil hunter, announced the discovery of what he claimed was the first-ever bird. He called it *Archaeopteryx*, and it was about the same size as a modern magpie. Although it had teeth like a reptile, it was

Palaeontologists have found *T. rex* dung with crushed bones in it. Bones have nutritious marrow inside them, so we know this giant predator used its powerful jaws and teeth to get every last bit of food from the animals it killed itself or leftovers from other predators.

definitely bird-like. Its feathers were arranged in much the same way as a modern bird's. It even had bird-like claws on its legs, and a wishbone like the one you find in a chicken. Von Meyer's fossil dated back some 150 million years, which means it lived at about the same time as the long-necked prosauropods like *Diplodocus* were munching the tops of trees.

For years, experts were baffled as to which creatures birds were descended from. How had they learned to fly? Where did their feathers come from? Knowing about just one prehistoric bird wasn't enough to understand what happened.

Then, in 1996, Chinese scientists announced that fossil hunter Li Yumin had found a dinosaur with feathers. *Sinosauropteryx* caused a sensation. This was a one-metre-long, two-legged creature with the jaws and pointy teeth of meat-eating dinosaurs. It had clawed fingers, and its legs showed it must have been a fast runner. Its simple feathers could help keep it warm but were not advanced enough for it to have flown. Later researchers showed it was also cute, with a 'bandit mask' face like a raccoon.

The puzzle of where birds came from had at last been solved. Feathers appeared on some dinosaurs. Then later, some feathers evolved into the kind that help birds fly. Many scientists think that all theropods (smart, fast dinosaurs including *Velociraptor* and *T. rex*) had feathers, especially when they were young. So what's the difference between birds and dinosaurs? Well, not much.

Actually dinosaurs are alive and well today. But don't panic. Only the descendants of dinosaurs with flying feathers are still alive. It's just that we call them birds.

Another bird-like dinosaur with feathers on the back of its head, body and arms was the *Sinornithosaurus millenii*. This fossil, found in China, dates to about 125 million years ago.

Theropods and birds

Date	Name	Characteristics
228 million years ago	*Eoraptor*	*Eoraptor* had five fingers on each hand and three toes on each foot. Birds today have three fingers in each of their wings.
220 million years ago	*Coelophysis*	*Coelophysis* had a wishbone. Birds today have a wishbone too, made up of two collarbones stuck together in a forked shape.
75 million years ago	*Oviraptor*	*Oviraptor* was discovered alongside some fossilised eggs, and it had feathers. Experts think it was probably keeping its own eggs warm the way a chicken does.
Today	Eagle	Eagles can fly. They also have feathers, talons, a beak and a wishbone. They have great vision and can spot prey from more than three kilometres away!

No one knows exactly how birds evolved from dinosaurs. But here are some examples of species and their characteristics that hint at the way today's birds emerged.

While dinosaurs ruled the land, other types of animals dominated the ocean and skies. Giant sharks, underwater crocodile ancestors and nightmarish marine reptiles prowled the seas gobbling up squid and fish. And in the skies, flying reptiles called pterosaurs swooped and glided. The smallest were the size of a pigeon and the largest were as big as a small aeroplane, with wingspans up to twelve metres. The best known of these monsters is *Quetzalcoatlus*, though new finds have begun to challenge it for the title of largest flying reptile of all time.

Dinosaur times were pretty exciting, but for a long time they were missing one thing we now take for granted – flowering plants. Today, they are by far the most successful plants alive. But for about 330 million years, none of the plants in the world had flowers.

Tylosaurus (below) was a giant twelve-metre-long predatory marine reptile with razor-sharp teeth. *Hatzegopteryx thambema* (right) is known from just two fossils found in Romania. Based on their size, scientists think this creature might been the largest pterosaur ever discovered.

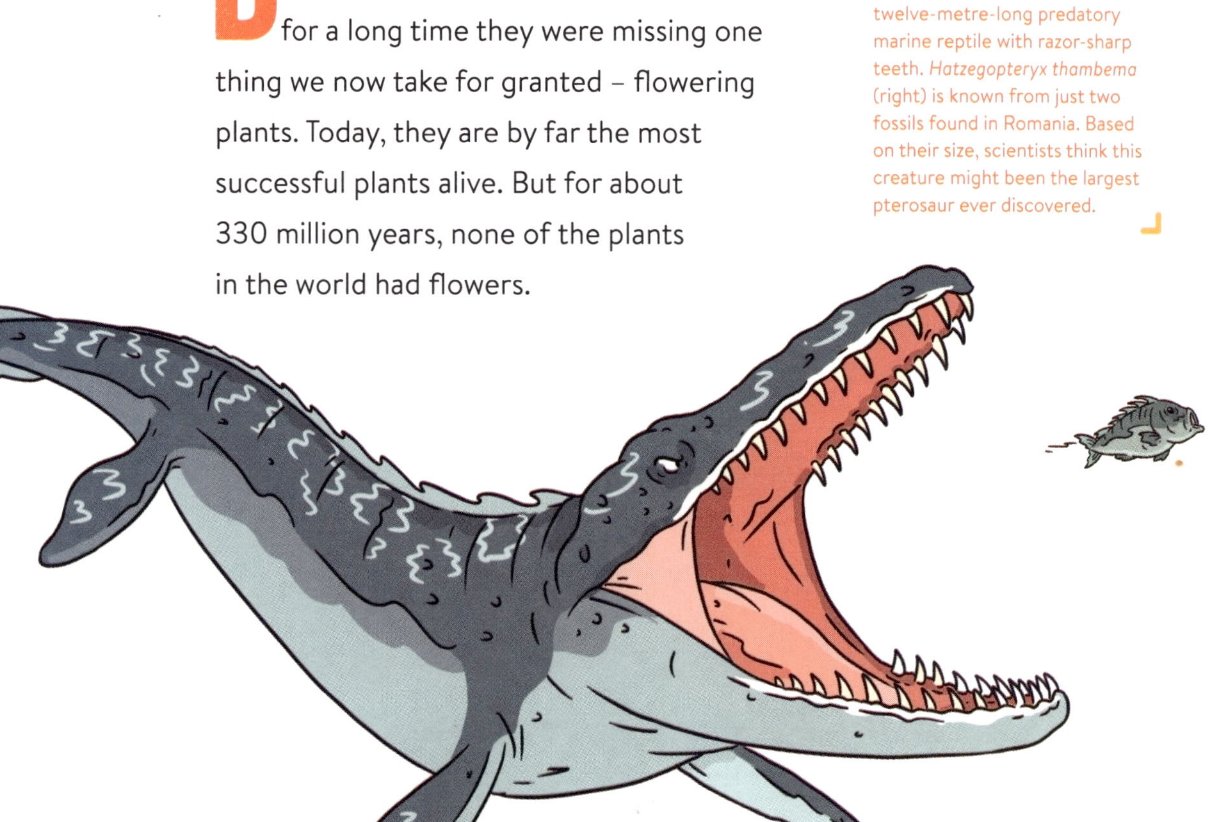

Many cone-bearing evergreens and spore-spreading ferns that were around during the Jurassic Period, before flowering plants evolved, are still with us today. This forest in New Zealand is home to many of them. So, when you go for a walk here, you can imagine you are about to meet a dinosaur!

The oldest flower fossils date back to about 140 million years ago. This was during the Cretaceous Period, when dinosaurs were at the height of their power. Since then, flowering plants have made a massive impact on life on Earth. In fact, most of what we eat comes from flowering plants and the animals that eat them.

Flowers are brilliant at helping plants reproduce more easily. To talk about how, we need to go back to between one and two billion years ago. At that time, a new form of reproduction started in the oceans. It is called sexual reproduction. It works by combining genetic information (called DNA) from the cells of two parents so that the baby has a combination of the parents' genes. That way, the baby is different from either of its parents.

Sexual reproduction is a great way of making sure all members of a species are different from one another. Variation in living things allows life to be more adaptable when the environment changes. That's why biodiversity matters.

But trying to mix DNA when you are a plant is quite tricky. How can two plants swap cells when they can't move from place

On one journey, a bee can travel as much as six kilometres from its hive.

to place? Flowers are a stunning solution to the problem. They spread reproductive cells called pollen from one plant to another in many different ways. Some release them to be carried by the wind. Others attract creatures known as pollinators – such as beetles, bees, moths and some mammals – that carry their pollen.

This is a two-way deal. Pollinators need flower partners as much as the flowers need them. The pollinator (usually an insect) eats some of the flower pollen and also drinks a sugary liquid called nectar that the flower produces. While it's eating, the pollinator gets the pollen all over itself, carrying it on its body from flower to flower. Everyone's a winner! That's why many flowers are so brightly coloured. It's so they can attract pollinators. It's like a form of TV advertising, saying, "Hey, look at me, over here! I have a sugary drink and, guess what, it's FREE!"

But even after successfully swapping their DNA, plants still have a problem. Their seeds now must be spread out so young plants don't compete for vital nutrients and water with their parents.

Some seeds travel on the wind (such as the helicopter-like seeds of a sycamore tree), some (such as coconuts) by water, and some (such as burrs) by sticking to an animal's fur.

But the most interesting method of all is to package seeds inside a tempting, ready-made meal. That's the real purpose of fruit, from strawberries and apples to peaches and even tomatoes. Fruits are designed by flowering plants to tempt animals to eat them and spread their seeds. When they've been digested, the seeds inside are randomly scattered on the ground in the animal's dung.

By the way, nothing is better for helping seeds grow than a shot of manure in the form of animal dung. It's another great example of natural teamwork in action.

We are now roughly one hundred million years from the present day. Let's see, that's about 11:29pm on our twenty-four-hour clock of Earth's history. That leaves only thirty-one minutes to go. Any sign of humans yet?

Actually, there is a hint of humans, although it's still millions of years before any sign of our ancestors can be seen wandering across the grassy plains of Africa.

Today, people live in vast sprawling urban areas. Some, like Tokyo in Japan, have more than thirty million people. But the idea of millions of the same animal species living close together first appeared long before humans. Welcome to the first insect 'cities' – the giant communities of bees, ants and termites.

Helicopter seeds – which are produced by field maple, Norway maple, sycamore and ash trees – spiral through the air, enabling them to travel out of their parent's shade.

> THE FOLLOWER BEES HAVE INTENSE ANTENNAL CONTACT WITH THE DANCER ... [WHICH] MAY ALLOW THEM TO EXTRACT INFORMATION ABOUT THE LOCATION OF THE FOOD SOURCE ADVERTISED BY THE DANCE.
>
> Kristin Rohrseitz and Jürgen Tautz, entomologists

There are about 20,000 different species of bees alive today. Some – especially honeybees – form highly social groups. It's fascinating to see the similarities between beehives and human cities. Honeybees pass on knowledge from one generation to another. They care for their young, and sometimes they even sacrifice their lives for the group. Also, these little insects do different jobs, dividing what needs to be done among them. These are good examples of how things we assume happen only in the human world can sometimes be seen in the lives of other creatures.

Honeybees also communicate. They talk to each other through the language of dance. When a bee returns to the hive, it tells the others where it has found food by performing a certain type of dance. The 'round dance' means that food is within one hundred metres of the hive and gives directions to get there. The 'waggle dance' can give directions to food as much as six kilometres away. Then there's the 'tremble dance'. This is used to let other bees know a lot of nectar is about to arrive at the hive for processing.

Ants are closely related to honeybees. The oldest fossils of ants' nests date from

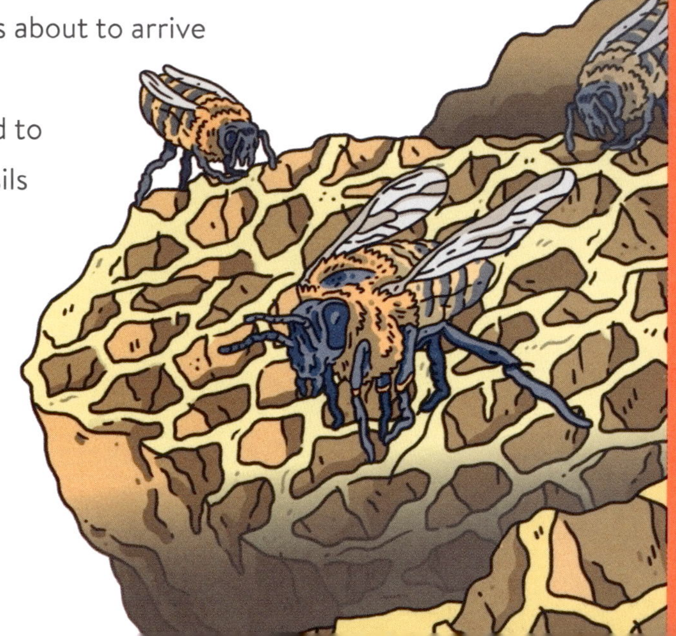

The queen bee lives at the centre of a hive. Worker bees are female and their job is to gather pollen and nectar to make honey. Drones are male and their job is to mate with the queen.

about one hundred million years ago. There are many similarities between ants' nests and honeybees' hives, but ants do not dance. Instead, they communicate through sound, touch and smell. When an ant finds food it will leave a trail of scent along the ground all the way home, to lead others to its source. It finds the way back by remembering certain landmarks, often using the position of the Sun as its guide.

But the prize for the first insects to work out how to live together in giant groups goes to termites. Fossilised termite nests date back 150 million years. Termites create some of the biggest insect cities of all. They often live in colonies that number several million. A queen can lay thousands of eggs a day. She gets so large (sometimes up to ten centimetres long) that she is often unable to move. If she needs more space, a team of worker termites heaves her up and pushes her to a newly built chamber.

Dinosaurs might have been the most successful land animals of their time and insects the most sociable, but there were plenty

Leafcutter ants are gardeners. They cut leaves from a plant and carry them back to the colony to feed a special fungus that grows in 'gardens' in their nest. The ants then dine off the fungus when it is ready to eat!

of other creatures around as well. Mammals are descendants of creatures related to *Dimetrodon* – the one with the sail on its back – and *Lystrosaurus*, the one that survived the Permian Mass Extinction.

Mammals went a lot further than *Dimetrodon* in controlling their temperatures. The ability to keep your body warm when it's cold outside is called being warm-blooded. The theropod dinosaurs were warm-blooded. That's why feathers worked for them. Mammals were warm-blooded, too, but instead of feathers they developed fur.

Many kinds of mammals evolved during dinosaur times. The earliest were mouse-like insect eaters, but by the end of the Cretaceous Period sixty-six million years ago, there were climbing mammals and burrowing mammals and mammals that glided from tree to tree. While one species was sucking down termites, another was digging the meat out of shellfish or munching tasty leaves.

All early mammals had one thing in common: They lived in the shadow of hungry dinosaurs that usually hunted by day and were always looking for their next meal. Probably for that reason, lots of early mammals were nocturnal, which means they were active at

night when it was safer to go out and slept during the day.

Most nocturnal mammals have eyes that contain lots of light-sensitive cells called rods. These help animals like cats see when there's very little light. Some of these same mammals have eyes that are great at detecting movement. They can see their prey darting around even in very low light. Our distant ancestors who shared their world with the likes of *T. rex* probably first developed eyes like this.

Mammals also developed excellent hearing. This allowed them to detect the faintest rustle of a possible meal in leaves and grasses. Much later, a few mammals, such as bats and dolphins, would develop this amazing hearing even more. They use a system called echolocation, allowing them to create a detailed mental picture of the world around them using sound.

Another way nocturnal mammals became pros at night hunting was by growing the smell-interpreting part of their brains. They used their noses to find the yummy food they craved. If you have a cat or dog, you'll know exactly what I mean.

“MOST DINOSAURS WERE ACTIVE DURING THE DAY AND MOST MAMMALS WERE ACTIVE DURING THE NIGHT. BUT IT'S PROBABLY NOT CLEAR CUT.”

Lars Schmitz, evolutionary biologist

The sabre-toothed squirrel was a shrew-like mammal with fangs.

Dinosaurs had dominated life on land for about 180 million years when disaster struck once again and they were wiped out. Only the birds survived. Pterosaurs, the flying reptiles, also vanished. So did the marine reptiles, except for turtles, which somehow survived. It was also the end of the road for the ammonites, those spiral-shaped creatures, relations of today's octopus and squid.

How could this happen? About 66 million years ago, a humongous asteroid about ten kilometres wide hurtled towards Earth. As this city-sized chunk of deadly rock and ice made its final approach, planet Earth would have looked like a sparkling blue and green jewel in the black void of space. Down came the asteroid, possibly splitting up into several pieces before finally smashing into an unsuspecting world.

It hit Earth with the force of thousands of nuclear bombs, blasting a crater more than 160 kilometres wide. Everything in a 1,000-kilometre-wide area was vaporised in seconds, leaving behind an enormous cloud of deathly hot, toxic gas.

The noise and sight of the impact would have deafened and blinded countless living creatures. Many of those not killed by the blast would have been drowned by giant waves created by the impact. Earth was plunged into darkness by thick heavy clouds of rock and dust lasting for as long as a year. Plants all over the world died from lack of sunlight and from a cooling climate. Even on the opposite side of the globe from the impact, animals died of starvation.

Dinosaur times were over, just like that.

Mammals, many of which were well-adapted for living in the dark, were quick off the block once the dinosaurs were gone. Well, it seems quick when you're moving through time as fast as we are. Within five million years, mammals of all shapes and sizes roamed the land. This period of time, from fifty-six to thirty-four million years ago, is called the Eocene (which means 'new dawn' in ancient Greek). Our twenty-four-hour clock of Earth's history shows it's between 11:42 and 11:49pm.

It's now that the ancestors of modern mammals come onto the scene. There were carnivorous predators such as *Andrewsarchus*,

> THE LARGEST MAMMALS EVOLVED WHEN EARTH WAS COOLER AND TERRESTRIAL LAND AREA WAS GREATER.
>
> Felisa A. Smith, biologist

which looked like a wolf but was twenty-two times bigger than its modern cousin. Even more amazing was the 'thunder beast' *Megacerops*. This was one huge plant eater that looked like a rhinoceros but was the size of a modern elephant. But not all Eocene mammals were gigantic. The ancestors of today's horses appeared then, too. One was *Hyracotherium*, which was only as big as a middle-sized dog.

One group of Eocene mammals is of very special interest to us. In fact, creatures from this group – primates – will become the main focus of the next part of our story. Modern primates include monkeys and apes, lemurs and aye-ayes. But the first primates looked more like squirrels. Early primate fossils have been found all over the world.

Around thirty million years ago, during the Oligocene epoch, monkeys emerged in Africa or Asia. Soon after, one or more groups of these monkeys somehow crossed the Atlantic. It's a bit of a

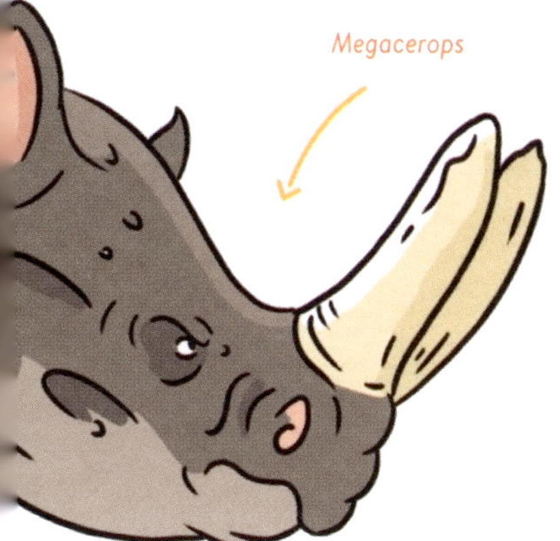

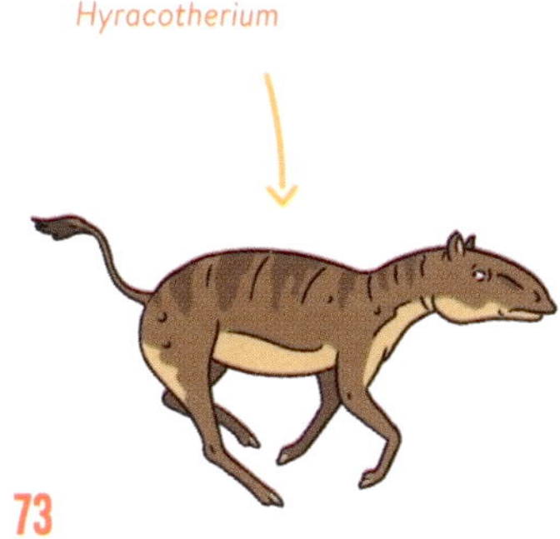

New World monkeys, including this spider monkey, have nostrils that point forward and can swing from trees using their tails.

mystery how they did it. Some experts think they found themselves bobbing on a raft in the middle of the ocean, eventually to be washed ashore on the coast of what is now Brazil. We call the descendants of the monkeys that made this journey New World monkeys. The ones that stayed behind in Africa and Asia are called Old World monkeys. These two main groups of monkeys still exist today.

The New World monkeys of South America use their tails to help them swing and balance in the trees. Some species can happily hang from a branch by their tail alone. It's as if they have an extra hand.

Apes and Old World monkeys evolved from a common ancestor, with apes probably branching off by about twenty-five million years ago. Palaeontologists have found fossils of early apes in Europe, Asia and Africa. So it's hard to figure out where they first appeared. Over time, these early apes evolved into today's great apes –

Old World monkeys, such as this baboon, have narrow noses with nostrils that point downward and sitting pads on their buttocks.

orangutans, gorillas, chimpanzees, bonobos and humans.

Yes, you are an ape! Biologists have discovered that the DNA in you and me is ninety-eight per cent the same as the DNA of other great apes. And they've worked out that humans and chimpanzees have a common ancestor that probably lived some time between six and eight million years ago. That's not long ago when you look at our clock. After all, it is only about two minutes before midnight.

Apes, such as this orangutan, have no tails and more complex brains than monkeys.

4

HANDS FREE

5 million – 12,000 years ago

Walking apes to migrating humans

4 MILLION YEARS AGO
The first human ancestors walk upright in Africa.

3 MILLION YEARS AGO
South and North America link up, changing the world's climate.

1.5 MILLION YEARS AGO
Early human species begin eating cooked food, likely using fire started by lightning.

300,000 YEARS AGO
Homo sapiens emerges in Africa as a new human species.

65,000 YEARS AGO
Modern humans reach Australia after rafting over shallow seas.

40,000 YEARS AGO
Neanderthals go extinct.

21,000 YEARS AGO
The last ice age reaches its peak.

About 23,000 years ago, during the last ice age, Siberia (in what is now Russia) was warmer than the surrounding areas. It is here that humans and wolves first worked together and wolves began to evolve into dogs.

A lot of people are talking about climate change these days. It's a big deal because the world is warming up and the ice caps are melting. This is especially bad news if you happen to be a coral reef or a polar bear.

But it's bad news for humans, too. The less ice at the poles, the more water in the seas. And that makes the water rise higher up on the land. One day there could be no ice left at all, and if that happens, the seas would be sixty-six metres higher than they are today. That means that if forty-two football players stood on one another's shoulders on a present-day beach, even the top one would need to be wearing scuba gear. Seas that high would swamp most of the world's coastal communities and some countries would disappear entirely. Millions of people would have to leave their homes.

But for Earth, being ice-free is pretty normal. For most of Earth's history there have been no ice caps at all and the seas have been as high as that sixty-six-metre level. Every so often, things would change and the world would get colder and the seas lower (remember Snowball Earth?). Then they would get warmer again.

About three million years ago, the world only had one big ice cap – on Antarctica. Then something pretty major happened. The tectonic plate that carries South America met the tectonic plate that carries North America. The two continents ended up attached by a thin piece of land that today is part of the country of Panama.

This new land connection forced Atlantic sea currents to flow northwards. As a result, a

Higher temperatures are causing ice to melt earlier in spring and refreeze later in autumn. That means it's harder for polar bears to find solid ice, which is crucial for resting, breeding and standing on while hunting.

4. HANDS FREE

5 million – 12,000 years ago

new climate system spluttered into life. It pumped warm air north and made winters warmer in north-west Europe by at least ten degrees Celsius. The warmer water in the North Atlantic started to evaporate more quickly. Water vapour travelling north collided with cold air in the Arctic, where there was probably already a little ice. The vapour fell as snow, landing on the ice and the cold water around it. Over time, the snow settled in layers and formed thick packs of ice. By about 2.5 million years ago Earth was wearing a second big ice cap, this time in the Arctic.

With huge ice sheets now on both poles, Earth plunged into a super-deep freeze. Colossal glaciers spread southwards from the North Pole. Sea levels plummeted because so much water was trapped as ice. Earth was in the grips of an ice age. And here's the

The Perito Moreno glacier in Argentina is mysterious. Experts don't understand why it is in equilibrium – with as much ice being added as being lost – while most of the other glaciers in the world are retreating because of warming temperatures.

amazing thing: it still is. This whole time, since the glaciers started forming almost three million years ago, Earth has been in a cool spell. It hasn't stayed exactly the same temperature all that time, of course. It's warmed and cooled and warmed again. Glaciers have crept onto the continents then pulled back then crept up again. But all that time, Earth has had two large ice caps. Just in case you were wondering, we're now in a warm time in the ice age. It's known as an interglacial period, and it's getting warmer fast.

Do you know what else happened over that time? Humans, that's what. Human ancestors had already appeared about a million years before the deep freeze started. But we modern humans evolved during this ice age, and that has made all the difference to our story.

Lucy was an ape who lived in what is now Ethiopia in Africa about 3.2 million years ago. She was discovered in 1974 by a team of scientists headed by Donald Johanson. They gave her a woman's name because her skeleton was small, which they guessed meant she was female. They called her Lucy because

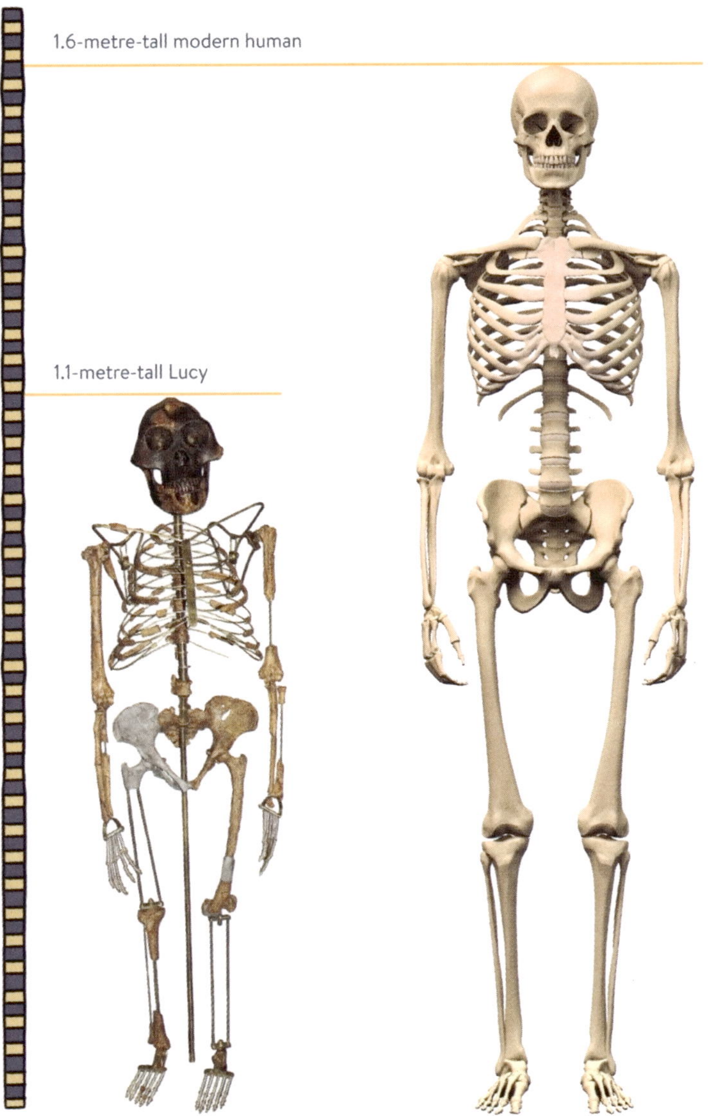

Lucy's bones suggest that she would have had much stronger arms for her size than a modern human so she might have lived a life that involved a lot of tree climbing. It has even been suggested that she died from a fall.

when they were celebrating the find, the team was listening to the Beatles song 'Lucy in the Sky with Diamonds'. Her species name is *Australopithecus afarensis*.

Lucy was about 1.1 metres tall and weighed about twenty-nine kilograms. When her discovery was announced to the world, Lucy caused a sensation. Why? Because experts could tell from the shape of her bones that she definitely walked on two feet, and humans are the only modern apes that do that consistently. Since then, fossils of 300 more individual *Australopithecus afarensis* have been found.

No one is quite sure what it was that made apes like Lucy stand upright, but it turned out to be a great advantage. With their hands free, they could carry food more easily, helping them survive even when times were tough. Being hands free means you can carry tools, too. And think how much easier it would be to hunt with a spear or to carry nuts wrapped in animal skin.

But was Lucy human? If being human means belonging to a group of apes that walks on two feet, then Lucy counts. But if it's about having big brains, then we must wait another million years or so for our sort of creature: *Homo*.

The first species that most experts feel comfortable calling human was *Homo habilis*. Its brain was 500–800 cubic centimetres, nearly twice the size of Lucy's (although still only half the size of our own brains). This species was very good at making tools. That's why *Homo habilis* marks the beginning of what is known as

> "NOW, WHEN WE IMAGINE LUCY WALKING AROUND THE EAST AFRICAN LANDSCAPE LOOKING FOR FOOD, WE CAN FOR THE FIRST TIME IMAGINE HER WITH A STONE TOOL IN HAND AND LOOKING FOR MEAT."
>
> Shannon McPherron, archaeologist

the Old Stone Age. It's about 2.4 million years ago and just forty-five seconds to midnight on our twenty-four-hour clock of Earth's history. The age of humans has finally begun.

Now let's fast forward about 600,000 years. Enter *Homo erectus*. Skulls of these humans show a second dramatic increase in brain size to about 750–1,300 cubic centimetres, almost as large as the brains of humans today. What on earth was going on?

There is an ancient Greek myth that tells the story of a divine being called Prometheus. He stole the fire of the gods and smuggled it down to Earth in the stalk of a plant.

The stone tool on the left was made by *Homo habilis* about 2.4 million years ago. The one on the right was made more than 1.7 million years ago by *Homo erectus*.

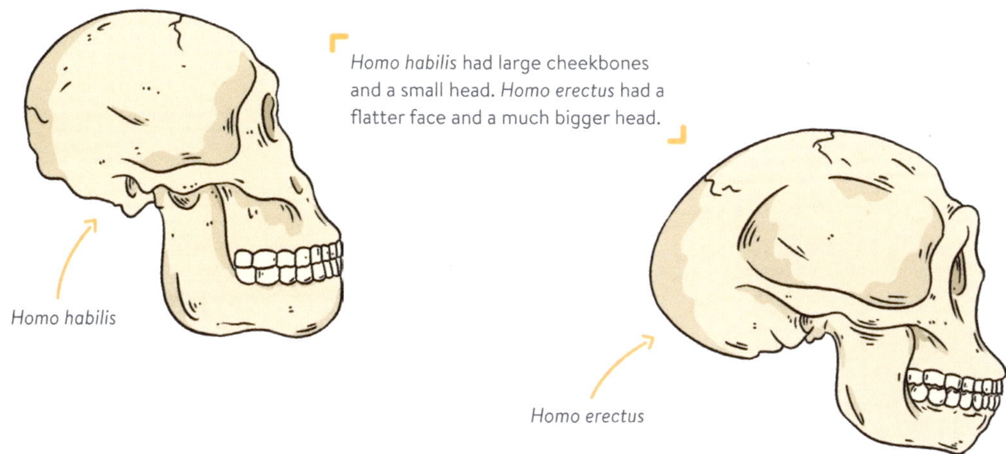

Homo habilis had large cheekbones and a small head. *Homo erectus* had a flatter face and a much bigger head.

Prometheus was severely punished for his crime. When the king of the gods, Zeus, found out, Prometheus was tied to a rock. Each day an eagle was sent to peck out his liver. Each night his liver would grow back so that it could be pecked out again when the eagle returned the next day.

The story of Prometheus is a myth. But to the best of our knowledge, it is a fact that no creature anywhere in the world other than human beings has ever been able deliberately to start a fire from scratch. We don't know when they began to do this or which species was the first. There is evidence from about one million years ago, but scientists think humans may have started intentionally using and controlling fires as long as 1.5 million years ago, or even more.

Fire scares away dangerous wild animals and provides warmth in colder climates. Perhaps that's why humans first wanted to control fires. But all the evidence suggests that, from the very beginning, fire served another, even more important, function in the lives of ancient humans.

Neuroscientist Suzana Herculano-Houzel studies the human brain. She has found a way to measure the number of brain cells inside our heads. It turns out that on average a modern adult

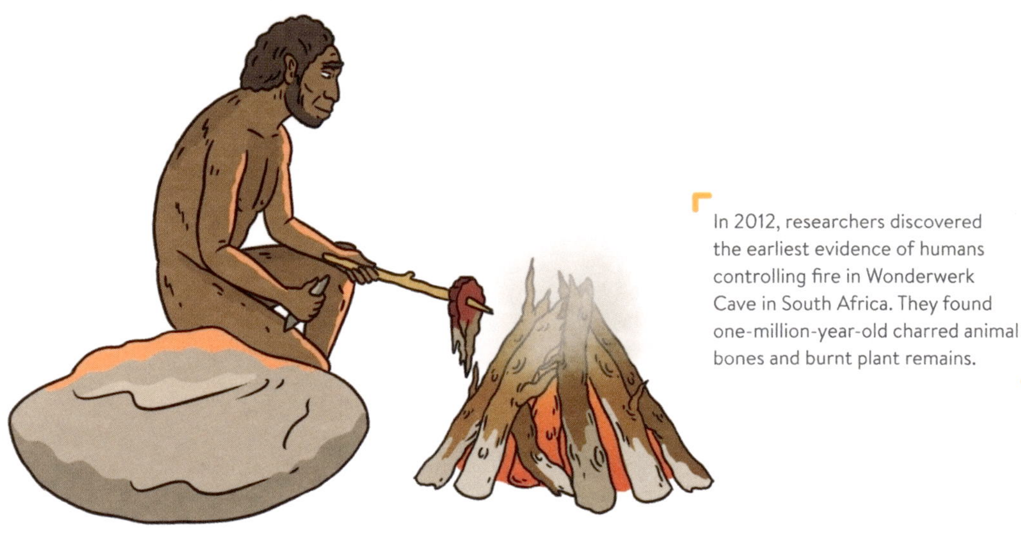

In 2012, researchers discovered the earliest evidence of humans controlling fire in Wonderwerk Cave in South Africa. They found one-million-year-old charred animal bones and burnt plant remains.

human has eighty-six billion neurons, the main type of brain cell. A chimpanzee has only about twenty-eight billion.

So the question is this: how come humans have so many brain cells? Dr Herculano-Houzel believes cooking is the key. That's because brains take a lot of energy. Modern humans use twenty per cent of all the energy we eat to fuel our big brains. Cooked food is easier to chew and digest, so it takes less energy from the body to absorb its fuel and nutrients. That means we could take in enough food to fuel a bigger brain. So the beginning of cooking was a gigantic breakthrough.

Here's a puzzle, though. What made these ancient people even think of the idea of cooking? A few modern animals make use of naturally occurring fires. They prey on small animals who run from the flames and eggs that are exposed when the grass around them burns. Some, including Australia's fire bird, will even pick up a burning stick from one fire and use it to start a new fire elsewhere.

> "IF WE STILL FED LIKE OTHER PRIMATES DO – WHICH MUST HAVE BEEN HOW OUR ANCESTORS GOT HOLD OF CALORIES – WE WOULD HAVE TO EAT [FOR] 9.5 HOURS EVERY DAY."
>
> Suzana Herculano-Houzel, neuroscientist

Some scientists think early humans were among those who hunted on the edges of brush fires. These people might have tasted some eggs made more delicious and digestible by having been heated by the fire. Maybe they even saw birds moving fire. Could some of that have given them the idea of taking a burning stick from a natural fire, transferring that flame to some wood or dry animal dung, and carefully tending this new fire in a ring of stones, ready to cook food when it was available?

The human brain is responsible for a huge variety of tasks, from movement to vision, memory to emotion.

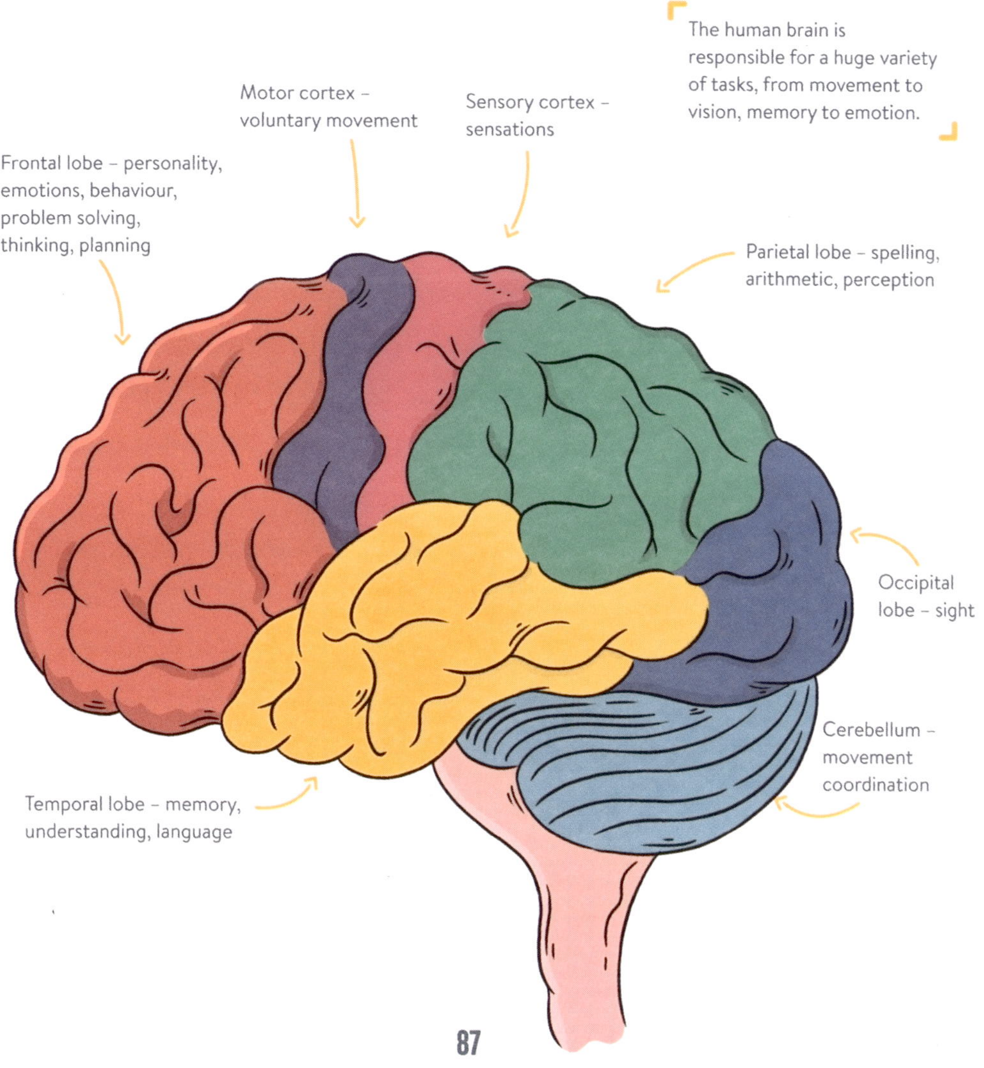

Homo erectus
1.9 million–140,000 years ago,
Africa and Asia

Homo naledi
335,000–236,000 years ago,
Africa

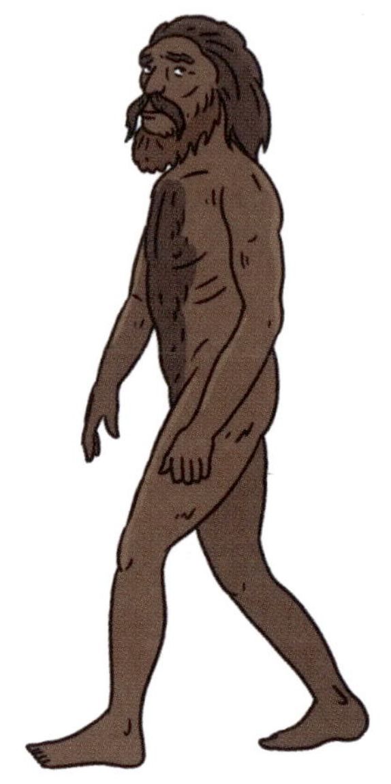

Homo heidelbergensis
About 700,000–200,000 years ago,
Europe, Asia and Africa

Around the time people started eating cooked food, ancient humans became big travellers. The earliest *Homo erectus* fossils are from Java, in what is now Indonesia. They date to 1.9 million years ago. So *Homo erectus* might have evolved in Asia from an ape that had travelled from Africa. But *Homo erectus* fossils have also been found in Africa, so maybe it evolved there and migrated to Asia. Either way we are talking about thousands of miles of travel. How could our early ancestors have gone all that way without roads and tracks, let alone cars, boats or planes? It is hard for us to imagine walking such enormous distances. But they did have one huge advantage over us today – they were not in a hurry.

In 1856, quarry workers in the Neander Valley in Germany found what looked like human bones. But they weren't quite like our bones. They belonged to another species of human, Neanderthals, which first appear in the fossil record about 400,000 years ago. Since then, many Neanderthal sites have been found.

Experts think that between 400,000 and 70,000 years ago, at least five different species of humans were living on the planet. There were *Homo erectus*, *Homo neanderthalensis*, *Homo heidelbergensis*, *Homo naledi*, *Homo floresiensis* (a small hobbit-like species) and *Homo sapiens* (that's us!).

Neanderthals are the extinct humans most like us. Their brains were at least the same size as those of modern humans. Some might have had even bigger brains. Neanderthals were stronger

Homo neanderthalensis
About 400,000–40,000 years ago, Europe and Asia

Homo sapiens
About 200,000 years ago to today
All over the world

Homo floresiensis 100,000–50,000 years ago, Asia

This museum exhibit of a Neanderthal family is from the Neanderthal Museum in Krapina, Croatia. It is based on remains found in a cave in southwestern France.

than we are and had big noses and foreheads that sloped back above jutting eyebrows.

Neanderthals built houses from animal bones and were great tool users. Recent evidence shows that their hands were at least as nimble as ours. And their stone tools have been found in many places we know they lived, including all over Europe and near Jerusalem, in Israel.

They often put precious objects in the graves of those they loved, maybe to help them on to the next life. They made art, too. In 2018, archaeologists discovered paintings on the walls of caves in Spain that date back to 65,000 years, before *Homo sapiens* arrived in the area. They think Neanderthals were the artists. Plus, in 2018 and 2021, archaeologists working on Neanderthal sites found animal bones with regular notches in them. Much later humans used this sort of tool to keep track of numbers. Perhaps Neanderthals did too.

And there's one more thing: in 1989, a Neanderthal hyoid bone was found in a cave in Israel. The hyoid connects our tongues to our throats and allows humans to speak and sing. So probably Neanderthals could speak.

Making weapons and tools, chatting, holding funerals and creating art are all things that require brainpower, creativity and skill. The evidence suggests that these ancient people were asking some very important and very human questions. Is there life after death? How do I care for the people around me? What brings me good luck? These are the questions of curious minds that feel very much like our own.

Sit still and do nothing at all for just four seconds. Go on. Do it now... Now sit still and do nothing for twenty-four hours. OK – I don't expect you actually to do that. But try to imagine it anyway.

It is now a bit less than four seconds before midnight on our twenty-four-hour clock. That long twenty-four hours is how much of Earth's history passed before the first *Homo sapiens* could be heard calling across the hot, dusty African plains. You see, compared with Earth, humans are *very* young indeed. We are called *sapiens* because in Latin the word means 'wise' or 'full of knowledge'. Once you have finished this book, you can decide if you think it's a good name.

Modern humans and Neanderthals lived near one another across Asia and Europe for many thousands of years. They mixed enough so that most modern humans of Asian or European descent have between one and four per cent Neanderthal DNA.

To find the origin of the rest of human DNA, we must look to other sources. But which one is still a matter of debate. Some scientists think we're mostly descended from *Homo erectus*. Others think *Homo heidelbergensis* was involved. However it happened, the first members of our species, *Homo sapiens*, appeared in Africa about 300,000 years ago. By between 200,000 and 160,000 years ago, they had become what is called 'modern humans', people who looked and acted like us.

We humans are a restless lot. Have you noticed that although most people live in one place, they don't stay there all the time? I am reminded of this every time I sit in a traffic jam or go to the airport. Why, oh why, do so many people spend so much time trying to

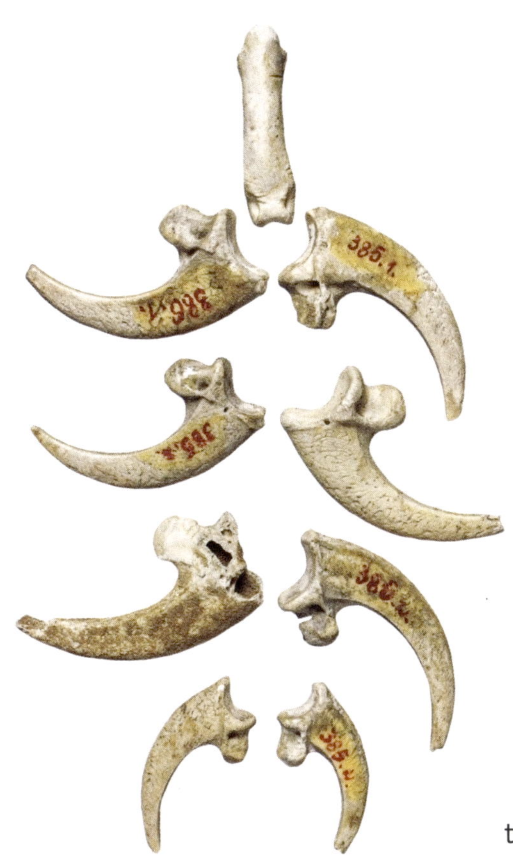

These polished eagle talons may well be a Neanderthal's necklace from about 130,000 years ago. They were discovered in present-day Croatia. *Homo sapiens* made jewellery at about the same time.

move from one place to another? Now I get it. Being constantly on the move is deeply woven into our nature.

We've seen that human ancestors travelled thousands of kilometres almost two million years ago. About 120,000 years ago, *Homo sapiens* started to do the same thing, with different groups migrating beyond Africa at different times.

DNA research shows *Homo sapiens* were quite diverse even before they spread out from Africa. They may have had slightly different face shapes, hair textures and skin colours. And they also had differences that were less easy to see from the outside, such as what diseases they might suffer from. Over time those differences would evolve to become the rich diversity of humans today.

Homo sapiens travelled all over the world. They trekked to the Middle East, where they started mixing with Neanderthals. Then they swept across the rest of Asia.

About 65,000 years ago, people first paddled ashore in Australia. The seas were much lower back then, thanks to water being locked up in ice sheets. So the distance they had to travel on rafts was far less than it would be today. People also headed west to

Europe, arriving about 50,000 years ago. They travelled around the edge of the Pacific ocean by boat, too, arriving in the Americas by at least 30,000 years ago.

As *Homo sapiens* settled around the world, other human species were vanishing. The last Neanderthals died out sometime between 40,000 and 28,000 years ago. No one is quite sure why other human species who lived at the same time as *Homo sapiens* went extinct. Did we kill them off? Did we eat all of the available food? Did some deadly disease come along that affected only them and not us? We don't know. But some experts think it all had to do with a volcanic eruption.

It was 74,000 years ago and Earth's inhabitants were going about their business when a volcano erupted in what is now Indonesia. This was no normal volcano. It wasn't even a normal supervolcano. It was the eruption of Mount Toba, the very biggest volcanic eruption of the past two million years. Ash filled the skies, global temperatures dropped, less rain fell. The climate bounced back in five to ten years, but that is a long time if you are struggling to find something to eat. Plants died and so did animals that ate them. For a long time, some scientists thought this must have been a time of disaster for humans, and it would have been if we were living in the Northern Hemisphere.

In 2021 a group of environmental scientists figured out that when Mount Toba erupted, it affected the climate in different parts of the world in different ways. It got much colder and drier in Europe, where most Neanderthals lived, and also in central Asia and North America. But *Homo sapiens* were lucky. Lots of us lived in eastern and southern

There are several ways to measure the strength of a volcanic eruption. One is to estimate the amount of material that is ejected by it, measured in cubic kilometres. That's a cube measuring one kilometre on each side. Mt. Toba ejected 2,800 times as much material as Mt. St. Helens.

Mt. St. Helens, USA
1980
1 km³

Mt. Tambora, Indonesia
1815
80 km³

Mt. Toba, Indonesia
About 74,000 years ago
2,800 km³

Africa and in India, where the climate changed only a little. We survived and thrived.

For most of human history, most people moved from place to place to find food. A person who travels all their life is called a nomad, and the way they live is known as nomadic. Such people don't own much. The more they have, the more they have to carry. Sharing makes for a better way of life.

The most important thing to carry with you on a long trek is water. You never know

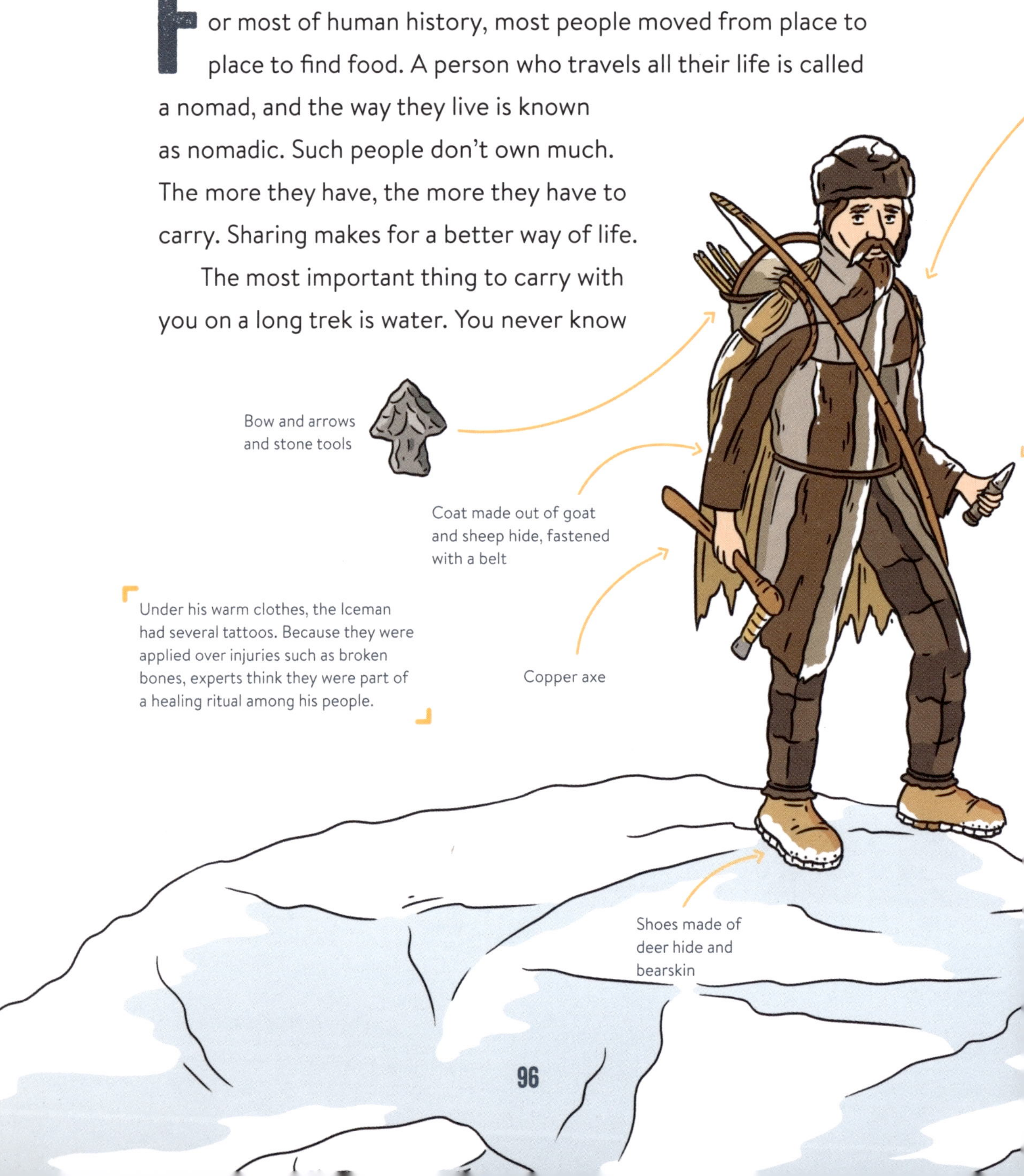

Under his warm clothes, the Iceman had several tattoos. Because they were applied over injuries such as broken bones, experts think they were part of a healing ritual among his people.

Rucksack

when you'll find a stream, but you know you are sure to get thirsty. To solve that problem, prehistoric humans dried gourds, vegetables belonging to the same family as pumpkins. When they're dried, their shells harden, and the seeds and fibre inside can be removed to leave a perfect water container. Prehistoric nomads used plenty of those.

They would also carry spears or bows and arrows for hunting. They had flint tools for skinning dead animals and lighting fires.

Dagger

One of the best-preserved examples of a prehistoric nomad is Ötzi the Iceman. Two German holidaymakers unexpectedly bumped into him while walking in the Italian Alps in the summer of 1991. It was quite a shock to find a dead body in the ice. However, it turned out that this wasn't a recent murder victim, but a body that had been frozen in the ground, on the edge of a glacier, for more than 5,000 years.

Now 5,000 years ago is a *lot* more recent than 30,000 years ago. But still, Ötzi provides some good clues as to what an ancient nomadic life might have been like.

Ötzi's body froze soon after he died, so it was preserved as a mummy. No one knows why he was walking in the mountains or where he was going, but close to his body was a prehistoric rucksack. It had everything he needed for his journey. There was a copper axe, arrows for hunting and a blade sharpener. He even had a birch bark tube for carrying embers to light fires. Ötzi was clearly an expert mountaineer.

Over the last 2.6 million years, glaciers have come and gone, sometimes covering the northern parts of the world for thousands of years at a time. Each swing of the climate, from warm to cool or cool to warm, changed the environment. With their homes and food sources changing, some species died out and others evolved.

When Earth was warming up from a frozen time called the last glacial maximum, the story should have been the same. But it wasn't. Dozens of large mammals were alive and well when the warming started. Some of them had existed for tens of millions of years. Yet, between about 13,000 years ago and about 8,000 years ago, most of the biggest died out. This disaster is known as the Pleistocene Extinction, named after the era when it happened.

In North and South America, horses, big cats, elephants, mammoths and mastodons, camels, great bears, giant beavers, peccaries (pig-like mammals), giant ground sloths and the glyptodont – an armadillo the size of a pick-up truck – all mysteriously disappeared. In all, about three-quarters of the large mammals became extinct. When the Pleistocene Extinction was over, very few animals in the Americas were bigger than a turkey. Even the beavers and bears that made it through the crisis were smaller cousins of those giants that once existed.

Pretty much the same thing happened in Australia, although the extinctions there started earlier. Victims included the giant kangaroo, a rhino-sized wombat and its relatives, and a fierce

Imagine bumping into a three-metre-long glyptodont. It had the heaviest armour plate protection of any ice age creature. By 10,000 years ago these giants had gone extinct like many other large animals around the world.

marsupial lion. Huge reptiles died off, too, including the giant horned tortoise and some gigantic crocodiles.

Large animals went extinct in other parts of the world as well. The southern half of Africa lost fewer than the rest. But even there about one in every six big mammal species went extinct.

Experts find this whole worldwide extinction event puzzling. What was going on? When scientists are working out a puzzle, they

THE GREAT TRAGEDY OF SCIENCE – THE SLAYING OF A BEAUTIFUL HYPOTHESIS BY AN UGLY FACT. ”

Thomas Henry Huxley, biologist

start with a hypothesis, a guess based on the evidence they have. One hypothesis to explain the Pleistocene Extinction is that a period of worldwide global warming caused large animals to lose habitat. But climate alone doesn't explain the timing of some of the extinctions.

Another hypothesis is that humans were to blame. Could humans like Ötzi have hunted all these giants to extinction? Or did we burn so many animal habitats so quickly that the animals couldn't adapt? This hypothesis might explain why elephants, rhinos and big cats survived in Africa when similar animals went extinct elsewhere. African animals and humans had evolved together over millions of years. Could they have found a balance that let both survive?

The point of having a hypothesis is to test it against other

Percentage of large mammals that went extinct after the Pleistocene Extinction

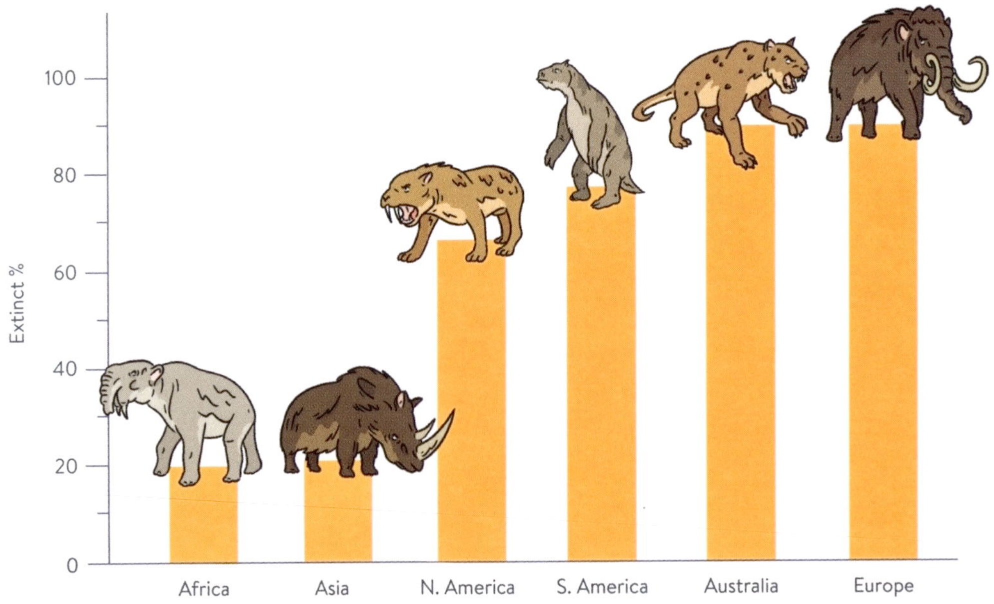

In 2018, palaeontologists announced the discovery of an 11,000-year-old fossilised human footprint right in the footprint of a *Megatherium*. The layered prints are evidence that humans chased this elephant-sized sloth.

evidence, to ask questions that might prove or disprove it. For example, if humans caused the extinction, why did Africa lose any animals at all? As often happens in science, we don't know all the answers. We just have to keep making hypotheses and questioning them. There could be more than one cause. Perhaps humans and climate change are both to blame for the Pleistocene Extinction.

The part we played at the beginning of the last second to midnight on the twenty-four-hour clock of Earth's history may have been our first big impact on Earth's environment. It was not to be the last.

When humans turned from hunting and gathering to farming and herding, one of their first herd animals was the goat. Those in the photo have climbed an argan tree in Morocco to eat its fruit.

5

SEEDS of CHANGE

38,000 – 2000 BCE
Farming, writing, and trade

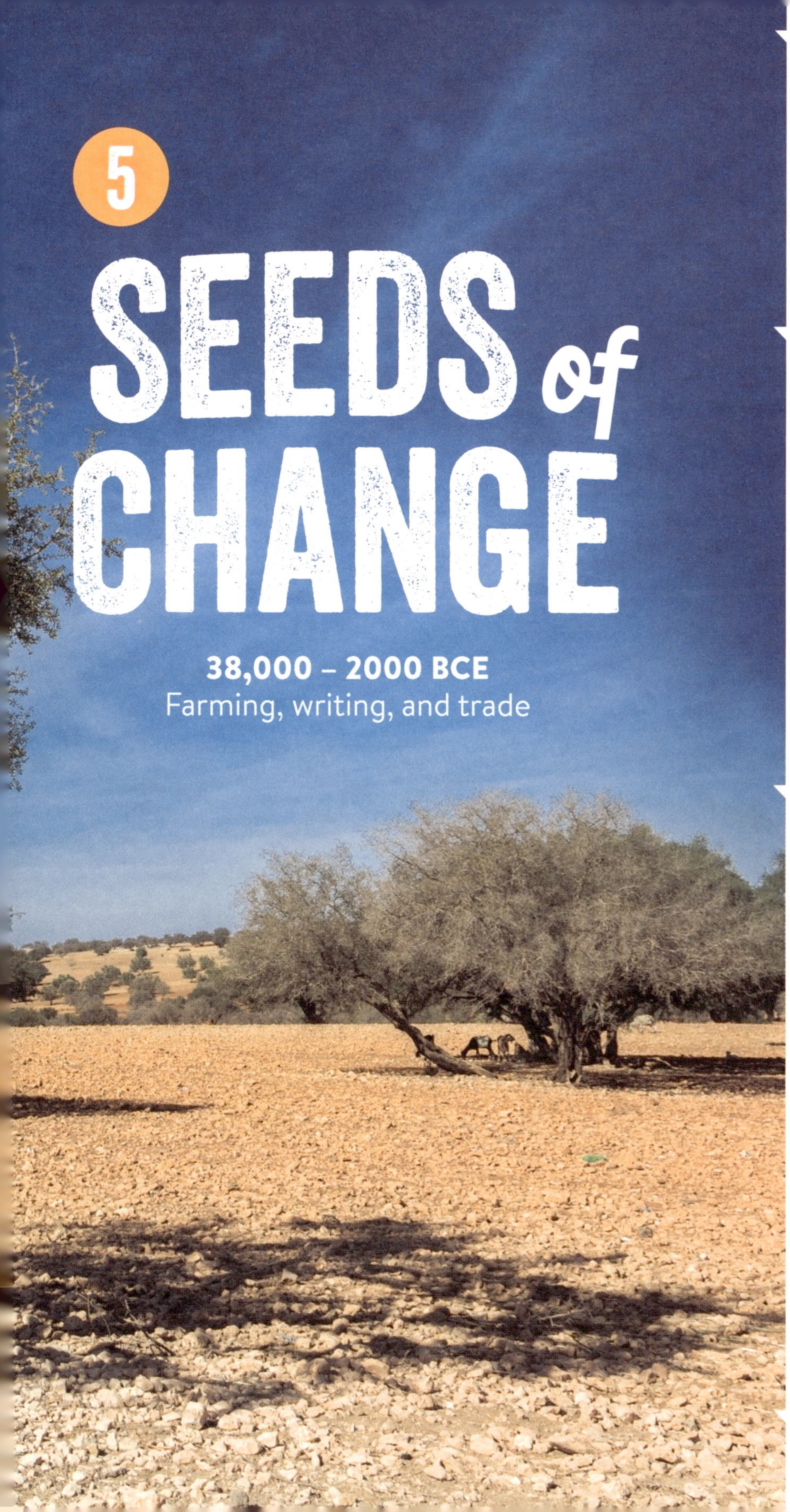

ABOUT 38,000 BCE
Humans and dogs started living and working together.

7000 BCE
People started farming.

5000 BCE
Nubians build the first astronomy observatory at Nabta Playa.

3400 BCE
First written languages.

3300 BCE
First wheeled vehicles.

2000 BCE
The Epic of Gilgamesh is written down for the first time.

Imagine living in a world where there are no shops selling food. In this world there are no fields or farms, no breakfast cereal, no cakes, no cauliflower. You and your family live off wild fruits, nuts, roots, and leaves. You scavenge leftovers from animals killed by predators. You roast meat or fish on a fire after a successful hunt or fishing expedition. This was the way people lived for most of human history.

At this time, most of the people in the world were nomadic like Ötzi the Iceman. Because they traveled around a lot, they owned no more stuff than they could carry. They didn't even have bags until 14,000 years ago, so they tied their belongings together in a bundle. Some people are still nomadic, but only a very few. That's because of a crazy new idea that first appeared about 11,000 years ago.

Some of the first people to try out a different way of life lived in an area of the Middle East known as the Fertile Crescent. This was a rich land with just the right amount of rain for growing things. Forests of oak and pistachio trees thrived. People known as Natufians had settled near the coast of what is now Syria, Lebanon, and Israel. The sea provided them with fish. They also went up into the nearby hills to gather the seeds of wild grasses.

There were so many good things to eat that these people didn't need to be nomadic. They settled in small villages in round mud and clay huts and hunted and gathered food from the land and sea around them. In some seasons they would hunt for wild animals, such as gazelles.

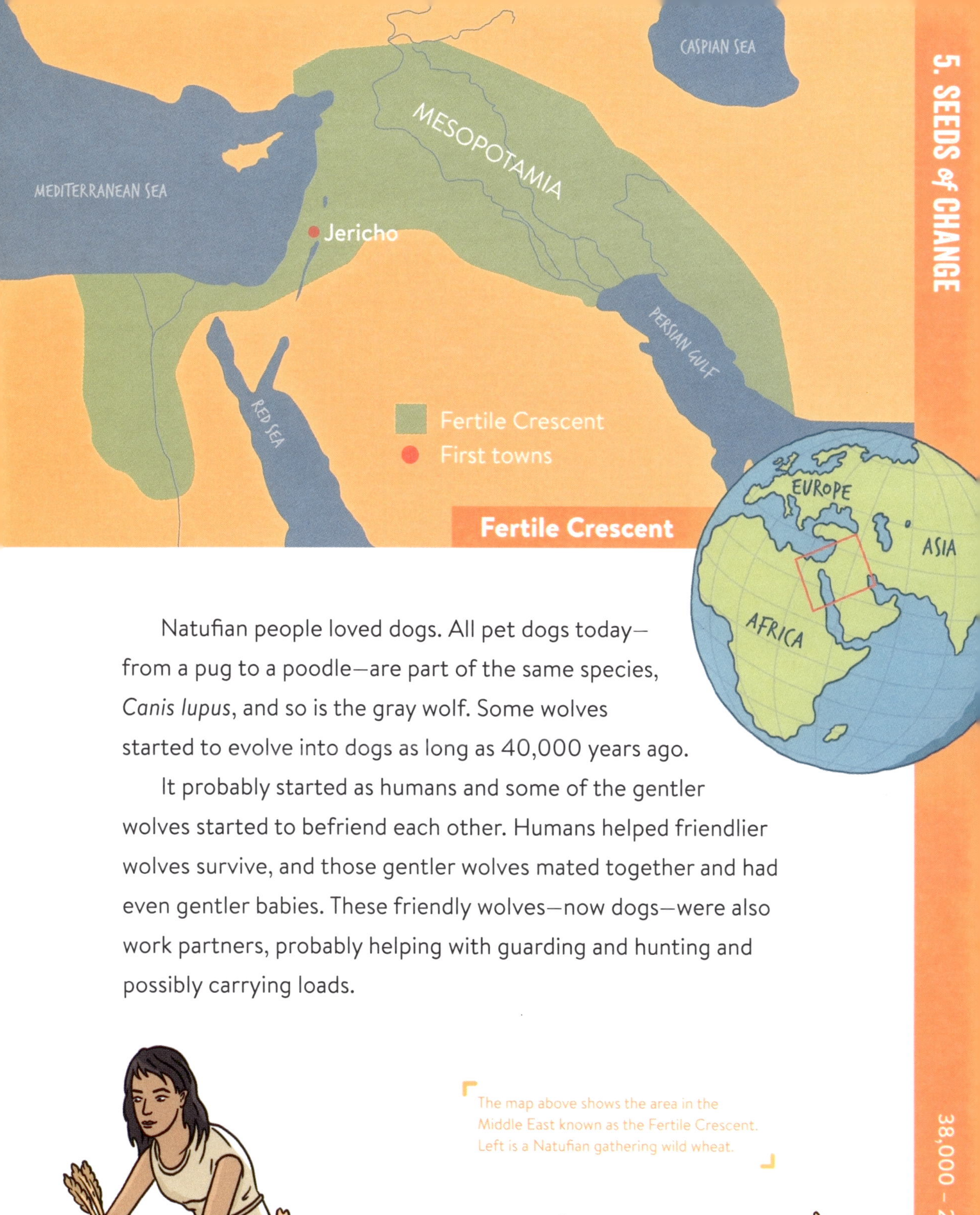

Natufian people loved dogs. All pet dogs today—from a pug to a poodle—are part of the same species, *Canis lupus*, and so is the gray wolf. Some wolves started to evolve into dogs as long as 40,000 years ago.

It probably started as humans and some of the gentler wolves started to befriend each other. Humans helped friendlier wolves survive, and those gentler wolves mated together and had even gentler babies. These friendly wolves—now dogs—were also work partners, probably helping with guarding and hunting and possibly carrying loads.

The map above shows the area in the Middle East known as the Fertile Crescent. Left is a Natufian gathering wild wheat.

We don't know for sure what work Natufian dogs did—or if they did any at all. All we know is that graves have been found in which dogs have been buried side by side with their humans. As a dog lover myself, knowing that makes me feel close to these people from the far distant past.

So there they were, living a fairly easy life for about 2,000 years, when somebody (we don't know who) had an idea. These descendants of the Natufians started intentionally breeding animals and growing plants, not just hunting and foraging for wild ones. This was a tremendously big deal. We call it agriculture, or farming. But the seeds they grew were very different from the seeds farmers use today.

Our pet dogs all evolved from ancestors of the Eurasian wolf (above). Humans likely didn't breed them on purpose. Instead, dogs and humans evolved side by side in a process called coevolution.

In the wild, seeds from grasses like wheat need to be as light as possible and loosely attached to the stalk. That way they have the best chance of being blown far and wide on the wind. But small seeds that fall easily to the ground are a nightmare for people gathering the seeds to grind, cook, and eat. Instead, they want big seeds that stay firmly attached to the stalk. If a grain of wheat gets blown away by the wind, you won't be able to use it for food because it's gone—poof! And once you start planting seeds yourself and not just relying on nature to do it, you need to be able to save

some seeds to plant for next year's crop, too.

So how did early farmers get bigger seeds? Looking back, it seems pretty simple, but of course somebody had to think of it. Over thousands of years, farmers saved the biggest seeds that stuck most firmly to the stalk and planted those the following year. Over time, this careful choosing changed the wheat.

This process is called artificial selection, or breeding. Almost all the foods we buy at the grocery store today are unlike their original forms. Animals and plants we use for food have been domesticated, which means humans have changed them from their wild forms. In most cases, our food has been changed to make it look better, taste more delicious, or just be easier to grow and store.

Once people in the Fertile Crescent started storing wheat, saving it to eat later or to plant the following year, mice began invading the wheat stores. And once there were mice, wild cats moved in to munch on the abundance of prey. That is the beginning of the domestic cat, which came to live near humans because that's where the food was.

Cats became human companions much later than dogs did. They earned their place in our hearts by getting rid of the mice and other pests that were eating our food.

Not long after the start of wheat farming in the Fertile Crescent, people began farming rice in southern China and India. Rice is an incredible crop. It can grow in both very wet and fairly dry areas, so that means different types of land can be turned into rice fields. Rice gave the people who grew it the ability to support large populations.

At about the same time that rice farming appeared in southern China, people along the Yellow River up north started growing millet, another grass. Chinese and Indian farmers bred rice and millet just the way farmers in the Fertile Crescent bred wheat.

Could any of these farmers have learned from or even taught one another? We cannot know for sure, but it's completely possible that these groups all invented farming independently. After all, at just about the same time, people in the Americas started farming, too. And we can be sure that nobody was traveling between the Americas and the rest of the world that long ago. People in these two areas didn't even know one another existed!

Rice is the most important crop for more than half of the world's population today.

So, what were ancient Americans growing? The first crops they farmed were potatoes, beans, squash, peanuts, and corn, which is also known as maize. Maize was probably domesticated in southern Mexico, starting with a grass called teosinte.

A teosinte ear has just five to ten seeds. Each seed is coated in a hard shell. That was great for wild teosinte seeds that could survive a journey through the insides of the most acidic animal stomach.

Teosinte, a wild grass, is the ancestor of corn.

It wasn't so great for people who wanted breakfast, though. So farmers chose those plants with an unusually large number of seeds as well as those with the softest shells. Eventually they were able to turn teosinte into the highly nutritious crop we know today as corn.

The farming of domesticated corn seeds spread north and south. People of the Andes Mountains in South America grew it. And so did people all the way up in what is now Canada. Today, people and animals both eat corn. It's the biggest seed crop in the world and is grown on every continent except Antarctica.

In the 1500s, the Spanish Franciscan friar Bernardino de Sahagún lived in what is now Mexico. Here are some of his illustrations of Indigenous corn farmers.

Another food we can thank ancient Mexicans for was chocolate. The Olmec civilization was the first to domesticate the cacao tree. Cacao seeds have a chemical called theobromine in them, which helps you stay alert. The word theobromine means "food of the gods." It was given this name because it was sacred to the Mesoamerican people, the cultural group that lived in southern Mexico and parts of Central America.

If you have ever sneaked a taste of unsweetened baking chocolate, you know that chocolate by itself is very bitter. That's how the Mesoamericans liked it. They drank it unsweetened for thousands of years before Europeans came along and decided to add sugar and extra fat and later to make it into bars.

How do we know what people ate in the distant past? Well, sometimes we are lucky enough to find their leftovers. Archaeologists working in Chiapas, Mexico, found pieces of 4,000-year-old pottery with the remains of a chocolate drink in it. And archaeologists working in China found a pot containing 4,000-year-old noodles.

Cacao seed pods are harvested twice a year. The beans and pulp inside are scooped out and left to ferment to develop the flavor. Next, the beans are dried out and roasted. Their shells are removed, leaving behind "nibs." Grinding the nibs results in cocoa mass and cocoa butter. Nowadays, additional ingredients such as sugar and milk (for milk chocolate) are then added to create chocolate.

Obsidian is natural glass that forms when lava from a volcano cools quickly. It was a very precious material because it was brilliant for cutting animal skins to make clothes. Obsidian occurs naturally in the rocky hills of central Turkey, but experts have found carefully shaped pieces hundreds of miles away in ancient Jericho. How did they get there?

Jericho is one of the world's oldest towns. It was founded by Natufians and has been lived in continuously for about 11,000 years. Round houses from 9,000 years ago had more than one room and open spaces for cooking and washing. These early buildings were built on solid foundations, with stone floors and walls made of clay bricks. Each home had its own special corner for storing food.

As farmers bred better crops, they were able to grow more than enough food to feed their families. This meant that even in places less rich in food than the Fertile Crescent, people could now swap extra food for useful or beautiful things other people had made. It even meant that some people didn't have to farm at all. Instead, people who made things could trade them to farmers in exchange for food.

Well, what if you had been a wheat farmer in Jericho at that time? Perhaps you might have thought about swapping some of your precious seeds

These super-sharp tools, dating from 5,000 years ago, are made out of a natural glass called obsidian.

for a knife made of that natural obsidian glass found only in some far-off land? And if you wanted one, maybe your neighbor did, too.

Merchants are people who buy goods and then sell them. This is called trade. When merchants started trading across long distances, they needed ways to transport their goods, usually with domesticated animals. And of course they needed plenty of goods to trade. Eventually, trade led to a form of exchange very familiar to us today. We call it money.

Though all of these changes were made possible by farming, the farmers themselves had a very hard life. There were no ploughs, tractors, or combine harvesters to help back then. Planting, weeding, digging, harvesting, and grinding seeds into flour between slabs of heavy stone were just a few of the many tasks that had to be done by hand. And because people were eating a smaller variety of foods, they were less well-nourished than their hunter-gatherer ancestors had been. Skeletons of early farmers tell the grim story. They are shorter than those who came before them and often have twisted toes, buckled backs, and knobbly knees.

Imagine someone said they had invented an amazing new mind-reading technology. This person claimed their system could transfer the thoughts from your brain into the mind of someone else. It would work from thousands of miles away. You could even use it to find out what somebody thought long after they were dead. Would you believe them?

The descendents of the Natufians were not just traders and farmers. They were also artists. This sculpture (from about 7000 BCE) is one of the earliest large-scale human figures ever discovered.

The Rosetta Stone, found in Egypt in 1799, contains the same text written in three scripts, including Egyptian hieroglyphics and Ancient Greek. Since historians knew Ancient Greek, they used the stone to figure out the hieroglyphics.

The name of Egyptian king Ptolemy V is inscribed in the Rosetta Stone. Here is his name in hieroglyphics.

Well, that technology really does exist. And, believe it or not, it was invented more than 5,000 years ago. Here's how it works. You take a thought in your brain, convert it into a code and put the code onto an object. Now you give the object to someone else who already knows the code. They read the code and, presto, your thoughts are now inside their brain!

This mind-reading technology is called writing.

If you were imagining some kind of fancy ancient helmet with wires sticking out of it, you may feel a bit disappointed. Sorry about that. But many of the things we take for granted as ordinary today are extraordinary achievements developed in the ancient past. Writing is just that. As far as we know, no other creature on the planet can do it. Only we humans.

Technically, history begins with writing. Historians learn about the past by reading what people have written down. If a people either didn't have writing or had writing that we haven't figured out how to read, we can learn about them from the objects and remains they have left behind, but it isn't quite the same as being able to read their minds.

No one knows who invented writing. Like farming, it seems to have been invented independently in many different places. But from about 3400 BCE, we see the first clear use of written symbols. That's about one-tenth of a second from midnight on our 24-hour clock.

If you're wondering what the BCE stands for, it means Before the Common Era. The Common Era begins at the year 1. Anything before is BCE. Anything after is CE. For example, my dad was born in 1936 CE. Pharaoh Cleopatra, who we'll meet later, died in 30 BCE. We tend to leave the letters CE off dates with four numbers in them, such as 1968, which is the year when I was born!

The earliest evidence we have for people writing things down was in Sumeria, an ancient civilization in the southern part of Mesopotamia, in the heart of what is now Iraq. In about 3300 BCE, merchants there began drawing simple pictures on clay tablets to represent the things they were buying and selling. Next to each picture, they made marks for how many of these things changed hands. These tablets were baked in ovens to make their marks permanent, creating a permanent set of records. This meant that merchants could trade without losing track of what they had bought and sold.

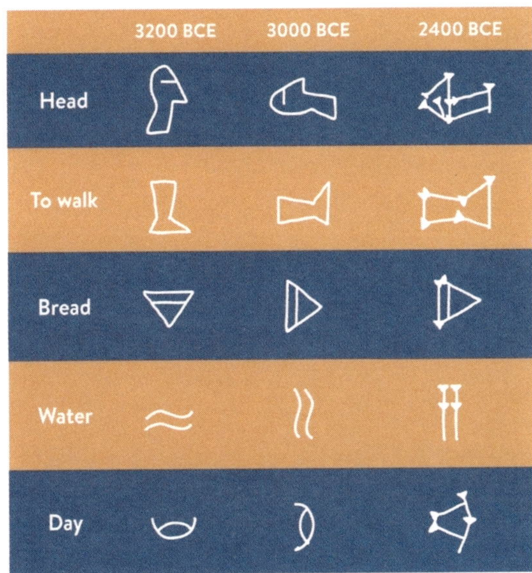

Sumerian script changed over time as you can see here. Also, first the direction of the writing went from top to bottom, but later it changed so it was read from left to right.

This clay tablet, carved by an Assyrian merchant, is written in cuneiform text. It says two men owe him about 7 pounds (3 kg) of silver and explains how he would like it paid.

Over time, wedge-shaped marks replaced the pictures. This style of writing is called cuneiform (which means "wedge-shaped"). It forms the basis for three of the oldest written languages in the world: Sumerian, Assyrian, and Babylonian.

Egyptians living at about the same time also had writing. They used a system called hieroglyphics, which was writing derived from pictures of objects combined with symbols for sounds. They might have got the idea of writing from the Sumerians, but nobody knows.

The Indus Valley civilization, in parts of what are now India, Pakistan, and Afghanistan, also had writing then, probably inventing it just after the Sumerians. But it's very different from any other language we know how to read, and nobody has yet decoded it.

At about the same time, in Peru, a civilization called Norte Chico kept records by tying knots in strings. A set of these knotted strings was called a quipu. And a bit later the Olmec (those chocolate drinkers from what is now Mexico) may also have had their own form of writing. In the late 1990s, road builders found a stone block engraved with 62 symbols that look like they represent animals, plants, insects, and fish.

Quipu could have up to 1,500 wool or cotton strings hanging down. The number of turns in each knot, their position, and the number of knots on the string add up to a value.

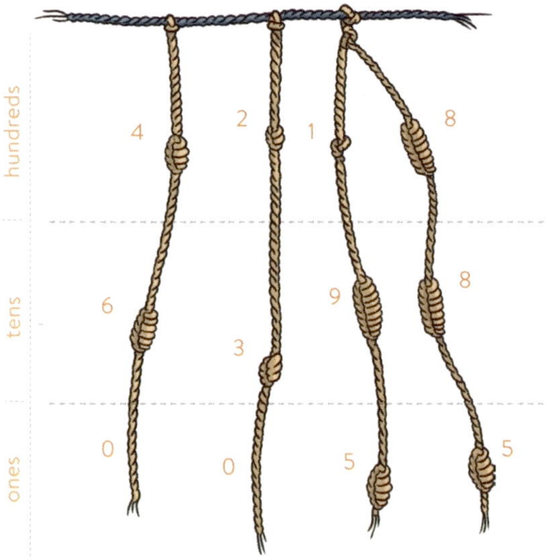

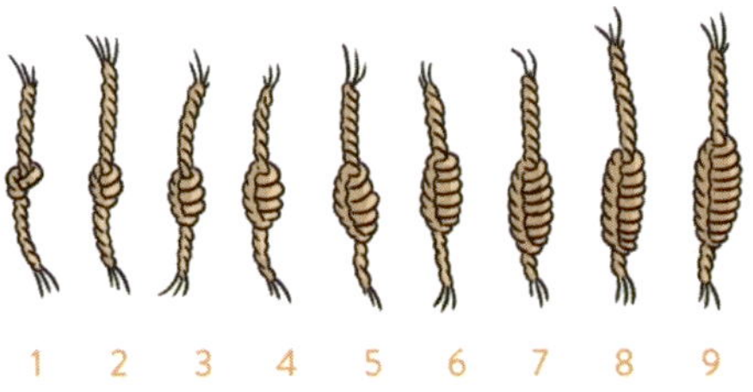

Over time, people all over the world began using physical coding (most of it written) to keep records and to communicate to people far away in space and time.

Trade and writing weren't the only ways people made use of the extra time farming gave their society. Another thing they did was to build massive structures. These were probably a sign that the culture had an elite, a group or family who was in charge and could get others to work hard for them.

In 5000 BCE a civilization in what is now Sudan and southern Egypt built a ring of huge stones called the Nabta Playa. It is the very first astronomical observatory (a place built to observe the night sky) we know of in the world. People from this area went on to become the biggest trading partner of Ancient Egypt.

Europeans of this time are also famous for building massive structures. These were usually made from enormous blocks of local stone. This is why this culture is known as megalithic (mega means "big" and lithic means "stone"). Many of these stone structures were set upright in circles like the Nabta Playa circle. Stonehenge, in England, was one of those. It dates to about 3000 BCE. In other places, people built temples to their gods, with altar tables at one end or in the center. One famous surviving example is Hagar Qim on the Mediterranean island of Malta.

When a lot of people live close together doing different jobs, trading with one another and with far-away cultures, and working together on major projects under the orders of an elite, you have what is called a civilization.

Sumeria, where writing was first developed, was the earliest civilization we know of. Fresh water from rivers meant the people could flood their fields. That made just the right conditions for crops to thrive.

The Tigris and Euphrates rivers also provided two long flowing superhighways. People could use boats made from reeds to carry themselves and their goods from one riverside city to the next. We know more about this very old civilization than we do about many others, in part thanks to an extraordinary discovery.

We don't know for sure what the many stone circles found around the world were used for. Some (including Stonehenge, shown in this picture) are lined up with the Sun in a way that allowed people to keep track of the seasons. They may also have been used for religions rituals and holiday gatherings. What we do know is that moving and standing up enormous stones is a lot of work, so they must have been very important to the people who built them.

It was the 1840s in England, and Austen Layard wasn't having any fun being a lawyer. So, he decided to go on an adventure. He headed for the distant island of Ceylon, now Sri Lanka, off the southern tip of India. But he never got there. His journey took him through the Middle East, where he got very interested in archaeology, studying the remains of ancient civilizations. He worked on several important digs and even wrote a book. Then, about ten years after he first left London, he decided to investigate what looked like a hill across the Tigris River from the town of Mosul.

The hill turned out to be the ancient Assyrian capital of Nineveh, which had been destroyed in 612 BCE and slowly buried in soil. Layard and his team uncovered a giant palace. Even more important, they found a staggering 30,000 clay tablets covered with cuneiform writing. We call this collection of writings the Library of Ashurbanipal after the ruler who we think assembled it. Historians even think he wrote some of the tablets himself. These tablets transformed our understanding of life in ancient Mesopotamia, including Sumeria.

The most famous tablets from the ancient library tell of the adventures of Gilgamesh, an early Sumerian king. Gilgamesh had been a real-life king who ruled one of the first Sumerian cities, called Uruk, located on the bank of the Euphrates River. Uruk was the largest city in the world at the time. As many as 80,000 people lived there.

The Epic of Gilgamesh, probably first written down in about 2000 BCE, is a poetic fantasy. It tells the story of a character called

Gilgamesh, who was two-thirds god, one-third human. Gilgamesh goes on an epic journey in search of a way to live forever. It is the very first written work of fiction that we know of.

The Sumerians also loved math. The Sumerian counting system was based on the number 60. It's a great number on which to base a math system because there are so many ways to divide it (by two, three, four, five, six, ten, twelve, fifteen, twenty, thirty). It's thanks to the Sumerians that we have 60 seconds in a minute, 60 minutes in an hour, and 360 degrees in a circle.

> "ON ALL SIDES, AS FAR AS THE EYE COULD REACH, ROSE THE GRASS-COVERED HEAPS MARKING THE SITE OF ANCIENT HABITATIONS."
>
> Austen Layard, archaeologist

As if that weren't enough, these ingenious people probably came up with the most revolutionary invention of all time—the wheel. The first wheels we know about were Sumerian potters' wheels, used

After his amazing discovery, Austen Layard made drawings of the palace of Nineveh. In 1853 architect James Fergusson used the drawings to create this painting of what it may have looked like.

to make clay pots. These were invented in about 3500 BCE, around the same time as writing. By about 300 years later, Mesopotamians had wheeled carts. People in what is now Slovenia and in several other places in Europe and the Middle East did, too.

Which culture made this giant leap from making pots on wheels to carrying pots on carts? We don't know.

Just like books and TV today, stories spread from one culture to another in ancient times. This stone block from a building in what is now Syria shows the hero Gilgamesh supporting two minotaurs who are holding up the Sun.

So, you can see how farmers working very hard led to crafts and jewelry and inventions and trade and money and elites. Those elites made

This partial wheel and axle are parts of the oldest wheeled vehicle ever discovered. They were found in what is now Slovenia.

sure the extra wealth created by farming went to build massive structures to show their power and to give themselves and their families beautiful houses and lovely things.

The Sumerian civilization didn't last forever. About 2200 BCE, a terrible drought lasting over 200 years devastated the region. Land around river mouths became impossible to farm because seawater made it too salty. In a bid for survival, the Sumerian cities were fighting among themselves and with their neighbors. Finally, in 1787 BCE, a nearby civilization, Babylon, conquered Sumeria and made it part of the Babylonian empire.

It's incredible to think that everything about that war, from the wealthy kings of Babylon to the weapons their armies used and the soldiers who specialized only in fighting, would not have existed without the invention of farming.

La Venta, a river island in what is now Mexico, was home to a major center of the Olmec culture that was built around 1000 BCE. Archaeologists have found a pyramid, burial mounds, and sculptures of all sizes. This one is known as "the governor." Archaeologists think it represents a leader, possibly a high priest.

6

NATURE SHAPES *the* ANCIENT WORLD

3300 – 1200 BCE

Rivers, wind, silk, and rubber

ABOUT 3300 BCE
People living in the Indus Valley start to build trading settlements that turn into towns and cities.

3300 BCE
Silk is first farmed in China.

3000 BCE
Norte Chico people build their first pyramids.

2550 BCE
The Pyramid of Giza is built in Egypt to house the tomb of the pharaoh Khufu.

1700 BCE
The Minoan civilization reaches its peak on the island of Crete.

1633 BCE
The Shang dynasty begins in China.

1200 BCE
The Olmec invent rubber.

We've just seen how people shape nature by farming crops and breeding animals. But it's just as true that nature shapes people, as we're about to see.

At approximately the same time as the Sumerians were living in Mesopotamia, the Indus Valley civilization (the one with the writing we haven't yet figured out how to read) was thriving in what is now Pakistan, India, and Afghanistan. It lay along the banks of a giant river, the Indus, which could be used to transport goods and people. The Indus Valley took up an area twice the size of Sumeria. At its height, it covered about 400,00 square miles (1 million sq km).

Archaeologists have found about 1,000 cities and settlements in the Indus Valley. They date to between 3300 and about 1900 BCE. The Indus Valley emerged about 200 years after Sumeria and lasted until about 300 years after Sumeria fell. And they seem to have survived all of that time without much warfare. Lots of toys and

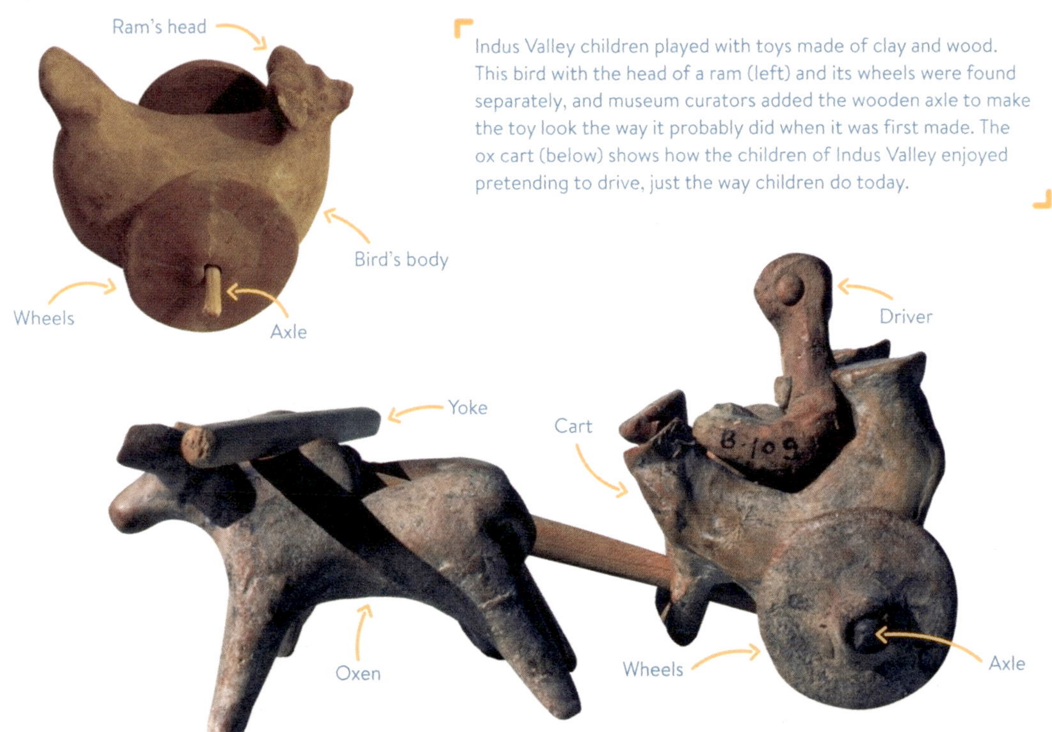

Indus Valley children played with toys made of clay and wood. This bird with the head of a ram (left) and its wheels were found separately, and museum curators added the wooden axle to make the toy look the way it probably did when it was first made. The ox cart (below) shows how the children of Indus Valley enjoyed pretending to drive, just the way children do today.

games have been found, but very few weapons.

These people wove cotton, made beautiful pottery, and crafted copper and bronze into fine jewelry and statues. Unlike in Sumeria, they didn't build fancy royal tombs or big palaces and temples. There is no evidence of a single all-powerful king or queen. But here's the thing—we don't know for sure.

TO JUDGE FROM THE NUMBER OF POTTERY MODELS THAT HAVE BEEN FOUND IN THE DRAINS, IT WOULD SEEM THAT THE CHILDISH HABIT OF TAKING PLAY-THINGS INTO THE BATH HAS PERSISTED FOR THOUSANDS OF YEARS.

Ernest Mackay,
archaeologist of Mohenjo-Daro

Having no fancy tombs might just mean that these people cremated their dead, as most people in India do today. Because we can't yet read Indus Valley writing, we only know what we can learn from the objects they left behind. But however they were ruled, we know they were very advanced and highly organized.

One of the two big cities was Mohenjo-Daro, which was laid out in regular blocks like some modern cities. Each street was connected to a water supply. Mohenjo-Daro even had flush toilets and sewers, things that weren't common around the world for another 3,000 years. Excavations have unearthed large public buildings, including a meeting place that could hold up to 5,000 people.

On the other side of the world from the Indus Valley, another huge and peaceful civilization was thriving in what is now Peru. The Norte Chico civilization, the one that used quipu, included dozens of cities, again along rivers. Each city included giant gathering places. And instruments made of animals bones show music was an important part of the lives of the people there. They had mummies and giant pyramids that served as tombs.

The Norte Chicoans built their first pyramids around 3000 BCE, before the Egyptians built theirs. The mummy of a leader we call the Woman of the Four Brooches was found inside one of the biggest pyramids. The brooches she is named after were made from animal bones and shaped like monkeys and birds.

We've talked a lot about farming for food, but there are other reasons to farm. Caral, the biggest city of Norte Chico, was

The Greater Pyramid (shown here) is the largest, most complex building in the 4,500-year-old Norte Chicoan city of Caral. Peruvian archaeologist Ruth Shady and her team examined the ruins and concluded that this is where the city's inhabitants practiced important rituals.

built on a high, dry plain. There, farmers built canals from the rivers to their farms to water their fields. This inland location surprised archaeologists because they were used to seeing major cities built closer to the sea. Then they realized why. This area was perfect for farming cotton, which could be traded to coastal groups for fish and other seafood. Fishers then used the cotton to make nets, with which they could catch more seafood.

Because cotton was so important, some experts think these people probably made beautiful textiles like later Peruvian cultures did and still do, though no one has yet found remains of these textiles. The Norte Chicoans decorated gourd containers with figures that might have been their gods.

The Norte Chicoans didn't have clay to make fire-safe pots for cooking, as other cultures we've met did. So they couldn't boil water directly over a fire. Most experts think they must have roasted their food. There are lots of ways to roast food. One is to wrap it in wet leaves and bury the packages in hot coals at the edge of a fire. But they also might have heated stones in a fire then dropped them into gourds filled with water to get hot water for cooking, something we know cultures such as the Haida of what is now Canada did with wooden pots.

Norte Chico traded with cultures all over South America. We know that because archaeologists have found plant remains and snail shells from far-away areas. And Norte Chico art includes animals such as monkeys, which lived hundreds of miles away. But, as in the Indus Valley, trade does not seem to have led to war. Archaeologists have found no signs of weapons, walls, or buildings created to defend against attack. They haven't found war wounds on any of the human remains from Norte Chico either.

Imagine you are a mighty ancient king and a genie pops out of a magic lamp.

"You can have as many wishes as you want!" says the spirit.

How would you respond? Would you ask for all the money in the world? To be able to boss everyone around? Or how about some all-powerful magic ring that would make you live forever the way Gilgamesh wanted to? History is full of stories about people who have wanted power and riches. But the first rulers who believed they could have it all came from ancient Egypt.

These all-powerful rulers were called pharaohs. More than 150 of them reigned over ancient Egypt from about 3000 BCE to 30 BCE. That's about 3,000 years! The Egyptian people believed pharaohs were living gods and that when they died they joined all the other gods in the afterlife. These divine rulers took full advantage of their power. They had some amazing palaces, temples, and tombs built for them.

Have you heard of the seven wonders of the ancient world? They are human-made structures ranging from temples to gardens to statues. Only one of them still survives today: the Great Pyramid of Giza. It was built as a tomb for one of the earliest pharaohs, called Khufu, who died in 2566 BCE.

This giant construction originally

Ramses II was one of the longest reigning pharaohs in history. He stayed in power for 66 years. In that time, he grew the Egyptian Empire and built an enormous number of buildings, many of them with images of himself on them. This sculpture in Luxor is 35.4 feet (10.8 m) high and weighs about 72 tons (65 tonnes).

6. NATURE SHAPES *the* ANCIENT WORLD

3300 – 1200 BCE

towered skyward for 482 feet (147 m). That's about as high as a 50-story building. It is made of more than 2 million blocks of stone, each one weighing as much as a large car. Experts are still puzzled at how these ancient people could have cut, transported, and hauled into place so many huge stones. They didn't have wheels until long after the pyramid was built. Scientists have estimated that it took 20,000 workers more than 20 years to build it.

We know a little bit about these workers. Archaeologists have found a workers' graveyard near the Pyramids and the remains of huge buildings that could have housed as many as 1,600 people at the same time. They also found some remains of their meals, including bread, beef, goat, sheep, and fish. Plus, the workers wrote on stones inside the pyramids, telling the names of their work groups and the places around Egypt where they came from.

The pharaohs may have believed they were gods, but their power depended on yet another giant river. The Nile is one of the longest rivers in the world. It flows north from central Africa into Egypt. Along the way, it picks up lots of fresh, nutrient-rich mud, which it dumps on Egypt's fields when it floods every year.

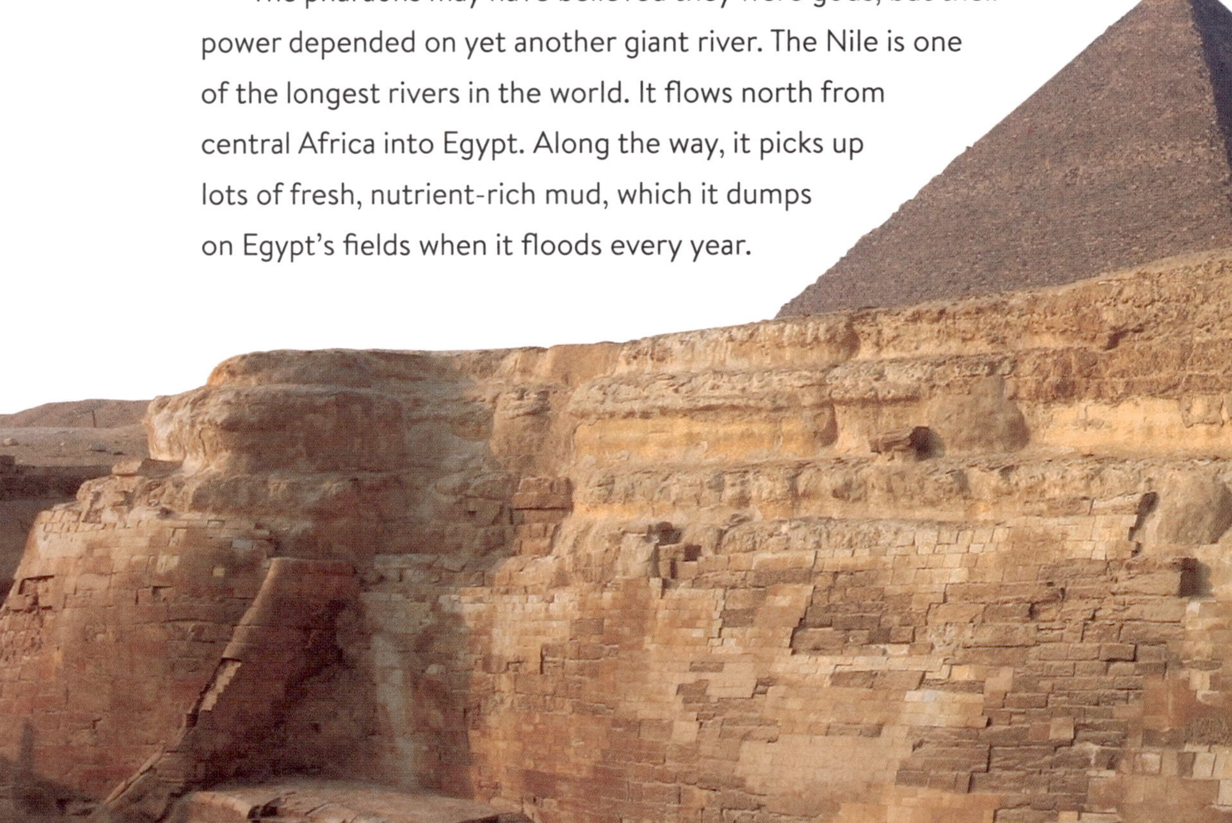

This mud is just the right stuff for growing a huge supply of food. And plentiful food made Egypt rich and the pharaohs powerful.

Another natural feature helped the pharaohs hold on to that power. The little strip of fertile land next to the Nile is surrounded by desert. Today we know this huge dry area as the Sahara. This giant desert protected Egypt from most invaders. The pharaohs didn't need fancy walls, towers, or castles to keep their country safe—with one exception.

Up the river lay Egypt's most regular trading partners, the Nubians. Egypt imported gold, ivory, copper, incense, and animals from people living in the tropical areas of central Africa. All of those goods came through Nubian traders. Nubians

More than 230 feet (70 m) long, the Great Sphinx has the face of a human and the body of a lion. Notice the pyramid of Khafre in the background? It's the second largest of the ancient Egyptian pyramids of Giza and was built for Pharaoh Khafre, son of Pharaoh Khufu, whose own pyramid is nearby.

were also famous as brave warriors who were brilliant shots with a bow and arrow.

At times the Egyptians conquered parts of Nubia. At other times members of the two countries' ruling families married. And once Nubia—sometimes called Kush—conquered Egypt. Their leaders became Egyptian pharaohs for 200 years.

Egypt's relationship with its southern neighbor was made easy (and sometimes dangerous) by a remarkable feature of the Nile. The river flows south to north, but the winds along it usually blow the opposite way, from north to south. That means people could

Ancient Egypt

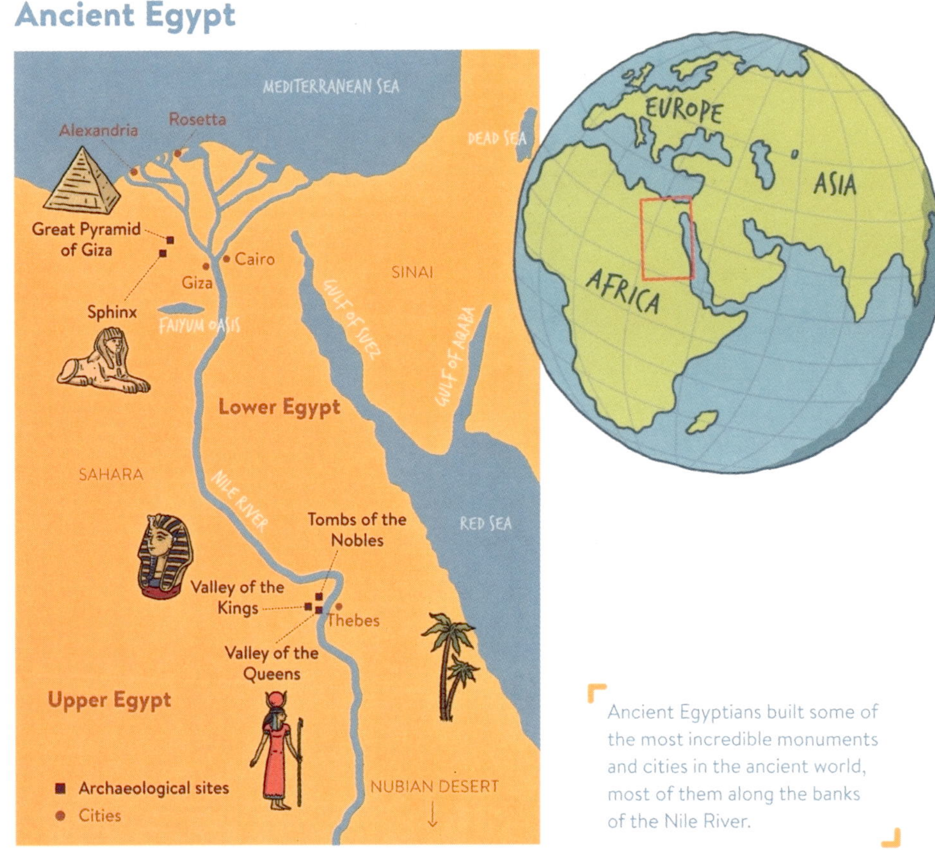

Ancient Egyptians built some of the most incredible monuments and cities in the ancient world, most of them along the banks of the Nile River.

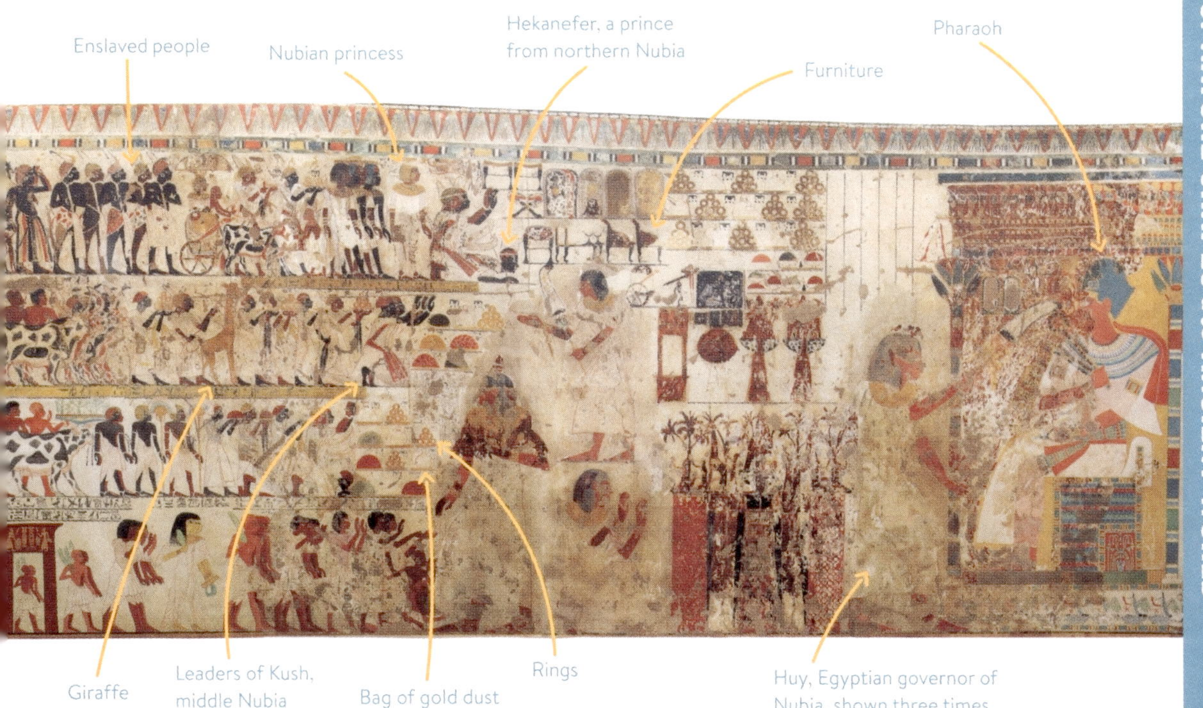

This painting shows a group of Nubian leaders bringing gifts (including gold, exotic animals, and enslaved people) for the Egyptian pharaoh. Nubia was very ethnically diverse, as you can see from the wide range of skin tones shown here.

float downstream in wooden boats. Then, when they wanted to return home, all they had to do was raise a sail and let the wind blow them back upstream. What could be more convenient?

Do you believe in life after death? How about your friends and family? If you ask them, I expect you will find some do and some don't. Those who do have lots of different ideas about what happens next. Some people believe that if you are good you go to a wonderful place called heaven and that if you are bad you go to an awful place called hell. Others believe in reincarnation. That's the idea that your spirit comes back to Earth in another person or even as a different living creature.

The Ancient Egyptians believed in life after death. They also believed they needed to pack some things to take with them when they went to the afterlife. A pyramid showed off how rich and powerful a pharaoh was. But it also provided a safe place to store all the things the pharaoh would need in the next life. And that included his or her body.

A rotten body wouldn't be of much use, though, even in a fancy tomb. So, the Egyptians preserved dead bodies by turning them into mummies. People all over the world (including Norte Chico, of course) have made mummies. But nowhere was the process more complex than in Ancient Egypt. It could take as long as 70 days.

Mummification wasn't just for pharaohs. Anybody in Ancient Egypt who could possibly afford it made absolutely sure they were mummified when they died. Some people even had their pets mummified.

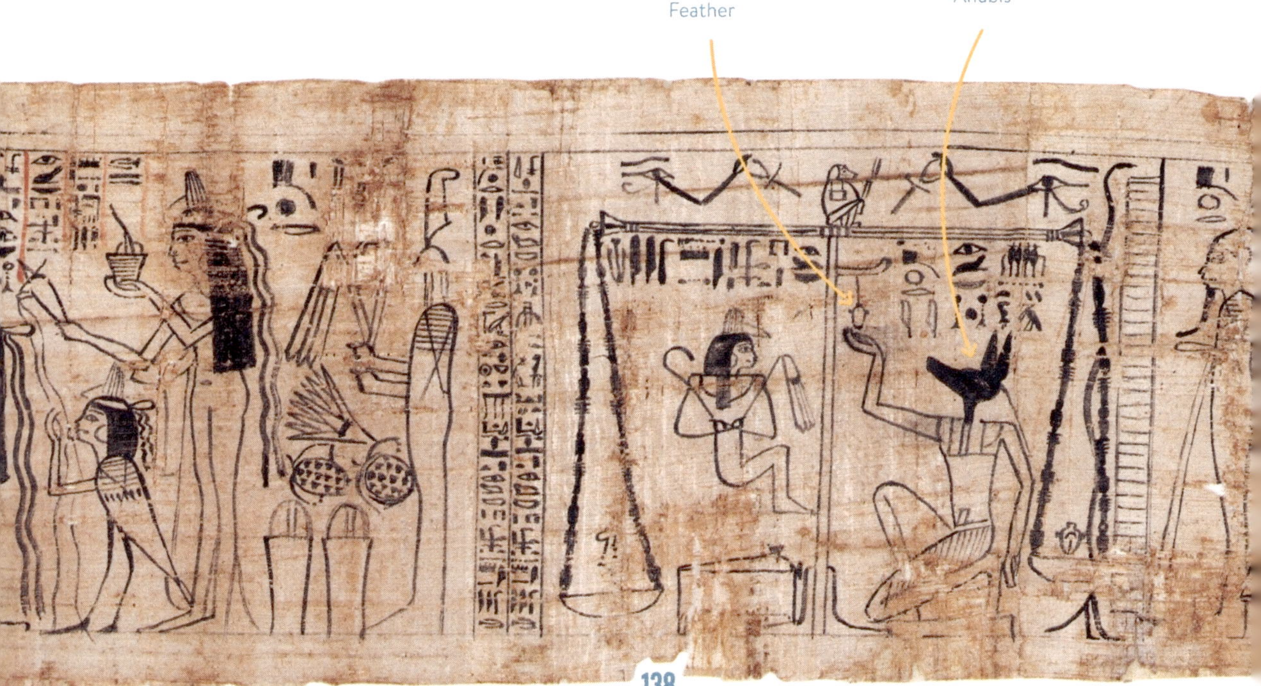

The expert who performed mummifications was a special priest called an embalmer. First, the embalmer removed the stomach, intestines, lungs, and liver from the body. He then dried them out and placed each in its own container called a canopic jar. Usually, the embalmer removed the brain, too.

Herodotus, an ancient Greek writer who saw a mummification, wrote that to get the brain out of the skull, the embalmer punched a hole from inside the nose into the brain cavity. Then he pulled the brain out with a hook. For centuries people thought this was how it was done. But now it looks as if Herodotus didn't quite understand what he was seeing.

You see, there's a problem with his description. Brains have the texture of jello, so a hook would pass right through it. Two American researchers, Bob Brier and Ron Wade, did an experiment in 1994

Anubis, the jackal-headed god of the dead, weighs a dead person's heart against a feather to see if the person's soul should enter the afterlife.

to figure out how the Ancient Egyptians actually removed brains. They tried pushing a stick through a hole in the back of a corpse's nose into its brain and giving it a good stir. When they stirred hard, the brain turned to liquid and oozed out through the nostrils. That's probably how the embalmers did it.

The heart was the only organ the embalmer left in the body. The ancient Egyptians believed that this was the seat of the soul, where people did their thinking and feeling. They thought that in the next life the gods would weigh it to judge if the person had lived a good or bad life on Earth.

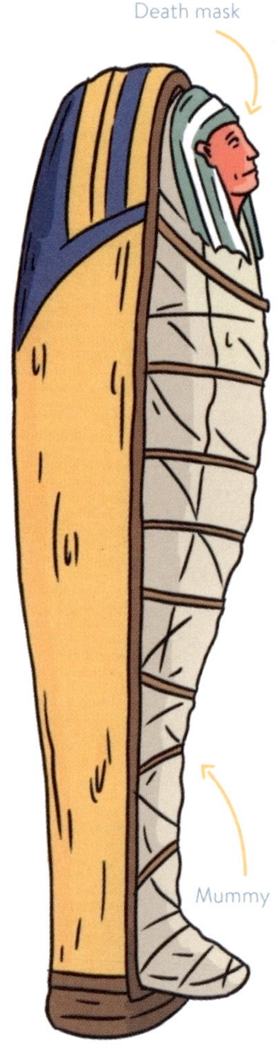

Once the organs were removed, the embalmer packed the corpse with a special salt called natron to dry it out. When it was dry, he stuffed the corpse with linen and sawdust, added fake eyes and wrapped it in strips of cloth. Sometimes he even replaced the tongue with a gold one. The finished mummy was packed inside a coffin called a sarcophagus and placed in a tomb. In the case of a pharaoh, that tomb might be a pyramid.

All around the body was everything that the dead pharaoh could possibly need in the afterlife. Archaeologists have found food, drink, crowns, tableware, weapons, clothes, books, pictures, and even games and toys in tombs.

The tombs of important people contained

teams of servants. These weren't real people. They were wooden or stone dolls, called shabti. Their purpose was to come to the dead souls of their masters or mistresses whenever they needed help.

A sarcophagus was a stone (or occasionally metal) container that housed a mummy to protect it from tomb robbers and animals.

Experts know a lot of this because the ancient Egyptians wrote down their burial rituals in *The Book of the Dead*. This collection of texts also includes magic spells, which were written and illustrated on scrolls and placed in tombs. The spells were meant to help the souls of the dead pass through the dangers of the underworld and into an afterlife of everlasting joy. You see, writing really does allow us to see inside the minds of people who have been dead for thousands of years.

In about 2040 BCE, the capital of Egypt was moved south to a city called Thebes. Here the burials continued, but there was one important difference. Pharaohs no longer built grand pyramids for all to see. Instead their tombs were carved into rock underground. They showed off above ground by building temples. Hundreds of underground tombs have been discovered in the Valleys of the Kings, Queens, and Nobles, near Thebes. Remarkably, some have survived almost completely intact.

Maybe you have seen a film or read a book about someone finding treasure buried in an ancient tomb? Most of these stories are fiction.

Sarcophagus lid

Here is one that is true.

Howard Carter was a British archaeologist who had been working in the Valley of the Kings on and off for 15 years. One day in November 1922, a member of his team found some steps leading into what Carter hoped was a tomb.

The team spent the next three weeks very carefully removing the sand and rock that covered the doorway. Once they got inside, they saw Carter had been right. They were standing in the burial chamber of boy-king Tutankhamun. King Tut had become pharaoh when he was only nine and died when he was 19.

A huge hoard of treasure was packed inside the chamber. The most famous object of all was the boy-king's funeral mask, made out of solid gold. It was placed on Tut's face underneath three layers of gold coffins inside a stone sarcophagus.

In the end, even the natural defenses surrounding ancient Egypt weren't enough to save it. The last true pharaoh, Cleopatra VII Philopater, is usually known simply as Cleopatra. She ruled Egypt mostly by herself from 51 BCE to 30 BCE, even

The Ancient Egyptians didn't think only humans deserved an afterlife. They mummified animals, too. Archaeologists have found cats like this one as well as dogs, birds, snakes, and even crocodiles.

though she was supposed to be co-pharaoh with her younger brother Ptolemy.

When her army was defeated by the Romans, she killed herself rather than surrender. The story is that she took her own life by letting a poisonous snake called an asp bite her. But maybe she killed herself some other way, though some think she was murdered. No one knows for sure. Once Cleopatra was gone, independent Egypt was no more.

TOWARDS SUNSET WE HAD CLEARED DOWN TO THE LEVEL OF THE TWELFTH STEP. HERE BEFORE US WAS SUFFICIENT EVIDENCE TO SHOW THAT IT REALLY WAS AN ENTRANCE TO A TOMB, AND BY THE SEALS, TO ALL OUTWARD APPEARANCES THAT IT WAS INTACT. ”

Howard Carter,
archaeologist and Egyptologist

Most ancient rulers we know about were men. And in most societies men had more power than women. So it's easy to assume that's always the way it was, everywhere and at every time. But that's not quite true. There were some women pharaohs in Egypt, like Cleopatra and the earlier Hatshepsut. Many early civilizations had powerful female gods. In Ancient Egypt and Sumeria, women were men's equals under the law and could run businesses and own property. We know from the way the Woman of the Four Brooches was buried in Norte Chico that women there held important roles in society, too.

Cleopatra was a brilliant politician. No one can be sure what she looked like because portraits of her done during her lifetime, including this 2,000-year-old coin, look very different from one another.

AT THE BIRTH OF SOCIETY AND CIVILIZATION I FIND A RELIGIOUS LANDSCAPE LITTERED WITH ... FEMALE DEITIES WHO MAKE WISDOM THEIR BUSINESS. ”

Bettany Hughes, historian

But nowhere in this period were women and men more clearly equals than in the Minoan civilization on the Mediterranean island of Crete from about 2000 to 1600 BCE. Accounts from ancient Greek historians and images on vases and wall paintings describe a society in which both men and women participated in all daily activities. There were no special roles for one or the other, and priestesses were some of the most important people in society.

One of the most striking examples of equality on Crete is sporting contests where women and men both competed. A favorite sport was bull-leaping.

A gymnast (a woman or man) would grab the horns of a bull and somersault onto its back. Then, in a second somersault, they would leap off and land upright back on the ground.

It's possible women were more important than men in Minoan society. And some experts think their goddesses were more important than their gods. If Minoan writing—the first in Europe—is ever deciphered, perhaps we'll know for sure.

Sometimes civilizations are shaped as much by other creatures as by humans. Silk is extraordinary stuff. It reflects the light, making it look shiny and glamorous, and it's very strong. So it's a perfect fiber for clothing. Do you know where these lovely fibers come from?

The caterpillar of the moth *Bombyx mori* is the key. It munches on the leaves of the mulberry tree for 20 to 33 days. Then it oozes out a continuous strand of silk more than half a mile (1 km) long, wrapping it around itself to make a cocoon. After ten to 14 days, the caterpillar has changed into a moth, and out it comes. The common name of *Bombyx mori* is silkworm, but it's not a worm at all.

Archaeologists have found evidence of ancient people using silk. It was being farmed in China by about 3300 BCE and in the Indus Valley very soon after (in addition to the cotton they grew). The very first writing in China talks about the silkworm spirit. Silk was very important even then, especially to those who cared for the caterpillars and who wove their cocoons into cloth.

Thousands of years after the beginning of the silk trade, a story began to be told in China about the origin of silk-making. It stars Leizu. She was said to be the wife of the legendary Yellow Emperor, who is supposed to have lived from 2697 to 2598 BCE. Here's how the story goes.

Leizu was out walking in the emperor's garden. There, she saw thousands of caterpillars eating their way through the leaves of a grove of mulberry trees.

Curious to know more about these creatures, Leizu collected some of the cocoons and sat down to drink a cup of tea. While she

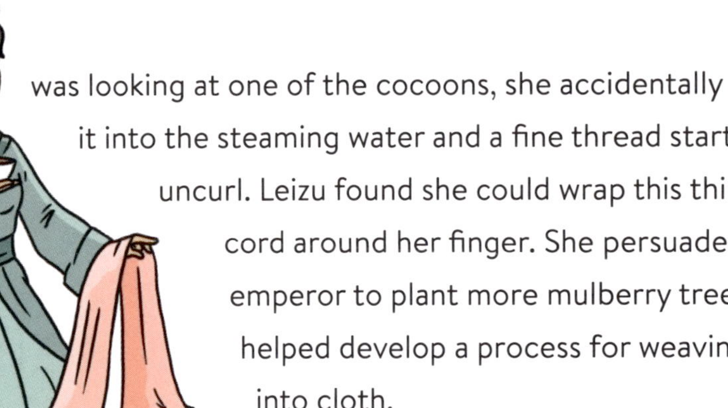

Legendary Empress Leizu

was looking at one of the cocoons, she accidentally dropped it into the steaming water and a fine thread started to uncurl. Leizu found she could wrap this thin, strong cord around her finger. She persuaded the emperor to plant more mulberry trees. She then helped develop a process for weaving silk fiber into cloth.

Silk-making declined in India after the Indus Valley civilization collapsed. That left China as the only place where people knew how to make this precious cloth. And for over 2,000 years they managed to keep it a secret. That way anyone who wanted silk had to buy it from China.

Silk became so popular that the trade routes connecting China to Central Asia, the Middle East, Africa, and Europe became known as the Silk Road or Silk Route. The cloth's fine texture and shimmer made it one of the greatest luxuries of the ancient world. A merchant might load up a group of camels with wool, gold, and silver in Baghdad, in what is now Iraq, and drive them thousands of miles to China. There he would trade them for silk and bring the silk back. He sold the silk at a profit and started all over again.

Of course, the secret of silk-making was bound to get out one day. As the story goes, in about 550 CE, some monks smuggled silkworms to Constantinople (now Istanbul, Turkey). From there it spread around the world, including back to India, which is now a major producer of silk.

When silk production started, the workers who unwound the cocoons and wove the fabric were mainly women working in their homes. As demand for silk grew, the government and nobles set up large silk workshops where both women and men worked.

The first rulers of ancient China who we know are historical rather than legendary belonged to the Shang dynasty (about 1600 to 1046 BCE). A dynasty is a series of rulers belonging to the same family. So in this period, China was ruled by the Shang family.

In the 1920s, archaeologists dug up a site called Yin Xu, about 311 miles (500 km) south of Beijing. There they found 11 major royal tombs and the foundations of a giant Shang palace. Inside were tens of thousands of beautiful bronze, jade, and stone objects. They also found weapons that had helped the Shang conquer the land for hundreds of miles around.

We know a lot about the Shang dynasty because they wrote things down. But in their case, the writing archaeologists have

Bronze is a strong metal made from a mixture of copper and tin. Skilled Chinese metal-workers made this axe blade in the 1000s or 1100s BCE. It was made by heating bronze until it melted and then pouring it into a mold. This process is called casting.

found isn't records of trades or long stories. Rather, it was a way to communicate with the spirits.

Here's how it worked. If you were a king and had a question for the gods, you could write the question on a piece of turtle shell or ox bone. You might ask, when will it rain? Will we win the next battle? Will we have a good silkworm crop this year?

Then you would hold a hot metal rod against the shell or bone until it cracked. You would interpret the length and direction of the cracks to reveal the gods' answers. Sometimes you would write down your interpretation on the same bit of shell or bone.

One of the Shang kings, Wu Ding, asked the oracle bones about all parts of his life. He wanted to know the weather, if he would win upcoming battles, whether he should give certain commands, and even the cause of his toothaches.

Archaeologists have found more than 200,000 pieces of turtle shell and ox bone. About a quarter have questions and answers written on them. They are called oracle bones. Experts have found it easy to read some of these inscriptions because they match up pretty closely to modern Chinese writing.

We've seen how important cotton was to Norte Chico and how much silk mattered to the culture of China. The Olmec, the inventors of chocolate who lived in what is now Mexico, used a material that was central to their way of life, too. The name Olmec means

"rubber people," and they got this name because they figured out how to make rubber by mixing rubber tree sap (called latex) with sap from morning glory vines.

If you mix equal parts of those liquids, you get a very flexible substance. Shape it fast, before it dries, and you have a great bouncy ball. Spread it on cloth, and you get a waterproof poncho. You can also mix 75 percent latex and 25 percent morning glory sap and get a very long-lasting, sturdy material, a bit like plastic, that can be shaped into waterproof containers.

The Olmec civilization lasted from about 1200 BCE to about 400 BCE. So they were around in King Tut's time and at the time of the Shang dynasty in China.

The Olmec were probably the first people in the Americas, and one of the first in the world, to use a symbol for zero. The zero symbol is important because we use it for more than just showing the idea of nothing. We also use it as a place holder. For example, if we want to write a symbol for one hundred and two things, we write 102. The 1 means "one hundred." The zero means "no tens." And

Rubber is extracted from the rubber tree by using a tool to scrape off a section of bark. Sap then drips out and is collected in a bucket, often tied to the tree.

This Olmec head was discovered near Lake Titicaca on the Peru-Bolivia border. Imagine how you would feel if you found this on a day out!

the two means "two ones." The zero keeps the tens place empty so we can understand what places the other numbers belong in.

The Olmec also sculpted what we now call colossal heads. These were huge portraits carved into boulders. Some were taller than a basketball player and weighed more than 22 tons (20 tonnes). But they looked like individual people. So archaeologists think they are portraits of powerful rulers.

No one knows why the Olmec built these heads. Did their rulers want memorials to themselves, the way the Egyptian pharaohs did? Were the giant faces intended to grab the attention of the gods?

The Olmec invented a ball game now called ulama, which spread throughout their area and north into what is now northern Mexico and the southwestern United States. Ulama was a combination of athletics and religious worship.

Major issues and disputes between rival kingdoms could be decided in a ball game, too. It was the gods' decision who would win and who would lose. Winning was very good news. Losing, not so much. That's because the losing side might be sacrificed to the gods and their bodies buried under the court.

The idea of sacrificing a team of ball players sounds awful. But it may have had an important purpose. Though there is evidence that the Olmec had soldiers whose job was to protect their trade routes, it doesn't seem as if they went to war over territory. So, it is possible that the ball game was used as a way to prevent war. And of course it was only possible because rubber trees and morning glory vines grew in that part of the world, and the rubber could be used to make balls.

From cotton to silk and from rubber to rivers, you can see how nature shapes people as much as people shape nature.

Ulama (which is still played in some parts of Mexico today) is like a mix between soccer and basketball. A stone ring hangs high above each end of the court, and each side tries to send the ball through the other team's ring and protect its own ring. Players aren't allowed to touch the ball with either their hands or their feet. They have to pass it using their hips, thighs, forearms and heads.

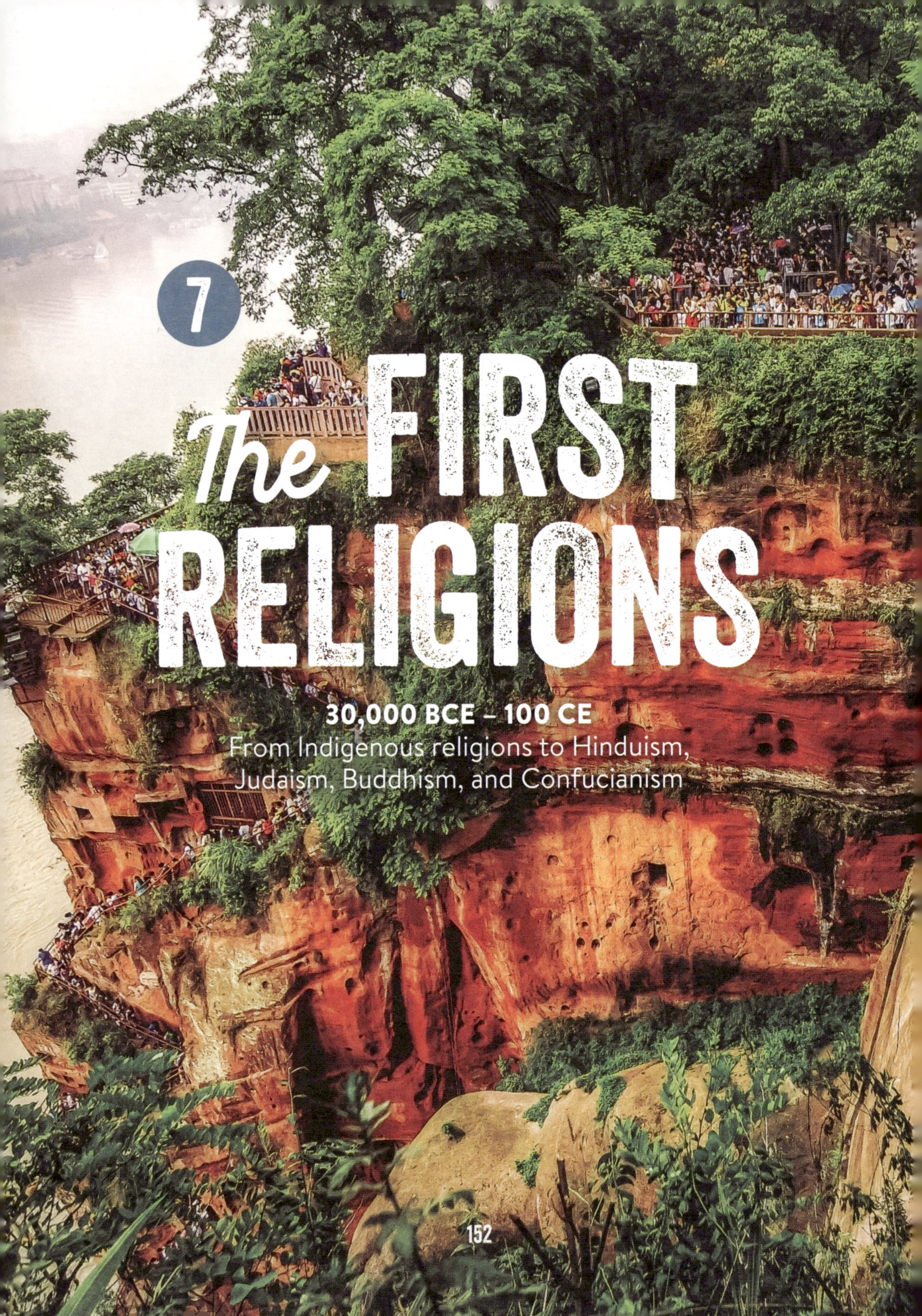

7

The FIRST RELIGIONS

30,000 BCE – 100 CE

From Indigenous religions to Hinduism, Judaism, Buddhism, and Confucianism

The giant Leshan Buddha was built in the 700s CE in Sichuan Province, China, overlooking the spot where three rivers come together. The largest Buddha in the world at 561 feet (171 m) tall, it took 80 years to carve into the rock of its hillside.

30,000 years ago
Burials show Indigenous religions were widespread.

2300 BCE
Babylonians are worshipping the goddess Ishtar.

1500–1200 BCE
The Hindu Vedas are written down for the first time.

1200 BCE
Israelites begin writing down pieces of what will become the Hebrew Bible.

586 BCE
The Judahites are enslaved in Babylon.

564 BCE
The Buddha is born in India.

551 BCE
Confucius is born in China.

100 CE
Buddhism reaches China.

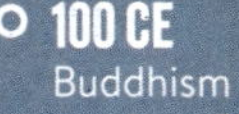

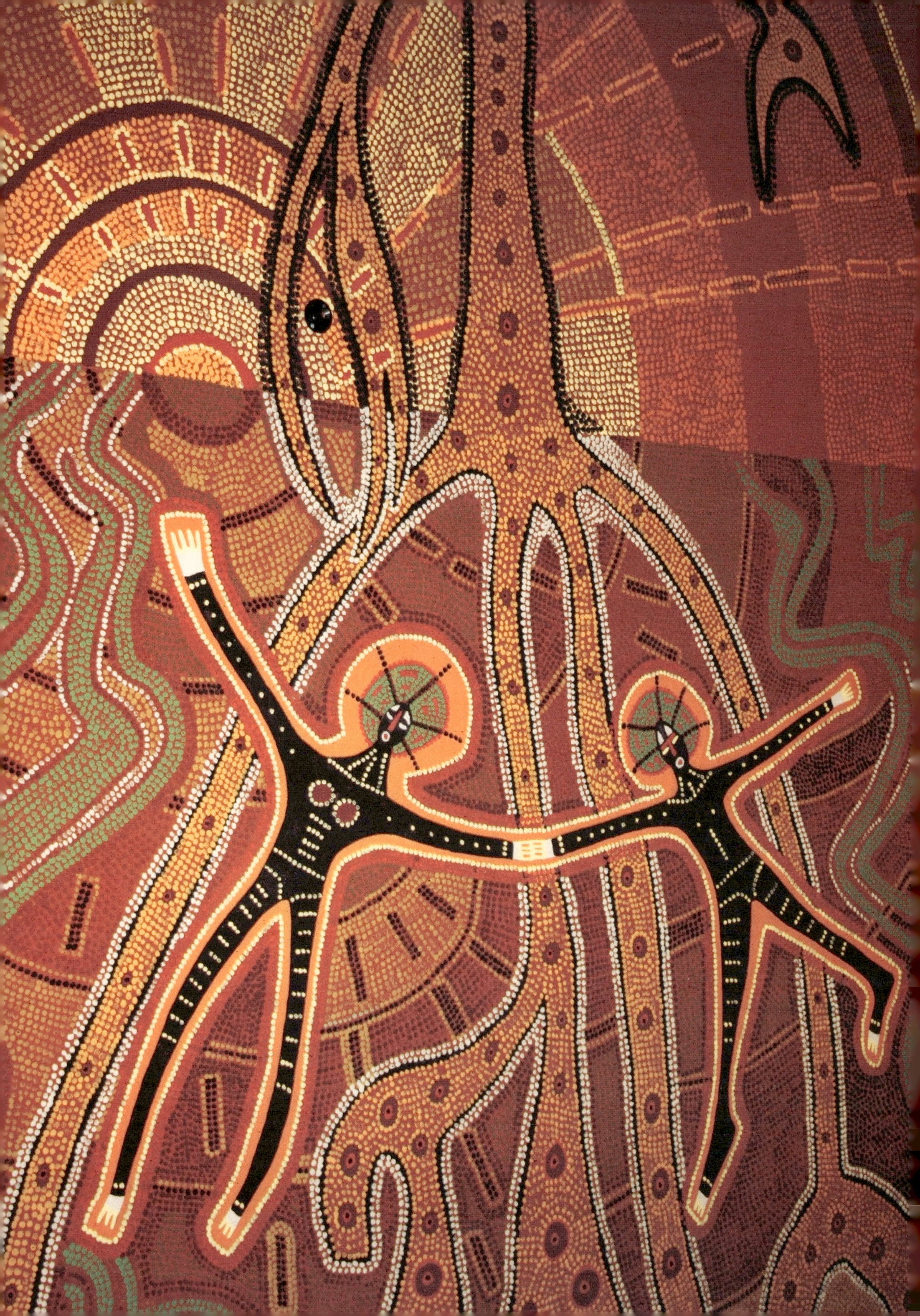

Inuit hunters, who live in the tundra of northern Greenland, Canada, and Alaska, traditionally hung up the skins of dead polar bears inside their homes for several days after they were hunted and killed. It's because they believed the polar bear, which they called Nanuq, had a powerful spirit even after it was dead. If the bear was male, the hunter offered the bear knives, harpoon heads, and rawhide ropes. If female, the hunter offered knives and sewing needles. Treat a dead polar bear properly and its spirit would share the good news with other bears so they would be eager to be killed by the hunter. But treat the polar bear badly, and it would warn other bears to stay away.

All around the world and from the earliest burials and tombs archaeologists have unearthed, there are signs that people have been shaped by religious beliefs. Why? Because humans seem to have a universal desire to explain the world around them through stories. We just can't help it.

Aboriginal Australian people's creation story tells of the Dreamtime. This was when the dramatic desert landscape of interior Australia was formed by supernatural ancestor beings who broke through the crust of the unformed Earth. These beings created everything from the Sun, Moon, and stars to mountains, trees, and water. They made people and animals, too. Because they were created by the ancestor beings, all things—living and non-living—are related.

Today, there are more than 4,000 religions in the world, although about two-thirds of the world's

One Aboriginal Australian origin story tells that in Dreamtime, a pair of lovers, Talwalpin and Kowinka, got trapped at sea by a fierce storm. The creator and sky god Baiame rescued them and turned them into trees that grew close together at the edge of the sea. Talwalpin became the cottonwood tree and Kowinka the red mangrove.

As part of a potlatch in Klukwan, Alaska, Tlingit dancers perform wearing masks that represent animals of the real and spirit worlds. The dance might tell a story, make fun of someone, or even offer an apology on behalf of the host.

people belong to one of the four largest—Christianity, Islam, Hinduism, and Buddhism. About 15 percent practice no religion at all, and the rest practice Judaism, Jainism, Taoism, and many, many others. Among those are thousands of local, or Indigenous, religions like those of Aboriginal Australians and the Inuit people of the Arctic region. If you add up all of the people who practice Indigenous religions today, they come to almost six percent, or about one in every 17 people in the world.

The history of religion starts from Indigenous cultures. From the very beginning, these religions have been as different from one another as the places where they are practiced. But they do tend to have one thing in common. Their beliefs are tied to the natural world surrounding them. Most Indigenous cultures see little difference between the physical world and the spiritual one. They believe that many parts of the environment, including animals, trees, rocks, mountains, and bodies of water, have spirits with as much personality as humans and often more power.

Religious leaders such as priests or shamans help people communicate with the spirits. About half worship ancestors, often treating their spirits as members of the community with great importance and power. And some also have high gods, including creator gods and gods who represent forces of nature.

As is common in many beliefs, Indigenous religions put great importance on the value of relationships. That means you should offer help and gifts to other people and to gods and spirits. And you must also offer thanks for gifts you have been given.

Members of several Indigenous nations who live on the Pacific coast of Canada held (and still sometimes hold) a ceremony called a potlatch. It is part party and part religious festival where a rich, powerful person hosts a lavish feast. At the feast they give away valuable items, such as canoes, beautiful carved boxes, and clothing, to the guests. The more generous the host is, the higher their status, the more power they have in the community, and the more the ancestors will smile on them.

All of the religions we've already talked about, including those of the Shang Chinese, the Egyptians, and the Olmec, are examples of Indigenous religions. That's because they were practiced in the place where they first emerged. But as the Shang were using their oracle bones, the Egyptians were worshiping their leader-gods, the Olmec were making their sacrifices, and an uncountable number of other peoples around the world were going about their spiritual business, something new was happening. A religion was developing in India that would go on to move beyond the landscape where it was created.

Hinduism probably started during the Indus Valley civilization. The first holy books of Hinduism are called the Vedas. They include praise songs to the 33 gods of the Vedas and instructions for performing religious rituals.

We don't know when the Vedas were composed, but we do know that they were passed from generation to generation. People memorized them and taught them to others for hundreds of years after the fall of the Indus Valley Civilization. As far as we know, the Vedas were first written down in India sometime between 1500 BCE and 1200 BCE.

> "RAISE THYSELF UP, GROW THICK BY THY OWN MIGHT, O GRAIN! BURST EVERY VESSEL! THE LIGHTNING IN THE HEAVENS SHALL NOT DESTROY THEE!"
>
> A blessing for the planting of grain from the Atharva-Veda

The central idea of Hinduism is that each person has an eternal soul or self that is reincarnated after death into another being. This being can be an animal or a person.

Hinduism includes a caste system. People are born into a particular caste, or level in society. They stay in that caste for their whole life. The highest caste, Brahmins, were priests during the time the Vedas were written, and it was their right to demand food and whatever else they needed to live from other

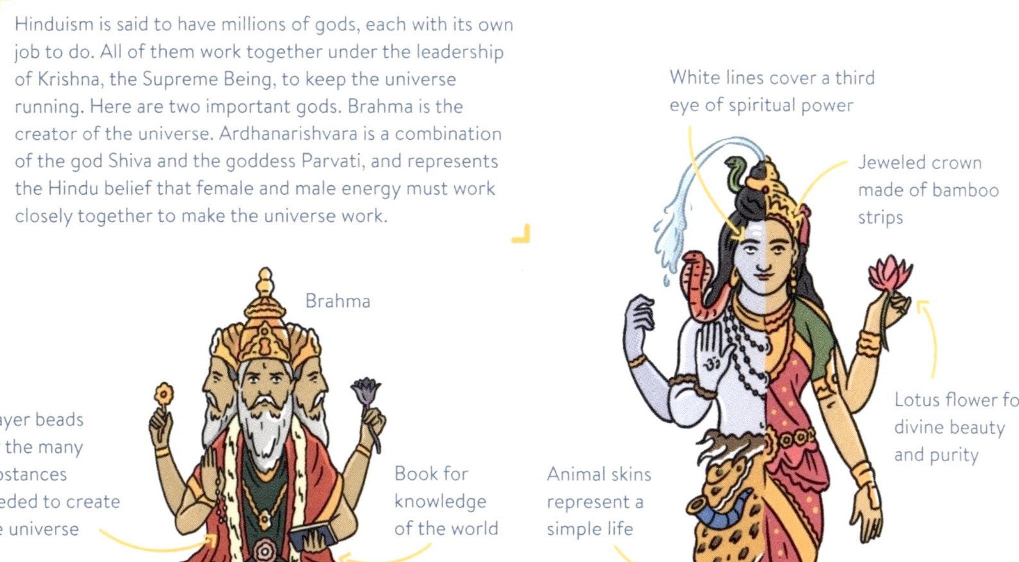

Hinduism is said to have millions of gods, each with its own job to do. All of them work together under the leadership of Krishna, the Supreme Being, to keep the universe running. Here are two important gods. Brahma is the creator of the universe. Ardhanarishvara is a combination of the god Shiva and the goddess Parvati, and represents the Hindu belief that female and male energy must work closely together to make the universe work.

people. The lowest castes then were servants or enslaved people. People in the middle worked in the government or were farmers, soldiers, or traders.

In Hinduism, everything you do in life creates karma, which is like a system of good marks and bad marks. If you follow the rules, then you collect good karma. And good karma allows you to be reincarnated at a higher level in the next life. The rules include being kind to others, performing rituals to the gods, and meditating. Over many lives, you can move up from being an animal to being a low-caste person to being a high-caste person. Finally, you reach moksha, when you are free from the hardships of the cycle of birth and death. For some Hindus, this means your soul is reunited with the soul of the whole universe or it becomes one with God.

By 1200 BCE, about when the Hindu Vedas were being written, something else important was happening on the eastern shores of the Mediterranean Sea. The region was known as Canaan, and it was home to city dwellers, farmers, herders, and nomads.

This was an important place at an important time for two important reasons. One is that the people of Canaan were developing the very first alphabet. Canaanites didn't write their language in symbols that represented words or ideas or syllables, the way the Ancient Sumerians, Chinese, and Egyptians were doing at the time. Instead, they came up with a system of symbols that represented the smallest possible sound units in speech. These first alphabets only included consonants, though. Cn y rd a sntnc wtht vwls?

This alphabetic way of writing spread like wildfire because Canaan was home to a major trading civilization. The Phoenicians (that's what the Greeks called them) took the alphabet with them wherever they went. Phoenicia was made up of self-governing cities. They had an incredible navy, which allowed them to conquer cultures all along the southern coast of the Mediterranean

Z W H D G B

' N M L K Y

T H T SH R Q

S P ' S

The alphabet developed in Canaan had just 22 symbols. This meant it was easier for people to learn than other alphabets, which had hundreds of symbols.

Sea to where it meets the Atlantic Ocean, over 1,500 miles (2,400 km) away. The Phoenicians traded and sometimes fought with the African and European cultures they encountered.

More than 1,500 small statues like these have been found in Phoenician temples in Lebanon. They were probably offerings to the gods.

One group of people who lived in Canaan was the Israelites. They started using the new alphabet to write down some of their beliefs. We know about these people mostly from their scriptures, which are now called the Hebrew Bible or the Old Testament. These texts are a combination of rules for how to live and stories that tell of the legendary founders of their culture and religion.

One of the most dramatic stories of the Hebrew Bible has to do with Egypt, which is right across the Sinai desert and the Red Sea from Canaan. It is called the Exodus. The story begins with the Israelites enslaved in Egypt. The Israelites followed only one god (called God). In the story, God helps Moses, the leader of the Israelites, convince an Egyptian pharaoh to set his people free.

To do this, God curses Egypt with a series of ten horrible plagues. The great Nile River—the source of Egypt's wealth—turns to blood. Frogs fall from the sky. Giant clouds of locusts eat all the crops in the fields. It gets dark in the daytime. All of the first-born sons of the Egyptians die in the same night. And more.

Once he understood that the Israelites had a very powerful god on their side, the pharaoh agreed to free them, though at the last minute he sent his army to chase them as they fled. God made a path of dry ground appear in the middle of the Red Sea so the Israelites could walk across. Then he let the sea flow over the path, drowning the Egyptian army.

The king of gods, Amen, giving Merneptah a sword, mirrored and shown twice

Khonsu, child god, son of Amen and Mut

Mut, mother goddess

The Merneptah Stele, a stone slab created in about 1230 BCE, is one of the ways we know that the ancient Israelites were real people, not legends. Under a picture of the patron gods of Thebes helping him in war, Egyptian pharaoh Merneptah brags about his conquests in Libya and Canaan, including saying that "Israel is laid waste and his seed is not," meaning that his army had completely wiped out the Israelites. This turned out to be quite an exaggeration.

The story of the Exodus from Egypt is a religious text. There is no archaeological evidence so far that the Israelites ever lived anywhere but Canaan. But a story that involves an escape from slavery makes sense if your people are enslaved at the time you're writing it, which these people were.

Some of the Hebrew scriptures had been written down already and the rest were being passed down orally when, in 586 BCE, the empire of Babylon (the same empire that had defeated Sumeria) invaded Canaan. Its powerful armies destroyed Jerusalem, the capital of Judah, one of the Israelite kingdoms. Many of the people of Judah, called Judahites, were enslaved and taken to Babylon.

The Babylonians had a rich religious tradition of their own, including the oldest known god for whom we have a name, a goddess named Ishtar. She was worshipped as far back as 2300 BCE. But as far as we know, Judahite captives were not interested in learning about Babylonian religion. They wanted to save their own beliefs and traditional ways of life.

Judahite scholars collected their scriptures in one place, writing down the Israelite beliefs and stories that hadn't been written down before, just the way the Vedic culture wrote down the Vedas. It was then that the religion of Judaism began to take shape.

A radical new belief emerged from this process—that there is only one all-powerful and all-knowing God.

Locusts—one of the plagues in the story of the Exodus—mostly live quietly on their own. But they can suddenly group together into a swarm of hundreds of thousands of individuals and destroy crops, leaving people to starve.

Babylon's Ishtar Gate was built in about 575 BCE, during the time the Jews were in captivity in the city. The gate was 39 feet (12 m) high and was covered in images of dragons and bulls. It led to a 0.6-mile- (1-km-) long street, called The Processional Way, with images of lions lining its walls.

As you can tell from the story of the Exodus, in the early days the Israelites were loyal to a single God, but they believed that other gods existed in the world. Only later, in Babylon, did they come to believe that only one single God exists, one who created everything there is and is actively involved in the lives of people everywhere. This belief is called monotheism. Judaism was the first religion that we know of to fully embrace it. It wouldn't be the last.

The Judahites spent about 40 years in Babylon and in other parts of the Babylonian empire. Then in 539 BCE, Cyrus the Great, founder of the Persian Empire of what is now Iran, conquered Babylon. In what is often celebrated as one of the ancient world's most profound acts of kindness, Cyrus decided to free the Jewish people from slavery and allowed them to return to Jerusalem if they wanted to. He also had a new Holy Temple built to replace one the Babylonians had destroyed when they invaded Jerusalem.

Around the time the Jews were enslaved in Babylon, another set of beliefs was emerging in China. The Zhou dynasty—which had taken over from the Shang in China—was falling apart. The Zhou had set up a system of regional noblemen—leaders of city-states outside the capital. These leaders were in charge of their states but loyal to the king. However, over time the nobles gained more and more power and began fighting the king and one another.

As the king's power fell apart, people who had once worked for the government lost their jobs. Some of them became philosophers. These thinkers traveled from city to city. They taught, and they also advised kings on how to rule wisely and on how society should work. The ideas they developed are known as the Hundred Schools of Thought.

One of these thinkers was Kong Fuzi, also known as Confucius. We don't know very much about Confucius as a person, but one story says he was minister of justice in a state called Lu. When he was in his fifties, he left his job and began trekking around the kingdoms of northern China. He taught his view of the right way to lead a good life and the best way to rule a kingdom. As fights between rival states got worse,

Extreme respect for parents and elders is central to Confucian philosophy. In one Confucian story (below), a tiger charges at a father and teenage son walking in the mountains. The son jumps in front of the father to protect him. Seeing the son's bravery, the tiger is so impressed that he doesn't attack after all.

Confucius made it his life's mission to try to sow the seeds of peace.

Confucius believed that a good society was one where everyone followed the rules and was kind to others. He advised kings that if they set a good example for their people, the people would obey them. He taught the same about parents and children, high-born people and ordinary people, men and women.

The leaders (kings, parents, high-born people, and men) should respect the people they were in charge of as human beings. In turn, their inferiors (subjects, children, ordinary people, and women) should always do what they were told even when they didn't agree. In the case of children, he included grown-up children. If you were 40 years old and your father was 70, you were still his child and should always obey him.

Confucius believed people were meant to live in this orderly way. And he believed that if you did right, heaven would reward you. As part of his rules about kindness, Confucius is quoted as saying, "That which you do not desire, do not do to others."

Do you recognize this saying? Often called the golden rule, this idea is part of nearly every religion in the world. It asks us always to remember that others are human beings and deserve to be treated as we would want to be treated in their situation, even when the other person is very different from us. You can see why he was, and is still, considered a very wise person. Millions of people practice Confucianism today, mostly in China and Korea.

Confucius is thought to have lived from about 551 to 479 BCE. His ideas about family, morality, behavior, authority, and traditions are still influential in Chinese society today.

Just about when Confucius and the other thinkers of the Hundred Schools of Thought were teaching in China and the Jews were writing down their sacred texts in Babylon, another very important thinker was teaching his ideas. His name was Siddhartha Gautama, and he lived on the other side of the great Himalayan Mountains from China, in India. His followers call him the Buddha.

Siddhartha was a Hindu, but he rejected some parts of Hinduism that he thought were wrong. We don't know much for certain about his life, but we think he lived somewhere between 580 and 480 BCE. And we think he was born in Lumbini, in what is now Nepal.

According to one legend, Siddhartha was born a prince. His mother, Queen Maya, died a few days after his birth. Siddhartha's father was very protective of him and had three palaces specially built in his son's honor. The idea was that Siddhartha would live all his life in these palaces. That way he would be hidden away from the poor, desperate lives led by most ordinary people.

But, at the age of 29, Siddhartha's curiosity to see the world for himself overcame him. So he sneaked out of his palace. He met old people and people with diseases and people who were dying. He was so upset by what he saw that he decided to leave his luxuries behind and join ordinary people in their suffering.

At this time, city-states covered the area of northern India along the Ganges River. The area was full of thinkers, much like the Hundred Schools of Thought in China. In Hinduism, a new idea was that you could live a holy life by becoming what's called an ascetic. Ascetics give up all possessions, pleasures, and family connections. They focus entirely on prayer and meditation.

Siddhartha decided to become an ascetic. At one point he ate no more than a single leaf or nut a day and almost starved to death. But eventually he concluded that starving himself was adding suffering to the world, not taking it away.

It is said that Siddhartha sat down under a tree to meditate for 49 days. After all of this time quieting his mind, he gained what is called enlightenment, or nirvana. He could see the truth of all things and felt lasting peace and joy. From then on, he was known as the Buddha, meaning "awakened one."

The Buddha said that all people are equal and that castes don't matter. He also stopped thinking about karma and earning good marks for the next life. But he continued to believe in reincarnation and the importance of meditation and selflessness. He taught a

Bodh Gaya, in India, where Siddhartha gained enlightenment, is one of the holiest sites in Buddhism. Pilgrims come from around the world to worship a direct descendent of the very tree Siddhartha sat under.

> “Good is contentment with just what one has.”
>
> The Buddha, from the *Dhammapada*, verse 331

middle way between a life of wanting more and a life of rejecting everything. He believed if you were kind to others, meditated, and lived simply, you could find your way to nirvana.

For the next 45 years, the Buddha walked along the Ganges River in what is now north-east India and southern Nepal. He talked to everyone who would listen, from kings and queens to robbers and farm workers and beggars. He explained to them that anyone can gain enlightenment. After attracting thousands of followers, the Buddha died at about the age of 80.

After his death, followers of the Buddha set up monasteries and continued to teach Buddhist ideas. Then something happened that started making Buddhism the major religion it is today.

About 200 years after the death of the Buddha, most of the area now called India was ruled by the Mauryan Empire. The third Mauryan king was named Ashoka. When he came to power in about 260 BCE there was just one undefeated kingdom left: Kalinga.

Of course, Ashoka attacked the Kalingans. The last battle of that war is known as the Battle of Kalinga. According to some stories, it left more than 100,000 people dead on the battlefield. The day after winning the battle, it is said that Ashoka walked out across the city. All he saw were burned out houses, dead horses, and scattered human bodies.

Ashoka was a very tough guy. His name even means “without sorrow.” But the sight of all this carnage is said to have made him weep and cry, “What have I done?”

Horrified at the loss of life, Ashoka decided to devote himself to peace. One thing he did was become a Buddhist.

The best information we have about King Ashoka is from a collection of instructions to his subjects that he had carved into pillars and rocks all around his kingdom. They are called the Edicts of Ashoka. In them, he asked people to be kind and generous, to work to improve themselves, to be honest, and to be grateful. He also promised that everyone in his kingdom could practice whatever religion they chose. He said that even though Buddhism was his own religion, he would respect all religions equally.

Following Ashoka's reign, Buddhism spread across Asia. His children Mahinda and Sanghamitra took Buddhist teachings to what is now Sri Lanka. By 100 CE, Buddhist monks had reached China. From China the religion spread to Korea, Vietnam, Thailand, and eventually into Japan. Nowadays, more people practice Buddhism in other Asian countries than in India itself.

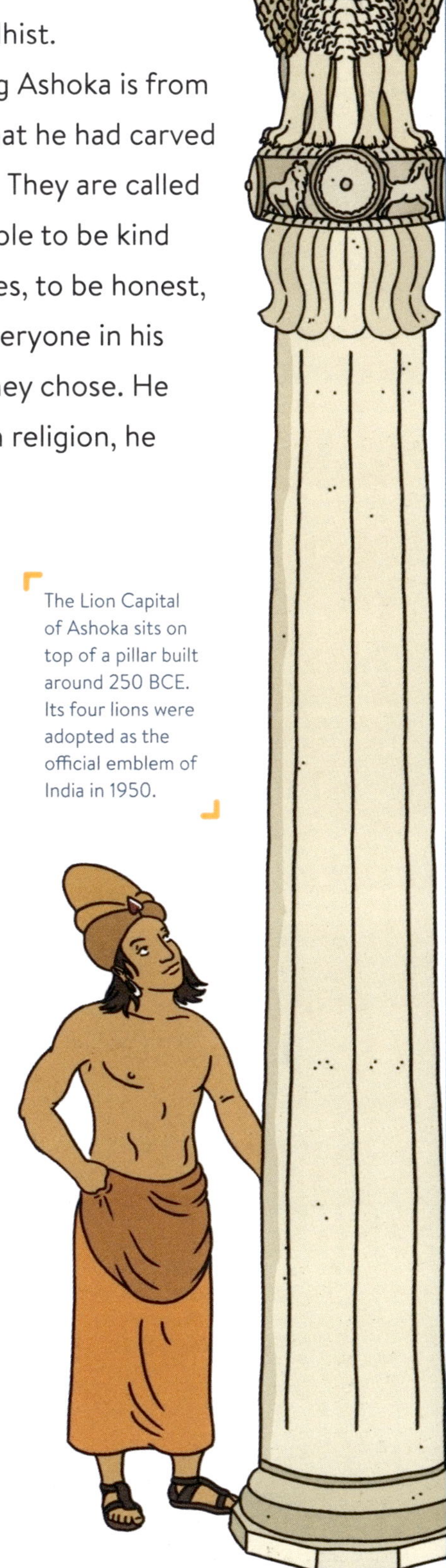

The Lion Capital of Ashoka sits on top of a pillar built around 250 BCE. Its four lions were adopted as the official emblem of India in 1950.

Tikal was a center of Mayan Civilization for 1,500 years, from the 500s BCE to the 900s CE. Located in the rain forest of what is now Guatemala, it was once home to as many as 120,000 people.

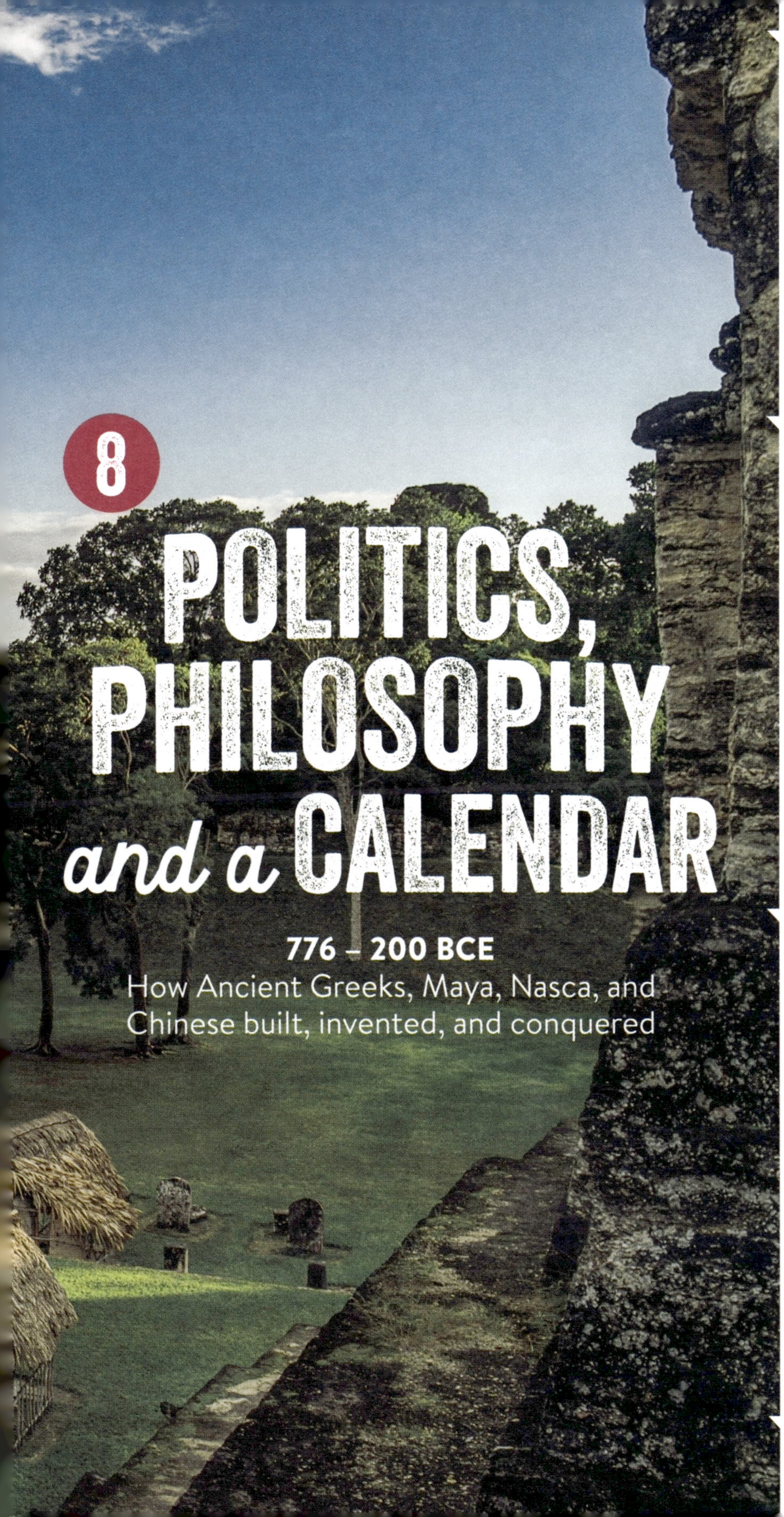

8

POLITICS, PHILOSOPHY and a CALENDAR

776 – 200 BCE

How Ancient Greeks, Maya, Nasca, and Chinese built, invented, and conquered

776 BCE
First Olympic Games take place.

600 BCE
The start of democracy (for rich, male citizens only) begins in Athens, Greece.

600 BCE
The Mayan civilization begins.

336 BCE
King Alexander of Macedon sets out to conquer the world.

221 BCE
Qin Shi Huang conquers and unites all of China and becomes Emperor.

200 BCE
The Nasca people create huge drawings on the desert of what is now Peru.

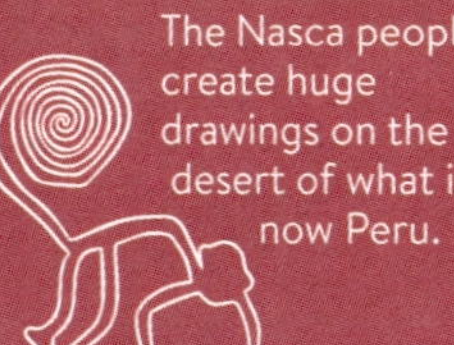

Do you like olives? When I was young, I used to stay at a fine old English house that belonged to my great-uncle and namesake. I remember he always offered us olives in front of his roaring log fire before dinner. I still love olives, maybe because they remind me of Uncle Christo.

Olives were first farmed by the people of ancient Greece. They were a very important crop, as important to the Greeks as wheat was to the Sumerians or cotton was to the Norte Chicoans.

That's because everyone wanted olive oil. It was as precious as gold is today. Squeeze out the oil from olives and you could use it for lighting lamps to see in the dark, for cooking food, or even as a base for perfume to make yourself smell good.

If you were a free person lucky enough to have some money, you could also trade your olives to buy something that meant you would never again need to work in the fields. And you'd never need to make your bed or even do the dishes after dinner. Can you guess what that incredible something was? The answer might be pretty disturbing. It ought to be. Because that thing that could do all your work for you was another person—an enslaved person.

In all of ancient Greece, we know the most about the city-state of Athens. That's because the Athenians left so much writing behind. They used an alphabetic script adapted from the one invented in Canaan but with vowel symbols added. The state of Athens included both the city itself and the surrounding countryside. In Athens (and probably in other places in Greece), two opposite ideas seemed to go hand in hand. One was democracy. The other was slavery.

It is one of the most unjust and offensive truths of human history that millions of people have had to spend their lives enslaved. This means having to work without pay and to be treated with harsh, often cruel, disrespect by people who think you are worth a lot less than they are.

In ancient Greece, enslaved people did all of the hardest work. If you were enslaved, you might have worked on a farm or in another family's house. Or you might have built roads, made pottery, or mined metals.

Every free family who could possibly afford it had enslaved people. In fact, if you were a free family, not having even one slave was a mark of extreme poverty. Not only families owned other humans. Businesses did, too. Even the government of Athens owned enslaved people. It rented them out to companies, and the money they made went to pay the government's bills.

To make olive oil, the ancient Greeks first washed the olives then used a crusher like this one to smush them into paste. Then they removed the seeds and put the crushed pulp into a press, which squeezed out the oil and vegetable juice. They let the oil rise to the top, skimmed it off, and bottled it.

At this point, slavery had been around for at least 6,000 years. We know Sumerians enslaved their prisoners of war. Egyptians did the same and also sent expeditions up the Nile River to capture and enslave non-Egyptians. Ancient Chinese, Indians, and Canaanites also enslaved people.

The reasons people were enslaved in the ancient world changed from place to place. In Athens, all you had to do was fall on hard times and take a loan you couldn't pay back. Or you might be traveling and be kidnapped and sold into slavery in another country. Or you could be captured in war. All this made free people very aware of their freedom and also very nervous when they felt it was being taken away.

In about 594 BCE, a new leader came to power in Athens. His name was Solon, and according to the stories told about him much later, he was a great warrior and a poet. Solon is famous for making some very big changes. One thing Solon did was to set up a system where all citizens could vote to decide exactly what the government should do. This is called direct democracy. Other Greek states also set up direct democracies. It was an exciting moment if you were a citizen of Athens.

But there was one catch. You only counted as a citizen if you were 1) free, 2) male, 3) Athenian, and 4) rich enough to own property. If you were enslaved, female, from anywhere else, or poor, forget it. So actually most people who lived in Athens couldn't vote. But the idea of elections in which the people had a say, the origins

Slavery was a part of many ancient civilizations. This stone panel from ancient Nineveh in Assyria shows enslaved prisoners of war being forced to work for their captors.

of democracy, did begin right there.

Because they had so many enslaved people doing all the hard work, Athenian citizens had something worth even more than olive oil. They had time, lots and lots of it. Free, rich Athenian men could use their time to learn, think, write, invent, and discover. They even had time to go to giant outdoor theaters to see plays performed and to listen to storytellers.

Some of the most famous ancient Greek stories were written by the poet Homer. In his two book-length poems, *The Iliad* and *The Odyssey*, he tells of the legendary Trojan wars, which are supposed to have taken place around 1180 BCE in what is now Greece and Turkey. You might know one of the stories.

According to Homer, Paris, prince of Troy (a city-state in what is now Turkey) kidnapped Helen, queen of Sparta. Sparta was a city-state of Greece, so Greece went to war with Troy to get Helen back, and they came up with a clever trick. They built a huge wooden horse and hid a team of skilled troops inside it.

Naturally, the Trojans were very curious about this giant horse parked outside their city walls. So they dragged it into the city to take a closer look. In the dark of night, the Greek soldiers snuck out of their hiding place, opened the gates of Troy and let the Greek army flood in to destroy Troy and its people.

You can tell this story was written by Greeks because it makes their enemies—the Trojans—look evil (they kidnapped Helen) and stupid (they were fooled by the giant horse). We don't know

In ancient Greece, soldiers used wooden devices called siege engines to break down castle walls. A siege engine could be as large as a small house and might be covered in damp horse hides to protect it against flaming arrows. Some experts think these machines were the inspiration for Homer's story of the Trojan horse.

Zeus

whether this war ever took place, but you can bet that if it did, the Trojans' version of the story would be different.

Athena

Homer's poetry and the work of other ancient writers also tell us about Greek religion. The Greeks believed in a group of gods known as a pantheon. Each of the gods was associated with some part of Greek life or the nature that surrounded them. There were 12 main gods.

Zeus was the king of the gods and the ruler of their heavenly home, Mount Olympus. Hera was queen of the gods and the goddess of women and family. Poseidon was the god of the sea. Demeter was the goddess of nature, farming, and the seasons. Athena was the goddess of wisdom, knowledge, science, literature, and war. Greek myths (the religious stories of Greek culture) tell of these gods and other spirits of the natural world and their interactions with humans.

Poseidon

Ancient Greek thinkers didn't always follow religious explanations, though. Just as Solon came up with a new way to govern, Greek philosophers were coming up with new ways to think about the world. Thales was a Greek philosopher who lived in a city called Miletus, on the west coast of what is now Turkey. It is said that in 585 BCE he stunned his neighbors by correctly predicting that the world would be plunged into pitch darkness right in the middle of the day on the 28th of May.

> "DURING THE BATTLE THE DAY WAS SUDDENLY TURNED TO NIGHT. THALES OF MILETUS HAD FORETOLD THIS LOSS OF DAYLIGHT TO THE IONIANS, FIXING IT WITHIN THE YEAR IN WHICH THE CHANGE DID INDEED HAPPEN."
>
> Herodotus, *Histories*

The obvious explanation back then was that the gods were angry. The not-so-obvious (and scientific) explanation was that there had been a solar eclipse. This happens when the Moon passes between Earth and the Sun, blocking out the daylight for a few minutes.

Thales is sometimes called the father of science. He believed that nature makes things happen, not unpredictable gods such as Zeus or Hera. And he taught that if you observe the world closely and make hypotheses and test them, you can better understand how the universe works.

In the ancient world, science and philosophy were closely related. They both involved thinking about how the world works. One famous philosopher was Socrates. Like the Buddha, Socrates thought a person's soul could be improved over time. But Socrates believed the best way to improve yourself was through problem-solving, discussion, and debate. It was an idea that would eventually influence the development of the modern world.

Not all Greek city-states were the same. While Athens was developing democracy and philosophy, Sparta was more interested in military might. There, baby boys were inspected to see if they were strong enough to become soldiers. The weakest were abandoned and left to die on the lonely slopes of a nearby mountain range.

If you were a boy who made it to the age of seven, you were sent off to a military training camp to learn how to become a fearless warrior. The camp leaders made sure you weren't fed enough at meals. The idea was that you learned to steal. However, if you were caught stealing, you would be punished because you were too clumsy to get away undetected.

Though women weren't considered the equals of men in Sparta, girls there had it better than boys. If you were a girl, you were well fed, given a lot of freedom, and encouraged to take part in sports and ride horses. You were educated at home and were supposed to grow up to be a good

Spartan fighters wore helmets like this one (below), with a crest down the middle. The small bronze statue (right) of a girl about to take part in a race was made in Sparta in about 500 BCE.

mother to strong future warriors. And because men were so busy fighting, grown-up women also had more power than they did in Athens and other places in Greece. They were equal citizens and could own property. The Spartan idea was to create a super-culture of strong, intelligent humans that would triumph over every other culture in the world.

All of the city-states of Greece competed in the original Olympic Games, which started as far back as 776 BCE. Like ulama in Mesoamerica, the Olympic Games were both sport and religious ritual. Athletes ran and jumped and rode horses in honor of their gods, the Olympians. All wars paused to let competitors pass through battlefields on their way to the games. Poems were written about the winners and statues made in their honor. The most prestigious prize was a crown made from the leaves of that most precious tree of all—the olive.

Prince Alexander of Macedon (a Greek city-state) was a good student and great with horses. At least he was great with his own horse, Bucephalus. His father, Phillip II, was king of Macedon and was busily creating an empire by defeating other states. So of course he could afford the best education for his son.

When Alexander was 13, his dad hired a great philosopher to run a small school for Alexander and his friends. That teacher was called Aristotle, and he ended up as probably the most famous Greek philosopher of all time. He thought and wrote about everything from nature to space and from city politics and public speaking to

> "THE PLEASURES ARISING FROM STUDY AND LEARNING WILL MAKE US STUDY AND LEARN ALL THE MORE."
>
> Aristotle, philosopher

poetry, music, memory, and logic.

Aristotle's thinking led him to a very important idea. He wrote that a basic set of natural laws could explain everything to do with everything. Understanding these rules was the key to unlocking the meaning of life. The best way to achieve this was using your senses to carefully observe the world around you. He probably taught some of these ideas to Alexander and his classmates.

Alexander's father was just getting ready to invade the Persian Empire to expand Macedon even more when he was assassinated. It was 336 BCE, and Alexander was 20 years old. Suddenly he was King Alexander. As king, his number one goal was to finish conquering the world.

Aristotle (right) taught Alexander the Great (left) when he was a boy at Mieza in Macedonia. Maybe it was Aristotle's teachings that inspired Alexander to extend his empire across parts of Europe and the Middle East and into Asia.

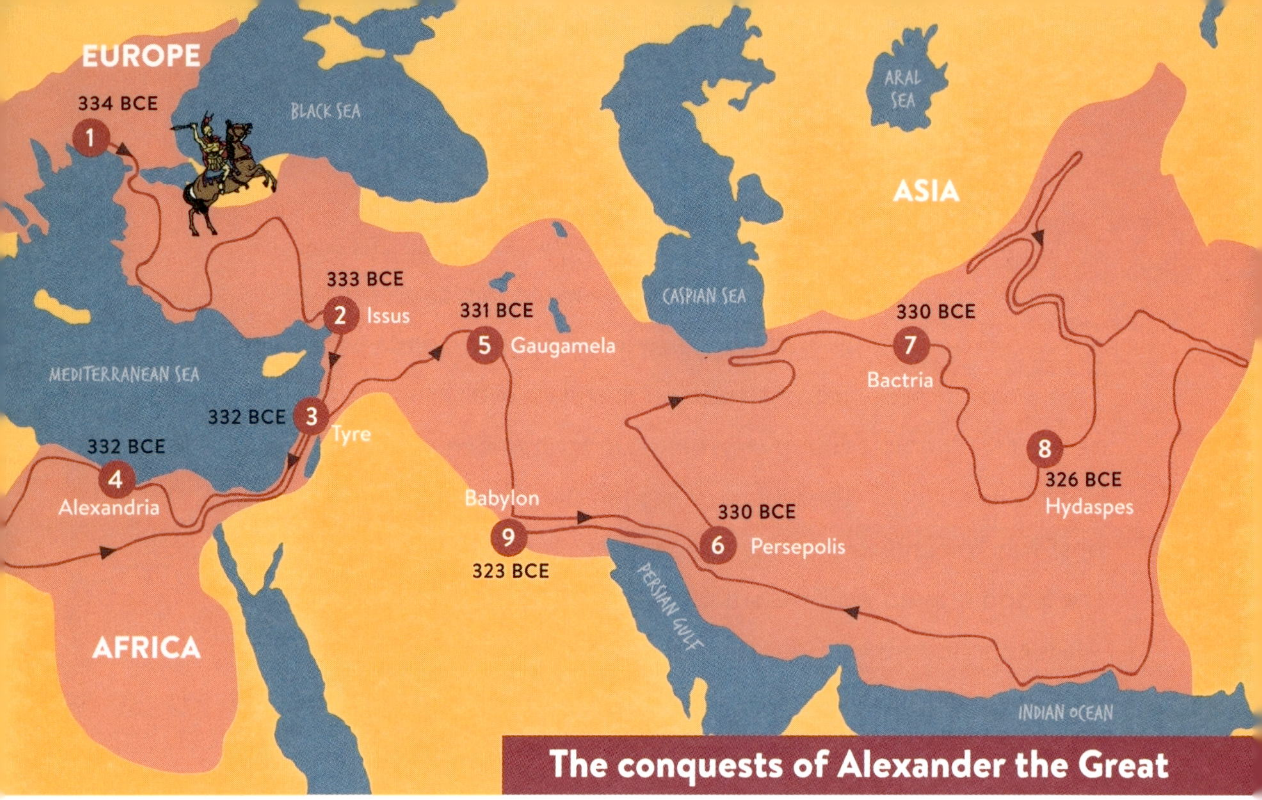

The conquests of Alexander the Great

 The Empire of Alexander the Great

Alexander the Great's route

1. Alexander set off with 48,000 soldiers
2. Victory at the Battle of Issus
3. Tyre captured after seven-month siege
4. Alexandria founded
5. Victory at Battle of Gaugamela against Darius III
6. Alexander storms the Persian Gates at Persepolis
7. Persian Emperor Darius III is killed in Bactria before Alexander reaches him
8. After battle of Hydaspes, Alexander conquers part of India
9. Death of Alexander in Babylon

Incredibly, he turned out to be really, really good at it. For the next 12 years or so, he led an army of something like 40,000 Greek soldiers. They crossed Persia, Egypt, and even parts of India, defeating any army that stood in their way. Alexander expanded the Macedonian Empire until it was almost as big as the Persian Empire had been.

Wherever he went, he brought Greeks with him. Thousands of them moved abroad, taking with them Greek ideas about drama, philosophy, politics, and science. Greek ideas mingled with Egyptian ideas and Persian ideas and Babylonian ideas and Indian ideas. As a result, a great wave of creativity broke over the empire.

Euclid, who lived in Egypt, developed a new type of math called geometry. Archimedes, who lived in Sicily, invented a water pump and a pulley system. And there was Eratosthenes, from Cyrene in what is now Libya. He calculated the distance around planet Earth using nothing more than a stick, a well, and a shadow.

Alexander died in Babylon at the age of 32. Some think he died of disease, others think he was poisoned. But it didn't take long after his death for those he had left behind to start fighting for power. By 320 BCE, the Macedonian Empire was in pieces. Still, within 100 years of his death, the Romans had started calling Alexander "the Great."

When Alexander was building his short-lived empire, the Mayan civilization was growing and thriving on the Yucatan Peninsula in what is now southeastern Mexico. When it reached its height 500 years later, it was made up of about 40 cities and extended across what is now Belize, Guatemala, and parts of Mexico, Honduras, and El Salvador.

Crops and farming lay at the very root of Mayan beliefs about the creation of the world. *The Popol Vuh* is a collection of Mayan mythology. Its name means "Book of the People," and it was passed down by word of mouth for nearly a thousand years before being written down.

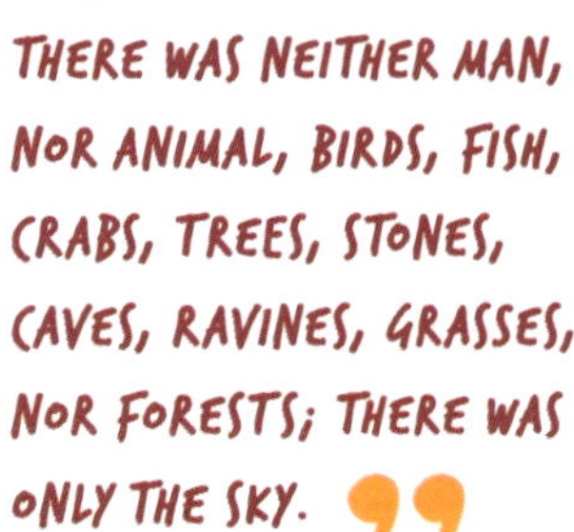

> THERE WAS NEITHER MAN, NOR ANIMAL, BIRDS, FISH, CRABS, TREES, STONES, CAVES, RAVINES, GRASSES, NOR FORESTS; THERE WAS ONLY THE SKY.

The Popul Vuh

According to *The Popol Vuh*, three gods, in the form of water-dwelling feathered snakes, created humans to keep them company. First they tried to make them out of mud, but that didn't work. Next they used wood, but that didn't work either. Finally, "true people" were modeled out of corn. Their bodies were made of white and yellow corn. Their arms and legs were corn flour. This story shows how central corn was to the Mayan way of life, just as it was to peoples up and down the Americas.

The Maya took Olmec culture and expanded it into a giant empire. Mayan cities were similar in size to the cities of Egypt, China, and Greece. They built huge pyramids and temples. Their strongly built forts suggest that they were involved in significant wars with their neighbors.

Mayan artists carved scenes from their mythology and inscriptions on the walls of important buildings. Mayan writing, which was decoded in 1981, is quite similar to Egyptian writing. In both, some symbols represent entire words and others represent the sounds of syllables. This is quite a coincidence as there is no evidence the two cultures had any contact at all. They were

The corn god, Hun Hunahpu, is one of the most important of the Mayan gods. He is associated with having plenty to eat and success in life. Here he appears in an ear of corn.

The Mayan calendar is really a combination of several ways to keep track of time. One—called the Haab cycle—tracks a year made up of 18 months of 20 days each plus one month with only 5 days. (18 months x 20 days) + (1 month x 5 days) = 365 days, or one year. New discoveries made in 2023 suggest the Mayan calendar was used as early as 1000 BCE.

thousands of miles and an ocean apart. It really is amazing how humans in very different places have come up with similar ideas so many times.

The Maya went well beyond the Egyptians in the way they kept track of time. They invented an accurate calendar that traced the time for 5,000 years, from 3114 BCE all the way to 2012 CE, the end of a great cycle.

After about 1,500 years, the mighty cities of the Maya were abandoned, maybe as a result of severe drought. (Some scientists think the Maya caused the drought themselves by cutting down too many trees, leading to climate change.) The Maya themselves didn't disappear, though. They stopped living in cities and instead lived in villages and small towns. They continued to work the land. They are there to this day.

The Indigenous people of Mesoamerica always knew they were living near the ruins of their past. But either they weren't telling outsiders about it, or the outsiders weren't listening.

Finally, in the 1830s, Juan Galindo, governor of Petén in Guatemala, paid attention. Galindo explored the ruins of several of the great Mayan cities and wrote about them. He also noticed that the people portrayed in ancient Mayan art looked very much like modern local people, so they were probably their ancestors. Once Galindo's writing made its way into the wider world, outside explorers and archaeologists started studying this incredible ancient civilization.

But not all ancient Mayan ruins were easy to find. Remember how Nineveh was hidden in what looked like a hill? Well, some of the Mayan cities had become so overgrown with jungle that not even the local people remembered them. Then, in 2015 archaeologists began using a new tool called LIDAR. This scanning technology allowed them to see through the jungle to what lay below.

What they found was astonishing. Stone houses, forts, and pyramids surrounded by networks of canals, fields, and roads show that around 15 million people had lived in this network of cities, towns, and villages and were part of a complex, highly organized civilization.

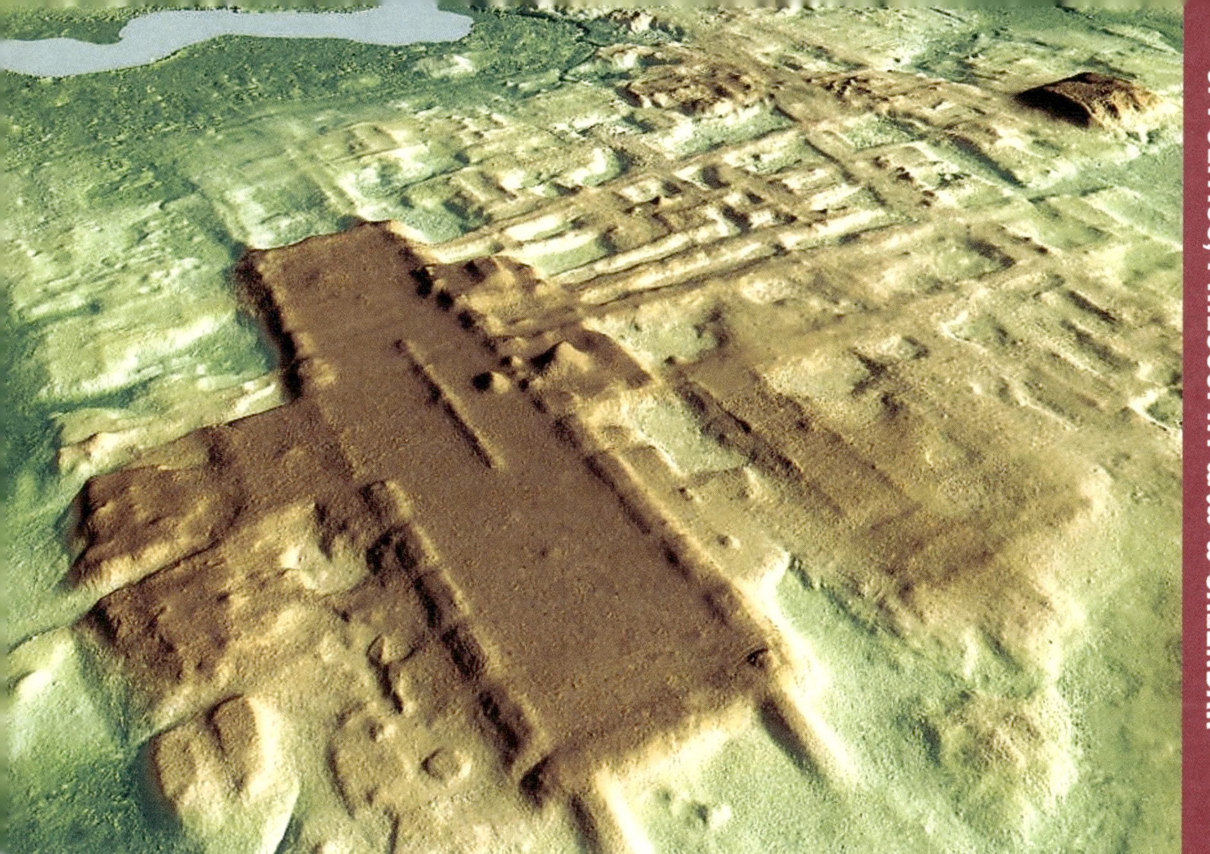

Aguada Fénix (discovered in 2020 and shown in the LIDAR image above) was a Mayan gathering place built between 1000 BCE and 800 BCE. The enormous earth platform stands 33–50 feet (10–15 m) tall and is nine-tenths of a mile (1.4 km) long. Archaeologists have found nine raised roads leading to it from the surrounding area.

About 100 years after Juan Galindo brought Mayan ruins to the attention of the world, Peruvians flying in airplanes in 1927 spotted the remains of another culture, one that remains a mystery to this day. The Nasca of the Andes Mountains in what is now Peru, created works of art we call the Nasca Lines, likely between 100 BCE and 300 CE.

If you look down on the Nasca Desert from an airplane or from the surrounding hills, you can see straight lines nearly 30 miles (50 km) long. You can also spot more than 70 enormous pictures of animals, insects, and humans, some of them as big as 1,215 feet

(370 m) tall, the size of three soccer fields. But look at them from the ground, and all you can see are paths in the dust.

When modern Peruvians first noticed these drawings, they couldn't understand how ancient people could have created them without being able to see the desert clearly from above. But archaeologists have since found wooden stakes in the ground at the ends of the lines. That suggests the Nasca people strung string between stakes to draw the figures.

But the big question is not how the Nasca people made these, but why? Some archaeologists believe the lines are related to astronomy the way Nabta Playa was and Stonehenge may have been. Others believe that they directed people to water in a desert where it only rains 20 minutes per year. And still others think they were gifts to the gods, offered in exchange for the hope of enough water to fill the Nasca people's irrigation canals so crops could grow.

The world is an enormous place, and lots of things are happening in it at the same time. While the Maya were living in their huge cities, the Egyptians were trading up and down the Nile, the Nasca were drawing their mysterious lines, and the Buddhist convert King Ashoka was ruling over all of India, another huge event was happening in China.

A warrior king named Ying Zheng led the Chinese state of Qin (pronounced "Chin") in defeating all the rest of China to create a giant empire. When Ying

The subjects of the Nasca Lines include monkeys, hummingbirds, lizards, and spiders (seen here).

became emperor in 221 BCE, he took the name Qin Shi Huang, which means "first emperor of China." Qin Shi Huang was a lot like Alexander the Great. He became king in his teens, took over the army at the age of 22, and finished building his empire by the time he was 38.

Qin Shi Huang wanted to make sure the country didn't fall apart again. He took back power from the nobles who had ruled the separate states and built up a strong army. He also ordered a set of walls to the north to be connected together. The idea was to defend the empire against attacks from nomads. This job took thousands of workers and continued long after his death. The structure is now known as the Great Wall of China. It is the largest defensive wall ever built.

Qin Shi Huang was a tyrant, but he was also very creative. He decided that China needed shared systems to make it easy for different parts of the empire to work well together. He created money that could be used all over the country. He ordered a system of standard weights and measures to make trade easier. He also created a written language that would allow educated people to

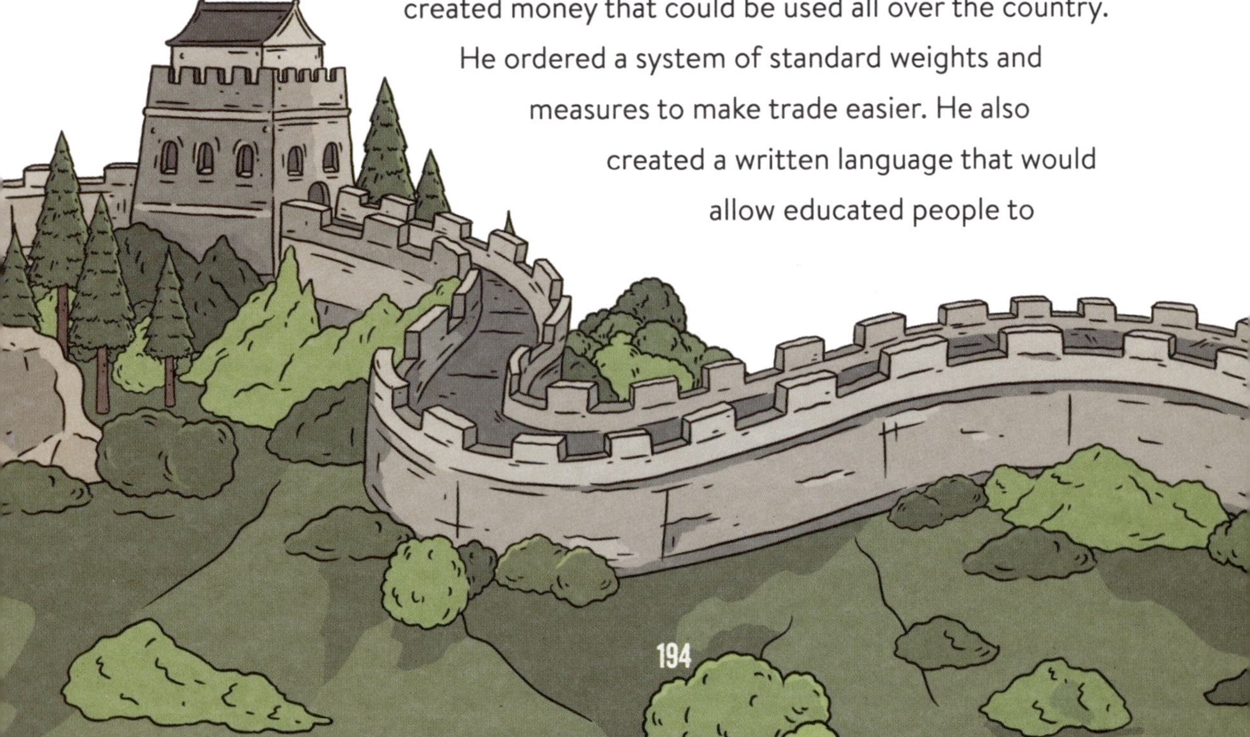

communicate clearly with one another.

Remember Confucious and the Hundred Schools of Thought? The emperor rejected almost all of their ideas. The one he kept was called Legalism. It worked for him because it upheld the emperor's right to harshly punish or even kill anyone who disobeyed him. Other ideas, including those of Confucius, were strongly discouraged.

> "I HAVE COLLECTED ALL THE WRITINGS OF THE EMPIRE AND BURNT THOSE WHICH WERE OF NO USE."
>
> Qin Shi Huang

As you might imagine, not everyone liked Qin Shi Huang. In fact, he survived several attempts to kill him. As he got older, the emperor became desperate to find a magic potion that would make him live forever. Remember the story of King Gilgamesh from Sumeria, who went in search of the same thing?

Qin Shi Huang was on a tour of eastern China, looking for this potion, when he died. It is thought that his doctors gave him some pills that they believed would give everlasting life. Unfortunately, they contained mercury, a highly poisonous metal.

For over 2,000 years, no one knew where Qin Shi Huang was buried. That is, until one day in 1974, when some farmers who were digging a well struck an unusual object buried deep underground.

About 5,500 miles (8,850 km) in length, the Great Wall of China is the longest structure ever built by humans. It was designed to protect against invasions from the north.

What they found led to an archaeological discovery as amazing as King Tut's tomb or Nineveh or the giant Mayan city buried in lowland jungles. It was a buried city spread out over 38 $miles^2$ (98 km^2). That's as big as modern Lisbon, the capital city of Portugal.

But this was not an ordinary city. It was a necropolis, a city-sized tomb. When archaeologists dug up a part of the necropolis, they found a huge army of clay soldiers. Like the shabti of the Egyptians, these figures were meant to help the emperor in the next life. But these aren't miniature figures. They are life-size statues, at least 8,000 of them. Each soldier is a separate work of art that looks like an individual person. They are made of terracotta, a kind of red clay. They carry bronze weapons and are lined up, all ready for battle. Along with the soldiers are 600 clay horses and more than 100 life-size wooden chariots. Qin Shi Huang's body lies somewhere in the necropolis, but it hasn't been found yet.

It's easy to think we know everything about the past, but that's impossible. There are still so many mysteries of ancient civilizations yet to be uncovered, so many inventions and new ideas still to be found and understood. Every new discovery reminds us there's always so much more to learn.

Experts think Emperor Qin Shi Huang employed as many as 700,000 workers over a period of 40 years to create the Terracotta Army, which he believed would protect him in the afterlife.

8. POLITICS, PHILOSOPHY *and a* CALENDAR

776 – 200 BCE

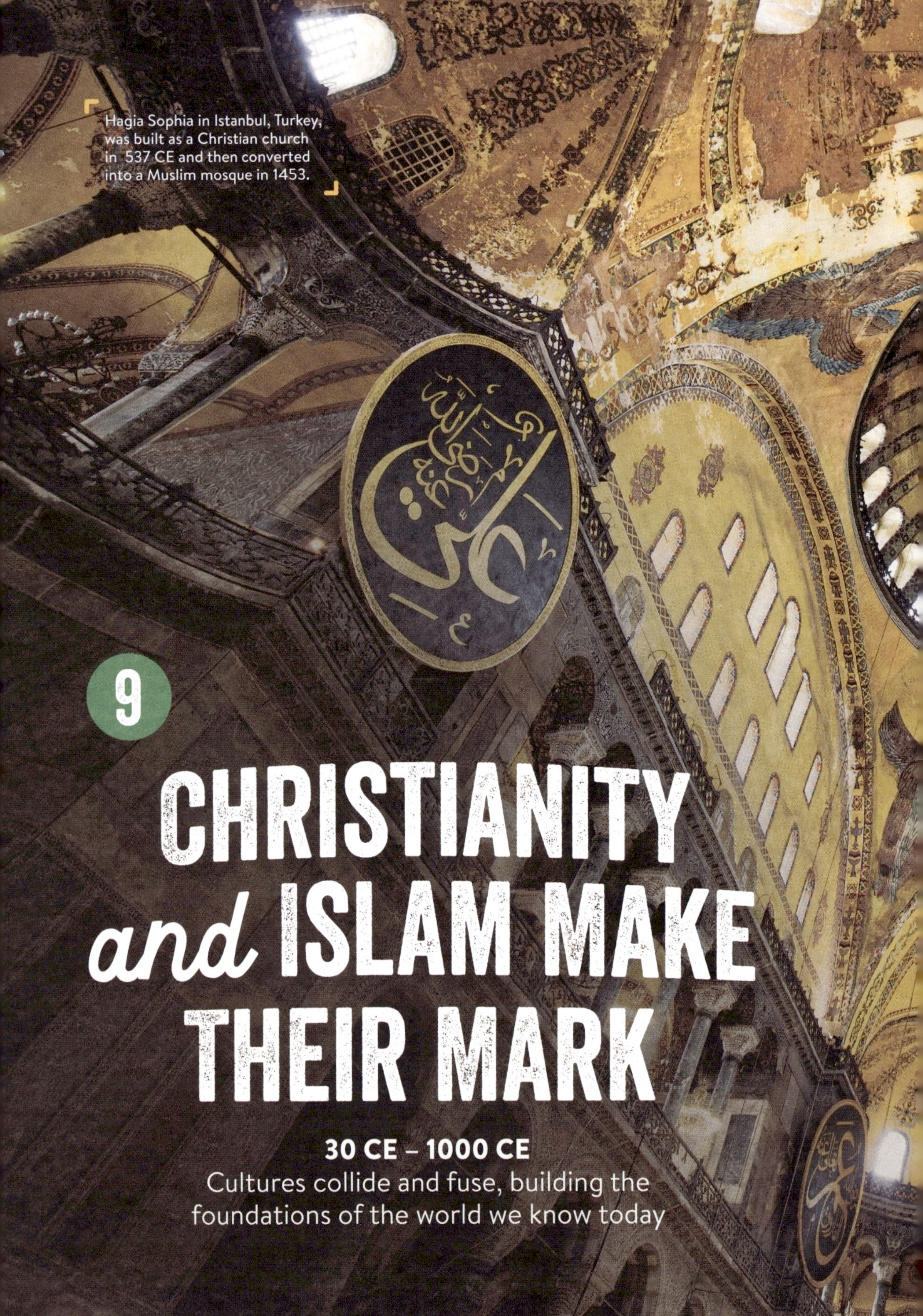

Hagia Sophia in Istanbul, Turkey, was built as a Christian church in 537 CE and then converted into a Muslim mosque in 1453.

9

CHRISTIANITY *and* ISLAM MAKE THEIR MARK

30 CE – 1000 CE

Cultures collide and fuse, building the foundations of the world we know today

30 CE
Jesus, the founder of Christianity, is executed.

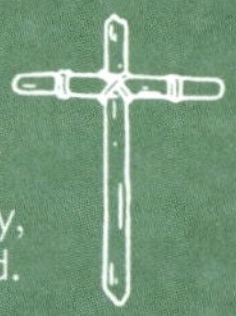

120 CE
The Roman Empire reaches its peak.

476 CE
The Western Roman Empire falls.

541 CE
The Bubonic plague breaks out.

570 CE
Prophet Muhammad, the founder of Islam, is born.

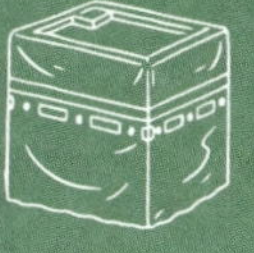

628 CE
Brahmagupta invents the symbol 0 in India.

751 CE
According to legend, the Muslim world learns the secrets of papermaking from captured Chinese soldiers.

1000 CE
Córdoba, in Muslim Spain, is one of the largest cities in the world.

History can be a little random about the way it celebrates certain leaders while hardly mentioning others. For example, though Alexander the Great built a giant empire, it only lasted his fairly short lifetime before collapsing. Yet he is one of the most famous people in European history. One reason is that he was a hero and role model to the Romans.

Adopting ideas from other cultures was a Roman speciality. For example, they picked up the Greek alphabet and changed it to work for Latin, their language. They also captured Carthage, a powerful city in North Africa. Carthage was a colony of Phoenicia, that seafaring civilization based in Canaan. They were hard to beat at sea because they had such advanced ships. So in 260 BCE, the Romans simply captured a Phoenician ship and studied it. Within about two months, they had built themselves an entire fleet.

By 200 BCE, the Roman war machine was expanding all around the Mediterranean. With each conquest they brought home huge piles of treasure and enslaved prisoners of war. By its peak in 120 CE, the Roman Empire was vast. It covered a large part of Europe, the Fertile Crescent, North Africa, and Turkey, connecting three continents, Europe, Asia, and Africa.

Of course, it's one thing to conquer a huge empire but quite another to keep it under control. Those who followed Alexander failed at that, and so did those who followed Qin Shi Huang in China. But the Romans managed it for nearly 1,000 years. One of the secrets of their success was sheer brutality.

In 73 BCE, enslaved people probably accounted for nearly half the population of the capital city, Rome. That year, Spartacus, an escaped enslaved gladiator, led thousands of other slaves in a rebellion. They fought hard, but they were no match for the Roman army.

When they were finally captured, the Romans decided to make an example of them. More than 6,000 rebels were nailed to wooden crosses and left to die. This form of execution is called crucifixion. The corpses of the rebels were left hanging on their crosses for years. It was a gruesome reminder of what could happen to those who rebelled against Roman rule.

Another way to keep people from rebelling is to keep them very busy. Ruins of huge building projects such as the Colosseum and Circus Maximus in Rome still stand as a reminder of the enslaved people of Rome who built them.

Experts think the ship the Romans copied from the Phoenicians was a quinquereme. It had 90 oars on each side and about 300 rowers to send it shooting through the waters of the Mediterranean Sea.

> THERE WAS LOTS OF BLOODSHED [IN THE AMPITHEATRE]. BUT THE COMBAT BETWEEN GLADIATORS WAS THE POINT OF THEM PERFORMING, NOT THEM KILLING EACH OTHER.
>
> Wolfgang Neubauer, archaeologist

These enormous buildings were designed to increase the power of the emperor, and to make him seem like a god. When the giant Colosseum was opened in 80 CE, the new emperor, Titus, celebrated by giving the people of Rome 100 days of spectacular drama in the form of mock battles, gladiator fights, animal hunts, and executions in the new stadium. He even had the building flooded so he could stage a sea battle.

The emperor came to the games so his people could admire him in all his glory. He was only too happy to see the most violent, bloodthirsty people of Rome all safely surrounded in one location under the watchful eye of his imperial troops.

People enslaved to the Romans also built Europe's first road network, which by about 100 CE criss-crossed over 3 million $miles^2$ (7.5 million km^2) of the empire. Most of the roads ran in straight lines. Everything that got in the way, from forests to farms, was demolished.

The Roman roads made the world feel smaller by vastly increasing travel speed. Horseback riders stationed along the roads could carry a message as much as 50 miles (80 km) in a day. That was an unheard-of speed in a time when most places had only rough paths or no clear path at all. But the Roman roads

Most gladiator contests were between two gladiators, but sometimes gladiators were forced to fight hungry wild animals. These contests were called *venationes*, which means "wild beast hunts" in Latin.

passed straight over mountains and through forests so riders could go at top speed. The roads also allowed the Romans to keep order, marching soldiers around the empire to subdue any rebellions.

It's not surprising that under this oppressive government people began to think about better ways to live. Jerusalem was humming with these new ideas. One of the rabbis there really grabbed people's attention. His name was Jesus.

Like the Buddha some 500 years before, Jesus's message was simple. Be peaceful. Love your neighbor as much as yourself. If someone hits you, do not hit back. And if you follow the rules, God will reward you. It might not happen today or even during your lifetime. But on Judgement Day at the end of time, everyone who has been good and faithful will be rewarded in heaven. Those who

The Colosseum could seat more than 50,000 spectators when it was open for public entertainment. It has survived more than 2,000 years, although earthquakes and natural erosion have caused parts of the building to collapse. This picture shows it as it stands now, in modern-day Rome, Italy.

A NEW COMMANDMENT I GIVE UNTO YOU … AS I HAVE LOVED YOU, THAT YE ALSO LOVE ONE ANOTHER. ”

Jesus Christ

haven't will end up in the fires of hell.

Some Jews came to regard Jesus as the son of God. They believed he would bring the end of the world as foretold in the Hebrew Bible. But others continued to practice the traditional Judaism of the Jerusalem Temple or belonged to other sects.

The people of Jerusalem were deeply unhappy with Roman rule, so there were a lot of uprisings. Of course the Romans cracked down on any possible rebels. At about age 30, Jesus was arrested and accused of claiming to be a king. This was an insult to Roman authority and therefore a crime. The Romans executed him by crucifixion in about 30 CE.

Most of our information about Jesus comes from religious texts written after his death. According to these scriptures, known as the

This famous painting by Leonardo da Vinci shows the last meal Jesus (center) had with his followers—known as apostles—before he was arrested and executed. Each of the apostles is reacting in his own way after Jesus predicts that one of them is about to give him up to the Roman authorities.

New Testament, his mother was named Mary but his father wasn't Mary's husband Joseph, but God himself. The New Testament also tells of many miracles Jesus performed during his lifetime. It is written that he walked on water, healed sick and injured people, and turned five loaves of bread and two fish into enough food to feed 5,000 hungry followers.

But the biggest miracle of all happened after he died. It is said that three days after his body was placed in a tomb, it disappeared. Then, his followers began to see visions of Jesus and believed he had come back to life. They called this event the Resurrection. And they set out to spread their good news about the son of God coming down to Earth to save humans.

About 40 years after Jesus's death, the Jews of Jerusalem rebelled against Roman rule. As usual, the Romans crushed the rebellion, and they burned down the Jerusalem Temple. Most of the ways Judaism was practiced in Jerusalem depended on the Temple, so when it was destroyed, so were those ways of worshipping God.

Two new religions emerged from the rubble. One was rabbinic Judaism, the kind most Jews practice today, where people worship at local synagogues, each with its own rabbi. The other was the one founded by Jesus. It is called Christianity and is now practiced by one-third of the world's people, more than any other religion.

Jesus's story went on to inspire millions all over the Roman Empire and beyond. It was particularly attractive to enslaved people who bitterly hated the cruelty of Roman rulers. The Roman government did its best to stamp out this upstart religion. Emperor Diocletian is famous for ordering in 303 CE that all Christians abandon their beliefs and instead pray to the traditional Roman gods. Anyone who disobeyed would be executed. And they were. As many as 20,000 Christians may have been killed for their faith at this time.

After he came to power in 306 CE, Diocletian's son Constantine stopped the killing. Then, in 380 CE, Emperor Theodosius I did for Christianity what King Ashoka in India had done for Buddhism. He made Christianity the official religion of the

The city of Constantinople (now Istanbul) was famous for its impenetrable walls. They were eventually breached by Ottoman invaders in 1453.

entire Roman Empire. Now it was against the law to worship the old Roman gods!

By now, the Roman Empire was falling apart. In 285 CE, Emperor Diocletian had split his vast territory into two parts. The eastern half was ruled from the city of Constantinople, now Istanbul in Turkey. The western half was ruled from Rome. Then, in the late 300s, Rome's northern enemies started chipping away at the western part of the empire, and by 500 CE it was no more.

Although the western Roman Empire was in ruins, the eastern empire—now called the Byzantine Empire—lasted for about another 1,000 years. But eventually it, too, got swept away by forces beyond its control, as we will see. Even though Roman rulers were gone, their roads, their language, their calendar, and any number of the other ideas they spread—either on purpose or by accident—have traveled farther than they could have imagined.

After the western Roman Empire collapsed and withdrew from Europe, the continent was a mess. Everybody was fighting everybody else. Germanic peoples known as the Huns, Vandals, and Visigoths, the Lombards, and even Byzantine Emperor Justinian I, were all competing for power and territory.

The real losers in all of these wars (as in all wars at all times and all places) were ordinary people. They had to deal with army after army

Odoacer was a warrior from Germany. His revolt led to the defeat of Romulus Augustulus in 476 CE, which is the date historians traditionally use to mark the fall of the western Roman Empire.

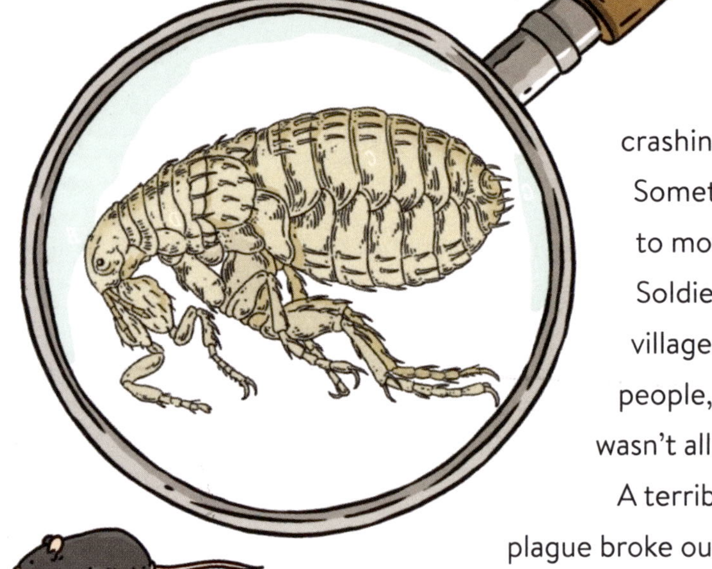

crashing through their homes. Sometimes, they were forced to move to a whole new place. Soldiers destroyed towns and villages, hurt and killed innocent people, and stole food. But that wasn't all the people had to suffer. A terrible disease called bubonic plague broke out in about 541 CE and reached Constantinople the next year. There, it killed as many as 5,000 people a day, leaving 40 percent of the population dead. It then spread across much of Europe. With repeated outbreaks over the next 300 years, this pandemic killed as many as 25 million people across western Asia, north Africa, and Europe. That's more than the entire population of Australia and New Zealand today.

Bubonic plague is caused by bacteria carried inside blood-sucking fleas. In the Middle Ages, the fleas traveled on the backs of rats and then bit humans, spreading the devastating plague.

All of this meant the number of people living in Europe was falling fast. There were about 27.5 million in 500 CE. By 650 CE, there were just 18 million. There weren't enough people to farm the fields, so forests grew up and covered them.

People who are sick and starving usually don't have time to make art or invent things. Maybe that's why there are very few records of new science, art, or writing from Europe during this time. Some kings and the people close to them were doing fine. But apart from them, life for people in Europe between 550 and 750 CE was nasty, brutish, and short.

About 1,400 years ago, during the time of misery in Europe and when the Maya civilization was at its height in Mexico and Central America, a merchant in the city of Mecca in what is now Saudi Arabia was seized by a series of visions. He told them to others, who found them so compelling that this merchant became the leader of a new religion. His full name was Abū al Qāsim Muhammad ibn 'Abd Allāh ibn 'Abd al-Muttalib ibn Hāshim. He is known simply as Muhammad, or the Prophet Muhammad.

Muhammad was born in Mecca in about 570 CE. He was orphaned at about six years old and later adopted by his uncle, Abu Talib, who was the head of their clan. The family were traders who bought, sold, and transported goods such as spices, salt, gold, and ivory. Abu Talib took Muhammad on trading trips to teach him the family business. When he grew up, Muhammad married, had children, and continued to travel and trade. He and his family practiced the local traditional religion, which had many gods believed to protect traders.

When he was about 40 years old, Muhammad began to spend a few weeks each year alone in a cave, praying. It was in the cave that he had the first in a long series of visions. The Archangel Gabriel revealed to him the final and absolute word of God, which was later written down as the Koran, the holy book of Islam. The God who spoke to Muhammad was the same one that Jews and Christians prayed to. Gabriel is an angel who appears in the Hebrew Bible and in the New Testament. He is said to have visited Mary, Jesus's mother, to tell her that she would have a child who would be the son of God.

In Arabic, the word for God is Allah. The angel told Muhammad

The Kaaba, a black building at the center of the al-Masjid al-Harām mosque in Mecca, Saudi Arabia, is considered by Muslims to be the house of Allah. Muslims all over the world face in its direction during their daily prayers. A pilgrimage to Mecca at least once in a lifetime is one of the five pillars, or requirements, of Sunni Islam.

that there was only one God, not many. He said that Allah was in heaven, not on Earth. He also said that Allah had revealed his word many times before, through prophets of the Jewish and Christian scriptures. These included Adam, Abraham, Moses, Jacob, Joseph, Elijah, Jesus, and more than 50 others. But, the angel said, over time humans had mistaken Allah's true words and as a result had created false religions.

Out of Muhammad's visions came a new religion called Islam, whose followers are called Muslims. There are branches of Islam, each with a slightly different set of beliefs and rules for life. The basic rules for Sunni Muslims (the largest group) are called the Five Pillars of Islam. Shia Muslims also have pillars, but some have more than five and others have five that are a bit different from the Sunni five.

Muhammad was a fierce defender of his new faith. Under threat from the tribes around him, who were happy with their traditional

Five Pillars of Islam	
Shahadah	Believe in Allah as the one and only true God.
Salah	Pray to Allah five times a day.
Zakat	Give generously to the poor.
Sawm	If you are a heathy adult, fast (don't eat or drink anything) between sunrise and sunset during the holy month of Ramadan.
Hajj	Make a pilgrimage to Mecca at least once in your lifetime.

religions, he raised an army of followers. First they took over his home town of Mecca. Then they went on to conquer the rest of the Arabian Peninsula.

After Muhammad's death in 632 CE, his followers went further, adding Mesopotamia and Syria. They conquered Egypt in 642, then marched west into an area called the Maghreb, which spread all the way along Africa's north coast from Libya to Morocco and down the Atlantic coast.

Why didn't they move on south to spread their message to the whole African continent? Well, in their way was the huge, hostile desert of the Sahara. But while the Muslim soldiers couldn't see a way to cross the sandy wastes of the desert, merchants did their job for them.

Many of the countries invaded during the Muslim conquests were

Muhammad's followers created a giant empire after his death, spreading out both east and west.

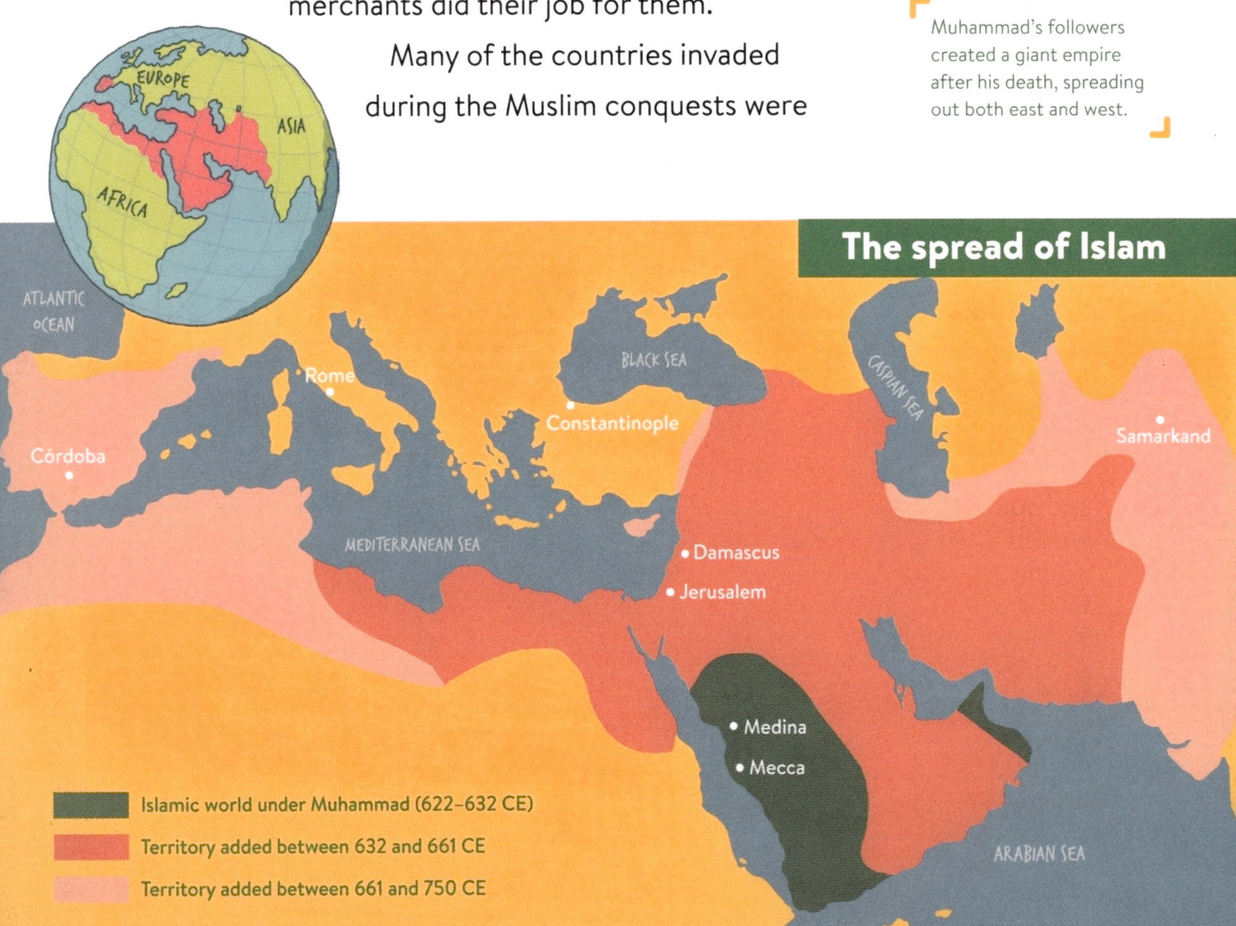

home to people called Berbers. The Berbers had been crossing the Sahara using camels since the 5th century and had established trade routes that stretched all the way to West Africa.

The journey took up to 60 days and, as there was little water to be found, was very dangerous. The Berbers knew where to look for water, though. And the risk was worth it to reach the wealthy Ghana Empire, which sold gold, ivory, ostrich feathers, and enslaved people to the Berbers. The merchants paid the Ghanaians in precious salt—and also passed ideas back and forth from one side of the Sahara to the other. Over time some Berbers converted to Islam, taking the parts that they were interested in and fitting them around their own culture.

Within 150 years, Islam had spread as far east as what is now Pakistan and west into Spain. Once again, vast swathes of Asia, Africa, and Europe were connected. By then, Islam was both a huge empire and easily the largest and fastest-growing religion in the world. Today there are more than 1.8 billion practicing Muslims. And Islam is the second most practiced religion in the world, after Christianity.

As the Muslim Empire expanded, it carried far more than the Islamic religion. Just as Alexander the Great had brought ideas both to and from the areas he conquered, so did Muslim thinkers and soldiers.

It's tricky to imagine a world without paper, isn't it? We use it today for everything from books and magazines to tea bags and toilet paper. Remember China's First Emperor Qin Shi Huang—the one who built himself that giant Terracotta Army? Well, after his death a new dynasty called the Han came to power in China.

Back in 140 BCE, Han Emperor Wu had ordered that 100 jobs as government officials be awarded based on how young men performed on a written test. But the jobs were open only to rich and well-connected families. So the system wasn't as fair as it seemed at first—a bit like the democracy of Ancient Greece.

More than 600 years later, in 693 CE, Wu Zetian, one of China's only female rulers, changed the system so that anyone (well, any man) could apply. Landing one of these high-paid jobs came to be a huge honor for the successful candidates' families and villages. But to study for and take these civil service exams meant reading written material and write things down. In much of the world, this would have been a huge problem because materials to write things on were rare, awkward to use, or expensive. Fortunately, that wasn't a problem in China. That's because the Chinese had paper.

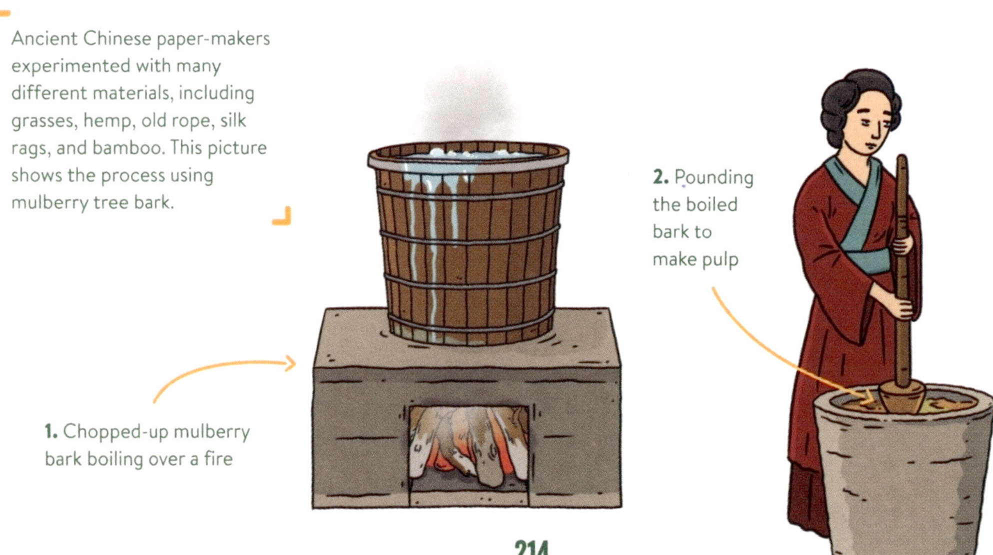

Ancient Chinese paper-makers experimented with many different materials, including grasses, hemp, old rope, silk rags, and bamboo. This picture shows the process using mulberry tree bark.

There's a legend that in about 104 CE a bright court official called Cai Lun came up with this brilliant new cheap material for writing on. He mixed hemp fibers, mulberry tree bark, and recycled cloth, and it is this mixture that made the paper smooth, flexible, and cheap. According to the story, the emperor at that time was very impressed by Cai Lun's paper-making system. He awarded Cai Lun with vast wealth and a nobleman's title.

It wasn't long before Chinese people began to use soft, inexpensive paper for almost everything, from wrapping up precious objects to making umbrellas. Wallpaper, kites, playing cards and lanterns all made their first appearance in China. Even the modern habit of using toilet paper started right here.

Wu Zetian was only able to expand the exam system because paper was available for students to use for studying. And the possibility of passing the civil service exams gave poor people more hope for wealth, privilege, and prestige.

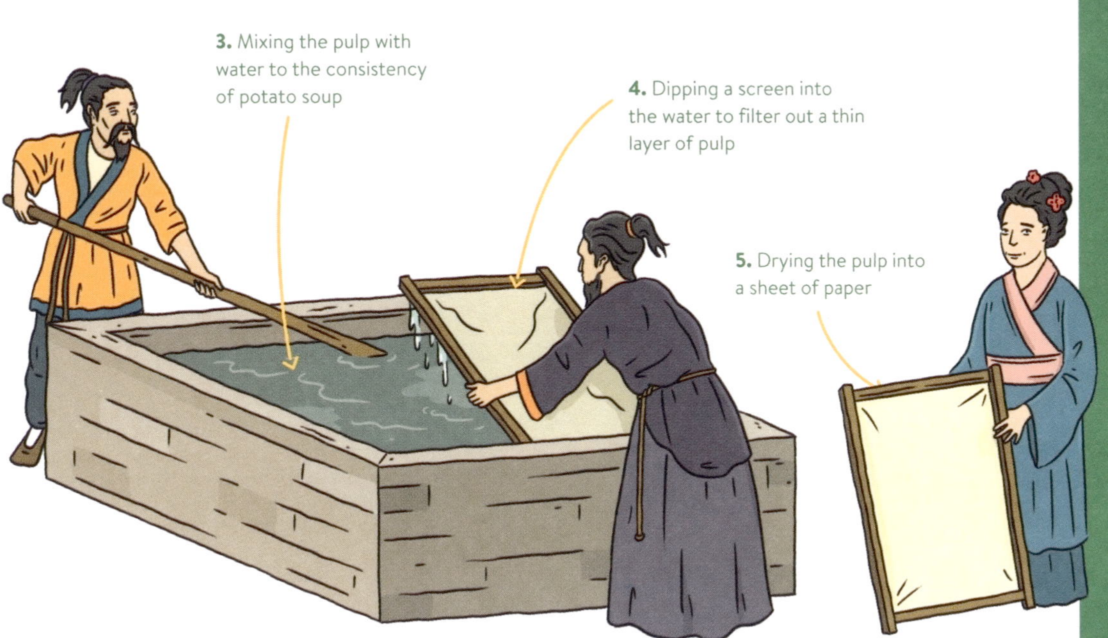

Civil service exams gave ordinary people the chance to get high-paid government jobs. A good education became the best route into Chinese high society.

Buddhist monks, originally from India, were paid by local people to pray for and educate their sons. That way people hoped to increase the chances of them passing the civil service exams. The range of subjects included everything from war strategy and law to farming and geography. And Confucius's ideas of loyalty and obedience to the family and the state were back in style. They ran through everything.

Paper was so simple and so useful that it spread to Vietnam, Korea, Japan, and India, but as far as experts can tell, it wasn't until the mid 700s that people outside east and south Asia knew how it was made. Which brings us back to the Muslim Empire.

A wonderful story is told about how the Islamic world got the secret of paper. Here's how it goes. In 751 CE, Muslim forces won a key battle against the Chinese on the banks of the River Talas, probably on the border between what are now Kazakhstan and Kyrgyzstan. In the battle they captured a lot of Chinese prisoners. Well, it turned out that some of the captives were experts in papermaking. Islamic forces had a policy of releasing any prisoner who taught at least ten Muslims something important. These captives bought their freedom by revealing the secret of how to make paper.

Islamic inventors changed the process to make it easier. And they designed new machines that allowed them to create a lot of paper at a time. By 794 CE, paper mills were opening in Baghdad, the capital of the Muslim Empire (now the capital of Iraq). From there, papermaking skills spread all across the Muslim world. Cheap, easy-to-make paper began to replace expensive papyrus, silk, and parchment.

Paper super-charged the spread of Islam by allowing its message to be received not just by word of mouth, but also through the holy book called the Koran, the record of what Muhammad had learned in his visions. So that everyone could know what the angel

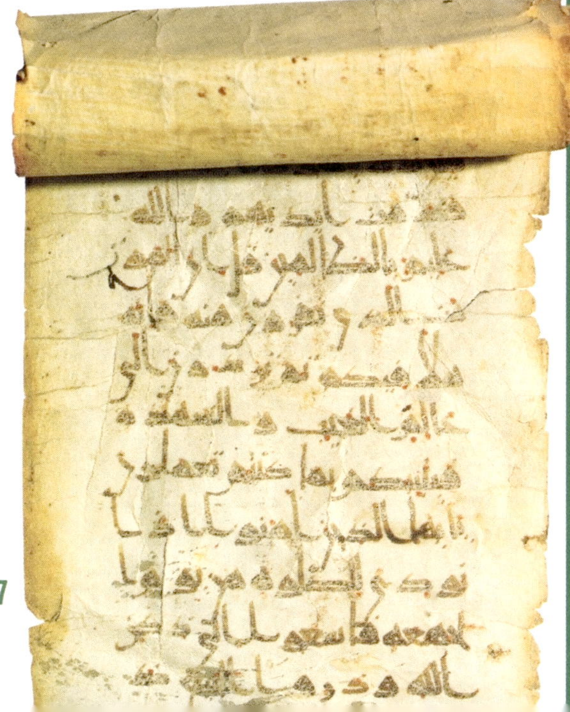

This is a fragment of one of the earliest examples of the Koran, written on a paper scroll. It was made in the 700s or 800s CE.

Muslim scholars met at the House of Wisdom in Baghdad. They translated ancient texts into Arabic and shared knowledge and scientific ideas.

had said to Muhammad, all Muslims were encouraged to learn to read, and schools were set up to teach them.

Muslim rulers valued learning of all kinds. This set off a blossoming of science and literature known as the Islamic Golden Age. Ancient texts, including works by famous philosophers like Aristotle, were respected, too. Hundreds of volumes were collected in the House of Wisdom, an enormous royal library in Baghdad.

The Caliphs (rulers) ordered that these ancient books be translated into Arabic from their original Greek, Latin, and Persian. They summoned translators, philosophers, and scholars to do the work. They even tried to merge the wisdom of philosophers like Aristotle with the divine revelations of Muhammad.

It's lucky for modern people that the Muslim Empire cared so much about learning. Over the centuries, many of the original books have been destroyed. But thanks to these learning-loving rulers, Arabic translations of them have survived and we can read important ancient books today.

Islamic courts like those in Baghdad, Córdoba (in Spain), and

Timbuktu (in Mali) propelled ideas and inventions around a huge area that connected the Far East with North and West Africa and Europe. World-changing ideas from India and China spread.

For example, an Italian merchant called Leonardo of Pisa (also known as Fibonacci) traveled to the Islamic city of Algiers in North Africa. There he saw the awesome power of doing math using a pencil and paper rather than an abacus, a sort of calculator made with beads strung on wooden rods.

The idea of number symbols on paper had come to Algiers from Baghdad. At the House of Wisdom there, two scholars named al-Kindi and al-Khwarizmi explained in about 825 CE how to do arithmetic using a new set of symbols—1, 2, 3, 4, 5, 6, 7, 8, and 9—that stood for numbers of things. Plus, like the Maya, they used the symbol 0, which stood for no things at all. These symbols could be arranged in rows and columns to allow fast calculation. They came to be called Arabic numerals. But they weren't actually Arabic.

So far there had been no contact between the people of the Americas and the people of Asia, Africa, and Europe, so there is no way the Mayan 0 could have found its way to Baghdad. But in about 628 CE, an Indian scholar called Brahmagupta had written a math book that showed how to use the digit 0 to write large numbers. For example, 2 can be turned into 20

Brahmagupta

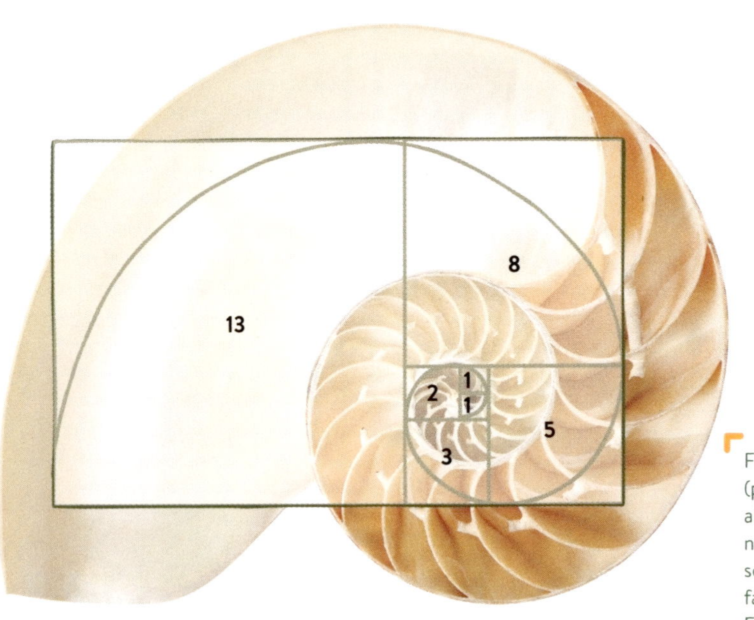

Fibonacci's book *Liber Abaci* (published in 1202) didn't just talk about the importance of Arabic numerals. It also explained number sequences and patterns, the most famous of which is called the Fibonacci sequence. This is a series of numbers where each new number is the sum of the previous two, as in 1, 1, 2, 3, 5, 8, 13 ... These ratios are often found in nature, as seen in the dimensions of this nautilus shell.

just by adding a single new digit, a zero. Or 2 can be changed into 200 with two zeros. It was Brahmagupta's 0 that had found its way to Baghdad.

When Fibonacci saw those Islamic merchants using numerals in North Africa, he decided he must take the ideas back to his homeland in Italy. The abacus was great at adding, but this new number system made subtraction, multiplication, and division much simpler. And it was far easier than Roman numerals such as IV, XII, and CVC, which were widely used in Europe at that time.

Within 200 years, Italian merchants and bankers had converted entirely to paper-based arithmetic using so-called Arabic numerals. This gave bankers more confidence to lend money, knowing they could easily keep track of loans and payments.

Modern medicine also owes much to scholars of the Muslim empire. The brilliant doctor Ibn Sina was born toward the end of the 900s in Bukhara, in what is now Afghanistan. He is said to have memorized the entire Koran by the time he was ten years old. He wrote about 450 books that we know of.

Just stop for a second to think of what it means to write 450 books. Ibn Sina only lived to about the age of 56. If we assume he started writing when he was 16 and kept it up without stopping until he died, that means he wrote over 11 books per year. That's almost one book a month for 40 years.

Ibn Sina's *Book of Healing* and *Canon of Medicine* were the most important medical textbooks in the Islamic world and Europe for more than 500 years. The five-volume work included the first detailed description of how the eye works. It even told surgeons how to treat cloudy eyesight, a condition now known as cataracts.

Ibn al-Haytham, who lived at about the same time as Ibn Sina, was a scientist who figured out the laws of light and lenses—about 600 years before

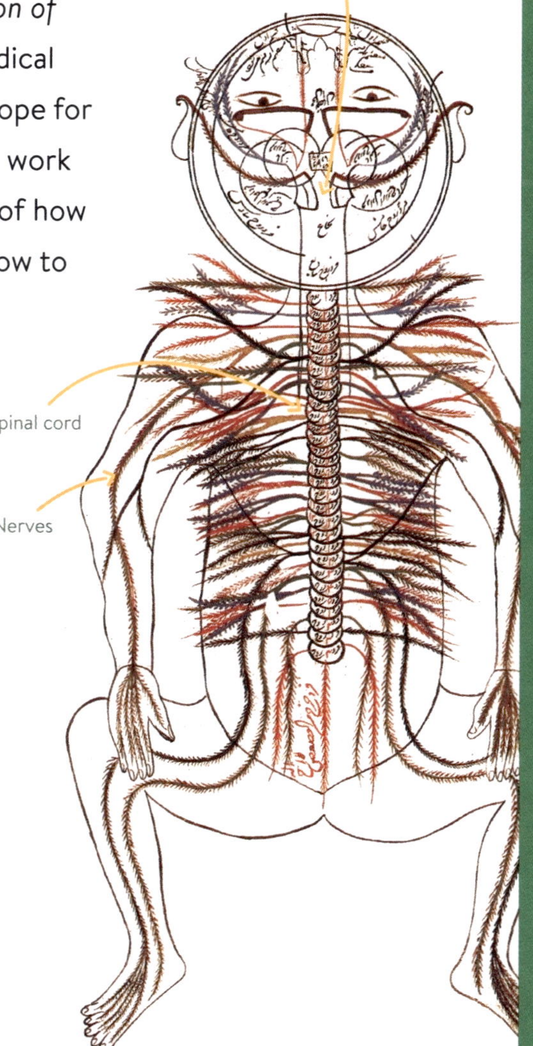

Ibn Sina understood that the brain is divided into parts with different functions and that the spine connects the brain to nerves that run through all parts of the body. This illustration is from his work *Canon of Medicine*.

Isaac Newton did similar work in England. Al-Haytham was born in Basra, in what is now Iraq, and spent most of his life in Cairo, Egypt. His book showed how rays of light can be reflected and bent, or refracted. It was later used by Italian scientist Galileo Galilei when he was building the world's first telescope designed for studying the stars and planets.

The Caliphs of Islamic Spain, which was called Al-Andalus, were determined not to be outdone by their rivals in Baghdad. They brought experts from all over the Islamic world to their capital city at Córdoba. Arabic knowledge of how to irrigate fields using underground canals and waterwheels transformed the countryside. Oranges, lemons, apricots, mulberries, bananas, sugar cane, and watermelons were all crops that had never been grown in Europe before. Muslim traders even introduced rice from India, making the popular Spanish dish paella possible.

Traders brought gold and ivory from across the Sahara. Córdoba's craftspeople turned them into coins, jewelry, and luxury goods for the Caliph and his court. Builders constructed a spectacular mosque called the Mezquita. With more than 1,000 columns made of beautiful stones, including jasper, onyx, marble, and granite, this giant house of worship could hold as many as 40,000 people for their five-times-a-day prayers.

By about 1000 CE, the number of people living in Córdoba had grown to more than 100,000. It was one of the biggest cities of its day. One enthusiastic chronicler claimed the city had 1,600 mosques, 900 public baths, 213,077 private homes, and 80,455 shops. Even if this was a colorful exaggeration, Córdoba sounds like it was a pretty bustling place.

One reason these ideas spread so easily is because all of those thinkers were able to write on paper. But making books, and especially making more than one copy of a book, was still an enormous amount of work. Scribes, who were educated people with great handwriting, worked all day long copying books. Imagine how hard it was not to make mistakes. But that was the only way to do it.

Well, that was until a new technology came along that prevented copying mistakes from being made. It also allowed that mind-reading power of humans—the written word—to spread so far and wide across the world that it began a total confusion of cultures, one that still reverberates today.

The Mezquita in Córdoba was one of the largest mosques in the world. It was converted into a Christian church after Christians drove the Muslims out of Spain in 1492.

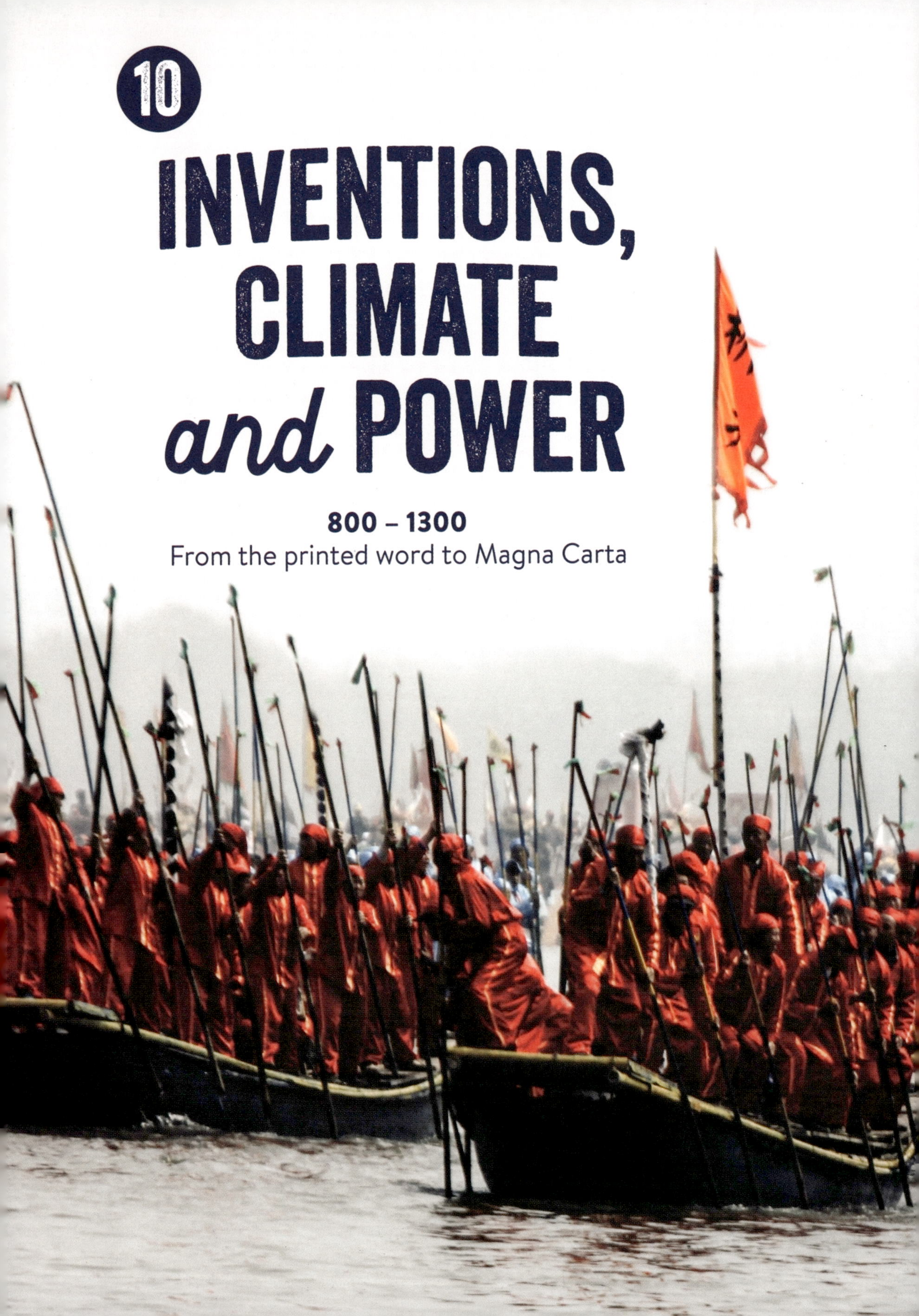

10

INVENTIONS, CLIMATE *and* POWER

800 – 1300

From the printed word to Magna Carta

This boat festival in Jiangsu Province, China, began about 3,000 years ago during the Southern Song Dynasty as a ceremony to remember those killed in war.

800 CE
Pope Leo III crowns Charlemagne the first Holy Roman Emperor.

868 CE
The oldest known printed book is made in China.

950 CE
Use of gunpowder weapons begins.

1006 CE
The Vikings try to settle in what is now Canada.

1204 CE
Christian troops sack Constantinople in the Fourth Crusade.

1127 CE
The Song dynasty is attacked by raiders from the north. China splits in two.

1215 CE
King John of England signs Magna Carta.

1279 CE
The Mongol Empire reaches its height.

The world's oldest known complete, dated, printed book is a Buddhist text called the *Diamond Sutra*, printed in 868 CE. It was made in China using a technique called woodblock printing. Printers carefully carved wooden blocks with words and illustrations. They brushed the blocks with ink and pressed them onto sheets of paper. It was hard work to carve the wooden blocks, of course. But once they had been created, the number of copies that could be printed was almost limitless.

Now China's golden age of advances in science and technology was ready for take-off. Printing helped ideas, designs and creativity spread even more easily

Over five metres in length, this scroll of the *Diamond Sutra* was printed to be given away for free. Diamonds are the hardest substance we know of. The Buddha believed these teachings would cut like a diamond through life's illusions and reveal universal truths.

This is how the technique of woodblock printing works.

1. Writing or a picture is carved into a block of wood

2. Ink is brushed on to the shape

3. Paper is gently laid on top of the ink

4. Any ink on raised areas sticks to the paper

5. Finished print

from one place to another. Which is exactly what happened after a wise emperor called Taizu seized the imperial throne in 960 CE and founded a new dynasty called the Song. One of Taizu's first acts was to increase dramatically the number of ordinary people who could take the exams to get government jobs – to about 30,000 a year.

THE LIFE OF MAN IS SHORT. HAPPINESS IS TO HAVE THE WEALTH AND MEANS TO ENJOY LIFE, AND THEN TO BE ABLE TO LEAVE THE SAME PROSPERITY TO ONE'S DESCENDANTS.

Emperor Taizu of China

Printers worked overtime. More than 500 classic texts, dictionaries, encyclopedias and history books were carved onto thousands of blocks of wood to provide mass-produced books for studying. At least a thousand new schools were opened throughout China to help prepare students for civil service exams.

An early Chinese rocket made from gunpowder and bamboo.

The ingenious Song government was rudely interrupted by violent gangs of people on horseback. Well, that is how the Song saw it, anyway. The invaders – a group called the Jurchens who came from Manchuria in the north – surely saw it differently. They might have pointed out that they were the recently united Jin dynasty and that they were just expanding their empire by taking land from their weak neighbours to the south. And while they were at it, they were taking over most of the rest of northern China.

However you tell it, the result was that China was split between the northern Jin dynasty and what remained of the Song dynasty. The Song were forced to move their capital south of the Yangtze River. They were now known as the Southern Song dynasty.

Rulers of the Southern Song were angry. They challenged their people's best scholarly brains to come up with every possible way of making new weapons, with the aim of guaranteeing victory if their northern enemies attacked again.

Charcoal, sulphur and a mixture of minerals had first been ground into a primitive form of gunpowder by Chinese monks during the Tang dynasty, in the mid 800s CE. These men had been ordered by their rulers to find a potion for bringing everlasting life. (Is this quest starting to sound familiar?) It's one of history's biggest ironies that during those experiments they stumbled across a combination of chemicals which could result in instant death.

Brilliant minds at the court of the Southern Song were able to build on that early gunpowder technology to create an arsenal of powerful new weapons, ranging from catapult bombs to flame-throwing cannons.

Can you see the devil with a snake weaving through his eye sockets to the right of the Buddha's head? He's about to throw a flaming bomb onto the Buddha. Above him and to the right, another demon is using a flame-thrower. This silk banner, dating to about 950 CE, is the earliest known illustration of the use of firearms.

They also pioneered the use of the most amazing navigation device of all time – the compass. Before the invention of the compass, sailors and travellers – like the Berbers who crossed the Sahara – had a rough idea of which direction was east because the sun rises in that direction, and they could look for familiar stars in the night sky. But in cloudy weather or inside dense forests, these methods didn't work, and it was very easy to get lost.

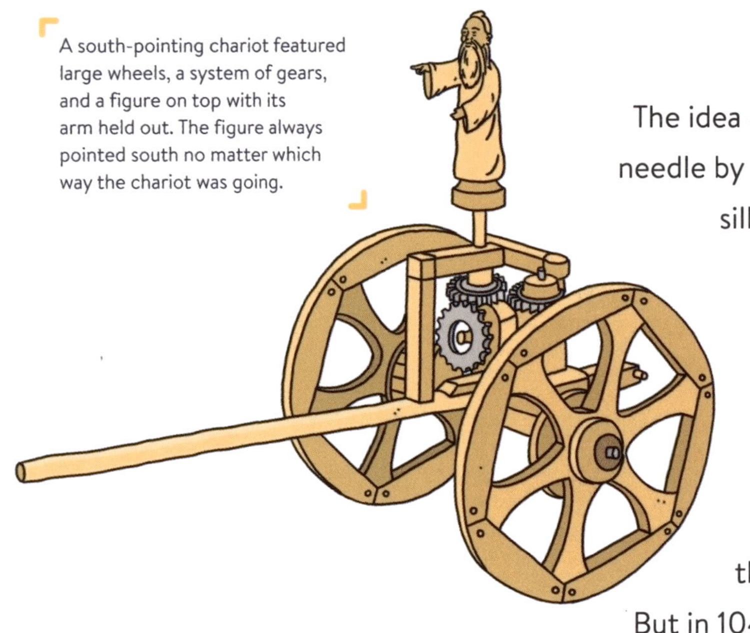

A south-pointing chariot featured large wheels, a system of gears, and a figure on top with its arm held out. The figure always pointed south no matter which way the chariot was going.

The idea of magnetising a needle by rubbing it against silk and then floating it in water to make a device that pointed north and south had been known in China since at least the first century CE. But in 1044, a Song dynasty military book called Wujing Zongyao described how this knowledge was used to create a chariot with an arm that always pointed south, to help guide troops in gloomy weather, on dark nights and in the middle of the day.

An even bigger breakthrough came a few years later. Song court scholar Shen Kuo worked out that instead of floating the magnetised needle in water, he could hang it from a piece of silk thread. Then it could be used for ocean navigation. Chinese ships carried his compass from around the year 1100.

If there's one thing that history has taught us, it is that no empire can last for ever – however ingenious its people. And as we've seen before, climate can play a part in their rise and fall. In this case the climate change that mattered was on the grasslands of central Asia, north and west of China – the land of the Mongols – and it wouldn't be long before it caused the rise of a new enemy that would come for the Song.

During the time of the European plague, the Carolingians (also known as the Franks) of northern France had started attacking their neighbours. By 800 CE, about when those Chinese monks invented gunpowder, the Franks had conquered and united the central part of Europe. This new empire included what are now Germany, Austria, the Czech Republic, Slovenia, Switzerland, the Netherlands and parts of Poland, Belgium, France and Italy.

At that time the Pope was the leader of all Christians and the people of Europe were mostly Christian. But Pope Leo III had problems. He had been accused of breaking his vows, and in 799 CE a group noblemen captured him and were trying to bring him to trial. He escaped but was still in danger. One person he went to see was Charlemagne, leader of the Franks and now of a huge European empire.

We don't know what arrangements Charlemagne and the Pope discussed, but we do know what happened next. The Franks marched into Rome in late November 800 CE. Charlemagne found Pope Leo III not guilty of the crimes he was accused of on 23 December. And the Pope crowned Charlemagne Holy Roman Emperor on Christmas Day, just two days later.

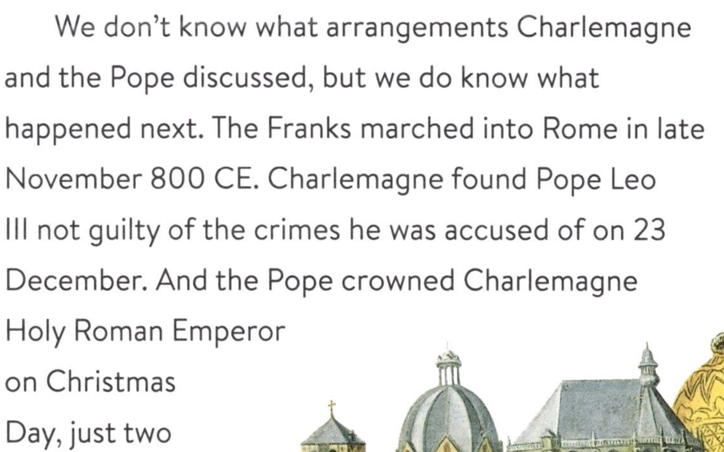

This is a portrait of Charlemagne painted in 1825. He is seen holding a model of the Palatine Chapel in Aachen, Germany, which is all that remains of a giant palace he had built for himself.

The idea was that Charlemagne was the heir to the glory of the old western Roman Empire. There were other kings in the lands across Europe, but they were all supposed to unite under Charlemagne.

Charlemagne kicked off a new era of learning, a lot like the ones in China and the Islamic world. Ancient books were copied. Schools were opened. Music was written. When Charlemagne died, there were wars for his crown. But things settled down again in 962 CE, when Otto I became Holy Roman Emperor.

And this brings us back to the climate. Because just about then the weather in Europe perked up. Cold, harsh winters gave way to what historians call the Medieval Warm Period. Between 950 and 1250 CE temperatures were even milder than they are today. Grapes grew as far north as Britain. Ice sheets melted, opening up routes across the northern seas.

A milder climate made for better crops. Better crops meant kings

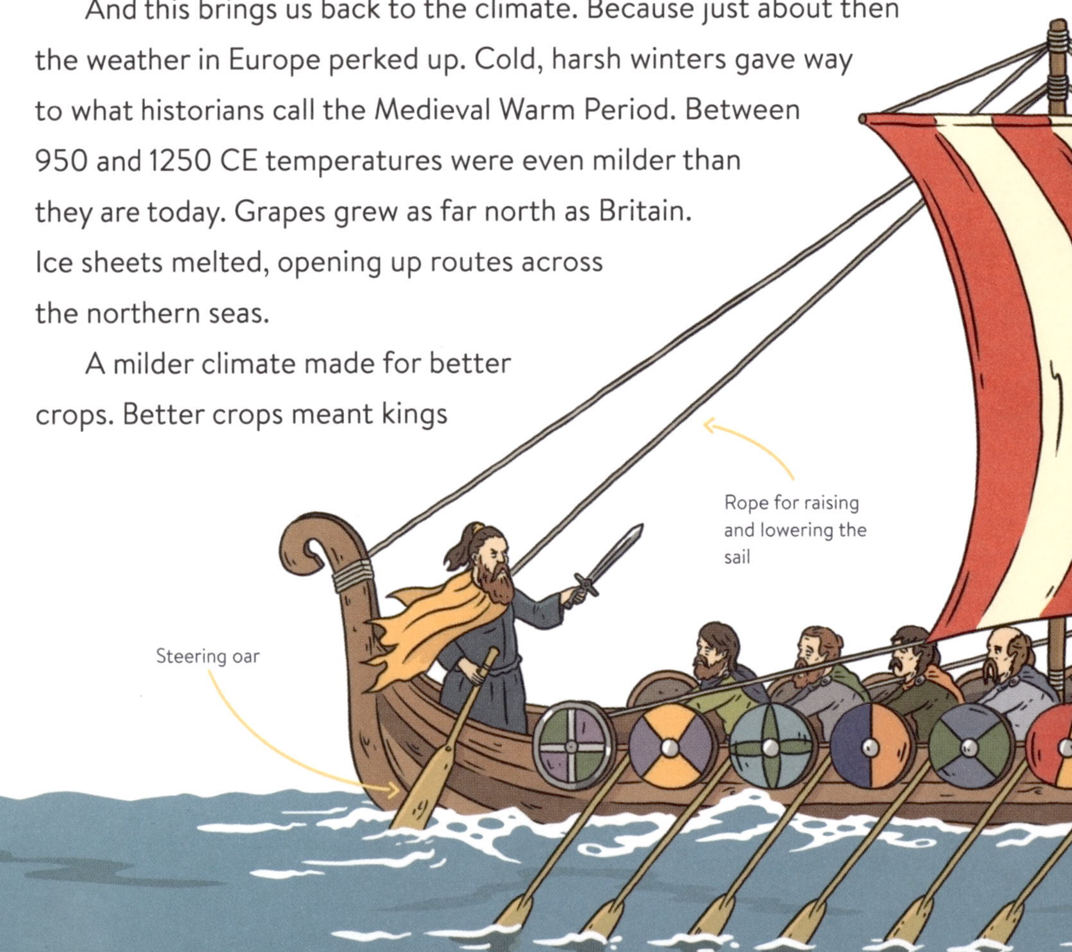

could make their subjects pay them more taxes. Richer kings started making a new kind of deal with their people. It went like this: come and join my army for a fixed number of days a year. In return, I will grant you land so you can grow food and make a living. This bargain is known as feudalism, and the people who farmed the land were called peasants.

Better weather helped northern European people expand into new lands. Enter the Vikings, people from what are now Denmark, Norway and Sweden. From as early as the 790s CE, the Vikings (also called the Norse) were excellent traders with brilliant shipbuilding and sailing skills. Starting in 793 they invaded large parts of England, Scotland and Ireland. By 839 they had sailed deep along rivers into the heart of Europe and settled in what are now Ukraine, Belarus and Russia. They called themselves the 'Rus', a word that is thought to come from an old Norse term, *rods*, meaning 'men who row'. The name Russia comes from these early Viking settlers.

Going the other way, the Vikings

Longships were the secret of the Vikings' success. These fast vessels allowed the Vikings to attack enemies quickly and nimbly. The thin shape was ideal for travelling on rivers as well as across the seas.

Viking mask

discovered a sea passage from Norway to Iceland and settled there in 874 CE. In a little over a hundred years, melting sea ice allowed them to get to Greenland. According to a series of Viking stories known as the sagas, explorer Erik the Red named the place Greenland because he wanted to make it sound like a great place to live. Actually it was a vast expanse mostly covered in glaciers, and there was very little green about it. It was populated by people related to today's Inuit, who traded with the Norse settlers.

Many cultures around the world carved masks out of wood, often for use in religious ceremonies. It was one of the things the Vikings and the Dorset culture had in common.

In about 1006 the Vikings reached the coast of what is now Canada. Erik the Red's son Leif Eriksson built a small town in what is now the Canadian province of Newfoundland. He called the area Vinland. This settlement, established nearly 500 years before Christopher Columbus's famous voyage in 1492, marks the first attempt by Europeans to make their homes in the Americas. That makes the Norse and the Indigenous people of Newfoundland the first Europeans and Americans ever to make contact. But the settlement failed.

No one is quite sure why. Some people think it had to do with an everyday part of the Scandinavian diet – milk. One of the Sagas tells how local people attacked the Viking settlers just one day after buying milk from them. That's weird, right? One day, you're trading happily. The next day, one group attacks the other.

Nowadays lots of people don't digest cow's milk well. In fact, more than eighty per cent of the Indigenous people of North America don't. The people the Vikings met didn't have cows, so they would never have tasted cow's milk before. Maybe the milk made them feel sick, and they thought the newcomers had poisoned them. Could that be why they attacked?

We don't know exactly which culture of Indigenous people looked up one day to see strange tall white people arriving in a ship, unloading unfamiliar animals and proceeding to build a town. The two most likely candidates are the Dorset culture and the Beothuk people. Viking records are no help. They called the people Skraelings, which was a Norse word and nothing to do with what the people they encountered called themselves.

The Dorset culture had been in the area (and also in Greenland) for almost 2,000 years. They lived along the coasts and mostly hunted sea mammals such as seals. They migrated from summer hunting areas to winter ones, dragging their belongings on sleds.

The Beothuk people were living in the area when British explorer John Cabot visited 500 years later. They built birchbark canoes and dressed

Dorset culture mask

in clothing made from caribou skins. They were possibly related to today's Mi'kmaq, and according to their tradition, they had been on Newfoundland for thousands of years. So perhaps they were the people who met, traded with and drove away the Norse. We may never know for sure.

The Vikings never did permanently settle in North America, but for hundreds of years they continued to visit and cut down trees for wood to bring back to Greenland and Iceland.

It's interesting that lots of people in history are known by names that other people gave them. The word Viking means 'pirate', so you can bet they didn't call themselves that. And though there are several ideas of what the word Skraelings means, one possibility is 'wretches', or 'poor, miserable people'. That wasn't a very nice name either.

The Bayeux Tapestry is a seventy-metre-long embroidered timeline, woven by hand in about the 1070s. It tells the story of William of Normandy's invasion of England. The scene below shows part of the Battle of Hastings in 1066.

Norman horses fall on sticks or stones set by the English to trip them

English soldiers defend a hill

Dead soldiers and horses

One of the biggest Viking settlements in Europe was around Rouen, in western France. Here they became known as Normans, which means 'people from the north'. (I bet they liked that better than Vikings.) The Normans' most famous ruler, William of Normandy, invaded England, winning the Battle of Hastings in 1066.

Like the Roman Empire before it, the feudalism of medieval Europe thrived on conquest. A king could give newly captured lands to knights and nobles, who in return provided weapons and soldiers for further conquest and war. As a way of trying to stamp his authority on England, William the Conqueror, as William of Normandy became known, ordered a survey of his adopted home. The result was the *Domesday Book* of 1086, which lists the lands and belongings of more than 265,000 families. It includes farmers, blacksmiths, potters, shepherds, enslaved workers and everyone else, too. It's an amazing snapshot of medieval life.

William of Normandy lifts his helmet visor to show his troops that he's alive after a fall from a horse

Bishop Odo waves a club to encourage Norman soldiers

Big data like this allowed William to let loose his tax collectors so they could extract as much money as possible from these newly conquered people. Domesday means 'doomsday', but William didn't call it that. The people did. That's because the book changed taxes from something that the lord might or might not remember to collect into something that was as sure as death.

The same warmer weather trend that opened up routes through the sea ice for the Vikings brought more food to Europe. By 1000 CE, the European population had recovered to more than thirty-seven million.

At this time, to the south and west, the first Islamic empire had broken into parts, and the parts were fighting one another. By

William the Conqueror stamped his authority on England by building a series of massive and intimidating stone castles such as the Tower of London.

about 1030, a new Muslim empire called the Great Seljuk Empire was rising. Based in Persia (now Iran), it ruled land from central Asia all the way to what is now Turkey.

The Seljuk Empire invaded the Byzantine Empire. Its soldiers even captured the Byzantine emperor himself at the Battle of Manzikert in 1071. Then they went on to take over much of what is now Turkey. They were getting perilously close to Constantinople, the capital of the empire, which used to be called Byzantium and is now Istanbul, in Turkey.

Europeans were getting nervous. Christianity had split in half in 1054 along similar lines as the Roman Empire had much earlier. Western European Christians became Roman Catholics. Byzantine Christians became Orthodox Christians. Even so, in 1095, Pope Urban II, head of the Roman Catholic Church, called for a single European army to come to the Byzantines' aid.

Christian crusaders carried shields depicting the cross of Christ.

Jerusalem, that city in Canaan that had played such a huge role in the beginnings of both Judaism and Christianity, had been captured by Muslim forces more than 400 years before, not long after the death of Muhammad. Jerusalem was, and still is, holy to Jews, Christians and Muslims, and they have fought over it for centuries. Pope Urban thought it would be a good idea for a new Christian army to retake this holy city while they were supporting the Byzantine Empire.

The Pope's call worked. Europe's Christian rulers united and set out to push back the Seljuks. This was the start of a series of wars called the Crusades. Knights in armour set out on horseback to fight people they thought of as infidels (or unbelievers). They were fighting in the name of God. Of course, the people they were attacking were fighting in the name of that exact same God. They just called him Allah.

When Pope Urban II said that any Christian who lost his life fighting the Muslims would be rewarded by God with eternal bliss in heaven, people took notice. The response was overwhelming. The effects of these bitter struggles rumble on as distrust and conflict between Christians and Muslims even today.

This First Crusade was surprisingly successful for the powers of Europe. They captured Jerusalem. In those days it was usual for conquering armies to do more than take over territory. They would kill the people whose territory they'd

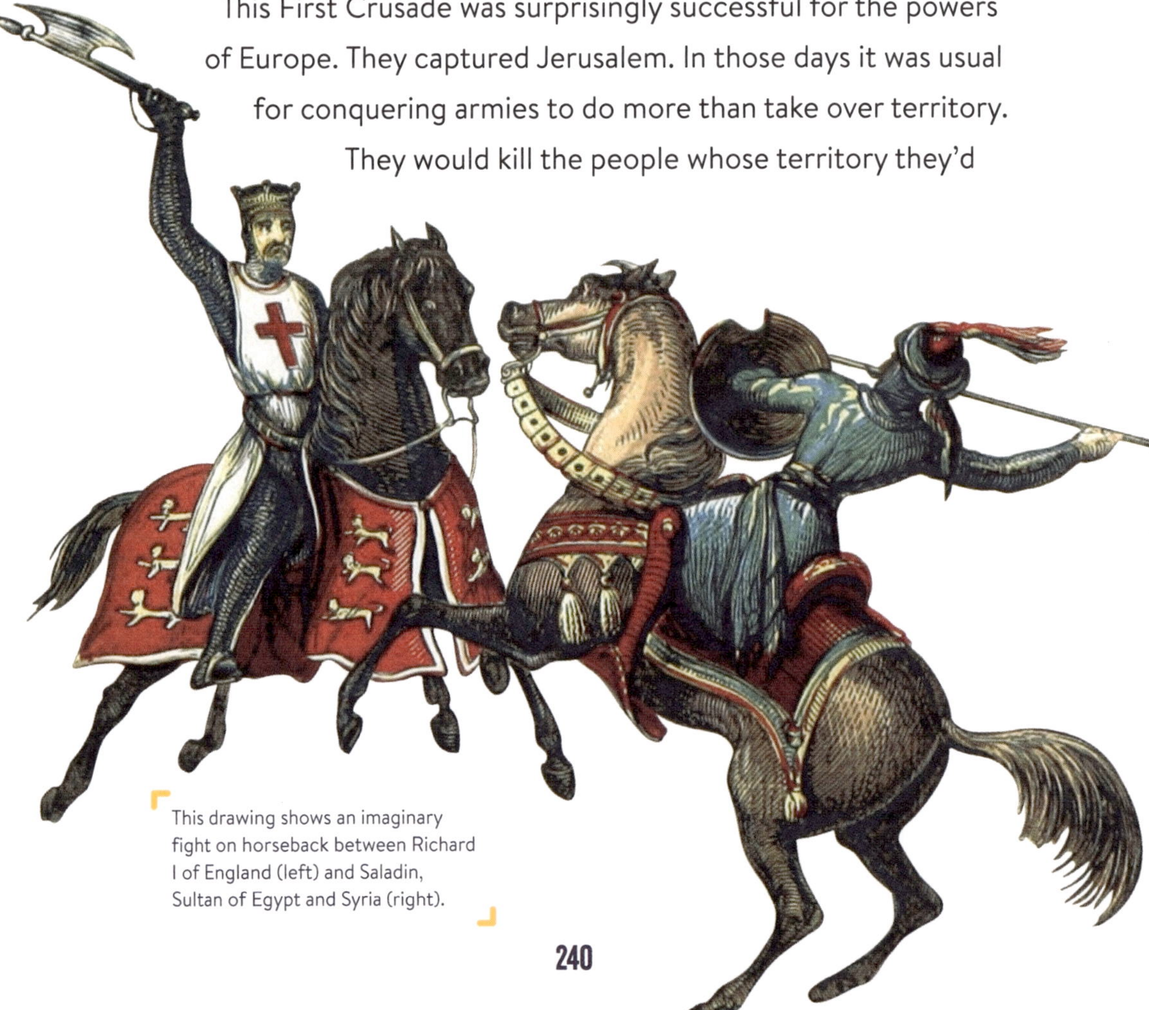

This drawing shows an imaginary fight on horseback between Richard I of England (left) and Saladin, Sultan of Egypt and Syria (right).

taken (sometimes this even happens today). When the crusaders captured Jerusalem, they massacred the Jews and Muslims who lived there. They didn't kill the Orthodox Christians of Jerusalem, but they accused them of helping the Muslims, and forced them to leave the city.

A new Roman Catholic Kingdom of Jerusalem was created, which lasted about eighty years. Because the Europeans had removed almost the whole population of the city, they spent much of that time trying to persuade Christians to settle there. Then in 1187 Saladin, the sultan of Egypt and Syria, recaptured the holy city, returning it to Muslim hands.

The loss of Jerusalem gave European leaders a reason to unite again. In 1189 an alliance of European kings including Richard I of England, Philip II of France and Frederick Barbarossa of the Holy Roman Empire, all supported by Pope Gregory VIII, marched to take back the Holy Land once again.

This would never happen nowadays. Rulers don't go to war themselves. They send their armies and keep in touch from a distance. But in the Middle Ages, kings and queens rode off to war. Often they rode right at the front of the army.

This crusade was not a success. Frederick drowned while crossing a river. Philip fell ill and returned to France. Richard made peace with Saladin after realising that his forces weren't strong enough to retake Jerusalem.

Richard was then captured on his way home by Leopold V, Duke of Austria. Leopold handed him over as a prisoner to the new Holy Roman Emperor, Henry IV. A huge ransom was paid for the return of the English king, who hurried home.

In 1204 another crusade set out for Jerusalem but never even got close. Instead, they turned their attention to the rich city of Constantinople, which was inhabited by fellow Christians, the very ones the Crusades were meant to be helping. On 12 April, these supposed soldiers of Christ broke in and did what they would have done to an enemy city. They stole treasures, destroyed property and attacked women. If they had done this exact same thing in Baghdad or Jerusalem, it would have been counted as honourable. But Constantinople was a Christian city. What happened was described at the time as one of the most shameful moments in all Christian history.

More than 300 years after the last crusade in 1204, the Italian artist Tintoretto painted this scene of crusaders swarming the walls of Constantinople.

> THE TRANSITION FROM EXTREME DROUGHT TO EXTREME MOISTURE ... MUST HAVE CREATED THE IDEAL CONDITIONS FOR A CHARISMATIC LEADER TO EMERGE OUT OF THE CHAOS, DEVELOP AN ARMY AND CONCENTRATE POWER. ”
>
> Amy Hessl, dendrochronologist

Just a few years after the last crusade, far to the north and east of Constantinople, changes were afoot. We know about year-by-year climate changes on the grasslands of Mongolia, north and west of China, because in 2014 scientists Neil Pederson and Amy Hessl worked out something quite amazing. If you've ever looked at the end of a log, you know you can see rings there. Each of those rings is the new growth of a particular year, so you can count the rings to learn how old a tree is. And you can see by the width of the rings how warm and wet (or cold and dry) each year was.

Pederson and Hessl looked at very old trees in Mongolia and found that there was an intense drought in the area from 1180 to 1190. During this time, we know that Mongol groups were fighting one another. These were people who depended on horses, and horses depend on grass. So maybe the drought at least partly caused the conflicts.

Then, from 1211 to 1225, there was a warm and rainy period, which would have made the grass grow better than ever before. Suddenly there was plenty of grass for all. And what happened then was astonishing. All those tribes united under the command of one man, Genghis Khan, and became one of the most successful conquering armies the world has ever seen. Did this happen at least partly because of good weather and plenty of grass? That's what Pederson and Hessl think.

Horses are still very important to the culture of Mongolia. This photo shows modern Mongolian children racing their horses across the very grasslands that may have made the difference for the Mongolian empire.

10. INVENTIONS, CLIMATE *and* POWER

800 – 1300

Grass or no grass, Genghis Khan was a brilliant and brutal military planner who demanded toughness, dedication and loyalty from all his people. Soldiers who performed well in battle rose through the ranks. Cowards were killed. Each unit of ten men had a leader who reported up to the next level. If one soldier deserted, his unit of ten was executed. You can understand why people never disobeyed.

The Mongols were ruthless, but they were also open to new ways of thinking. They promoted people when they did a good job, not because they were from powerful families or even because of what country they were born in. The Mongol Empire was one of the most ethnically diverse in history, and this policy of promoting the talented meant people of many cultures were included in government. Of course there was just one exception. Genghis Khan and his family were always in charge.

The Mongols created an international postal system. They also did research to improve farming. Careful planning in military councils (called *kurultai*) and excellent spying using speedy horses

The modern country of Mongolia honours Genghis Khan as their founding father. This sculpture of him sits outside the nation's Parliament building.

The Mongol Empire as of 1279

1 **Battle of Mohi (1241)**
The Mongols defeat Polish, German and Hungarian forces.

2 **Battle of Yamen (1279)**
Genghis Khan's grandson Kublai defeats the Song dynasty.

Genghis Khan and his children and grandchildren created the Mongol Empire. It was the largest empire composed of one land area that the world has ever seen.

were the keys to Mongol military success.

Whenever Genghis Khan faced an enemy city, he gave them a simple choice: surrender or die. As you can imagine, he was a man of his word. By 1215 the Mongols had besieged and sacked the Jin Chinese capital at Yanjing (now Beijing). Genghis Khan then headed west, where his forces split into two and conquered areas that are now Georgia and parts of southern Ukraine.

On their way back to Mongolia they defeated a Russian army led by six princes. As was the Mongol custom, the defeated princes were crushed to death under the weight of a banqueting platform while the Mongol generals ate their victory feast on top.

Genghis Khan died in 1227 – no one knows how. Some say he fell off a horse. And there is a legend that he was stabbed by a Tangut princess from northern China in revenge for the murder of so many of her country's people.

Genghis Khan's children and grandchildren expanded the massive Mongol Empire deeper into central Asia, across Russia and all the way to Hungary. Even the Southern Song dynasty with its gunpowder weapons could not hold out for ever. It was one of Genghis' grandsons, Kublai Khan, who eventually defeated them.

The Song's last stand took place at the battle of Yamen in 1279, just outside what is now Hong Kong, China. When a loyal court official saw that the Song fleet had been destroyed, he knew what he had to do. Grabbing the nine-year-old Song emperor, Zhao Bing, he lifted the boy up off his feet and together they jumped from a cliff to their deaths in the sea below.

Meanwhile, Europe was tearing itself apart with revolt and unrest. King John of England was so unpopular that on 15 June 1215 he was forced to meet with a group of noblemen in a field near Windsor, by the River Thames. They demanded he agree to a charter that would limit his power. No longer would he be able to do anything he wanted because he believed his power came from God. Instead he would have to obey a list of sixty-three rules. The list was known as Magna Carta.

These rules included not taking people's money to pay for his wars without asking them first. He was not allowed to throw people

King John of England agreed to the rules in Magna Carta by stamping it with his Great Seal. He didn't stick to his promises, though, making him one of the most unpopular kings in English history.

in prison without a fair trial. And he was also not allowed to take all the best fish for himself out of the River Thames. The Pope declared Magna Carta illegal soon after. But for some historians, this moment marked the beginning of a new age in which the rule of law began to take control from moody kings and upstart warlords.

But that process took a long time. And there are some parts of the world today where rulers still make up their own laws and exercise almost limitless power. It's a theme in our history book, like climate change and the human appetite for inventions, that just seems to go on and on.

TO ALL FREE MEN OF OUR KINGDOM WE HAVE ALSO GRANTED, FOR US AND OUR HEIRS FOR EVER, ALL THE LIBERTIES WRITTEN OUT BELOW, TO HAVE AND TO KEEP FOR THEM AND THEIR HEIRS, OF US AND OUR HEIRS... ”

King John of England,
Magna Carta

11 The GLOBAL MIDDLE AGES

1220 – 1521

Rich cultures around the world

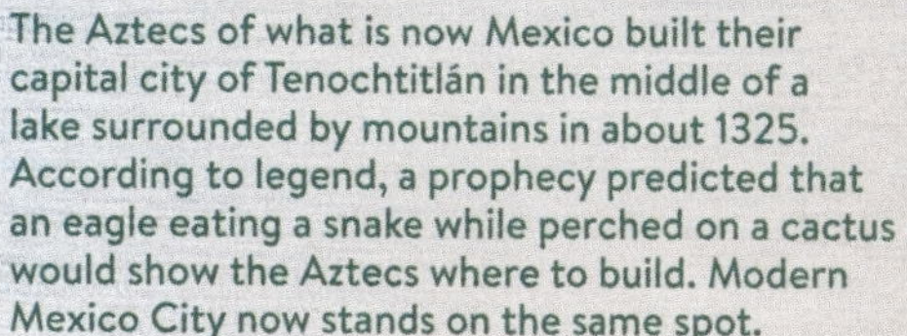

The Aztecs of what is now Mexico built their capital city of Tenochtitlán in the middle of a lake surrounded by mountains in about 1325. According to legend, a prophecy predicted that an eagle eating a snake while perched on a cactus would show the Aztecs where to build. Modern Mexico City now stands on the same spot.

1220
The Zimbabwe Kingdom completes construction of their royal walled city.

1324
Mansa Musa sets out on his pilgrimage.

1325
The Aztecs build their capital Tenochtitlán.

1350
The city of Cahokia is abandoned.

1350
The Black Death kills 40 million people in Europe.

1453
Ottoman forces capture Constantinople.

1521
A cooling climate prevents Suleiman the Magnificent from taking Vienna.

1550
The Italian Renaissance is at its height.

While Genghis Khan was building his enormous empire in Asia, two other major empires were thriving in Africa. The ancestors of the Shona people of what is now the country of Zimbabwe were part of the Kingdom of Zimbabwe. Their capital of Great Zimbabwe, built in about 1100, was on a hill and well defended by high stone walls.

Only royalty lived in the city itself, but as many as 10,000–20,000 people lived in houses made of mud brick in the valley just below. Archaeologists believe this royal city was the largest human-made structure in Africa south of the Sahara desert at that time.

The people of Zimbabwe made their living through farming, gold mining, and trade. They had an extensive trading network stretching from their circular stone city all the way to China, more than 6,000 miles (10,000 km) away. Shards of Chinese pottery as well as coins and glass beads from the Middle East suggest that the Zimbabweans were thriving until about 1450, when their trading hub fell into decline and parts of the huge empire began to fight one another for power.

The Mali empire, in West Africa, was founded by leader Sundiata Keita in the early 1200s, about 100 years after Zimbabwe. It grew very, very rich from trading gold with the Arab world on the other side of the Sahara.

Among the ruins of Great Zimbabwe were several birds carved from soapstone. This one might be a bateleur eagle, which the Shona people believed to be a messenger from the creator god Mwari.

The enormous riches of Mali are wonderfully told through the empire's most famous king, Mansa Musa. Musa was probably the richest person of all time, richer than any person in the world today. He was also Muslim, and all good Muslims make a pilgrimage to Mecca at least once in their lifetime if they possibly can. So in 1324 Mansa Musa set off for that holy city, taking with him more than 80 camels heavily laden with gold.

Mansa Musa's Mali Empire was one of the biggest in the world at the time. He is said to have remarked that it would take a year to travel from one end of it to the other.

Musa was very generous, making donations to the poor and to governments along his route. He stopped on the way to do some shopping in Cairo, Egypt. According to historians of the time, he spent so much gold and gave so much away that gold was worth less in Egypt after his visit than it had been worth before.

Mansa Musa's second reason for visiting Mecca had been to meet learned people and invite them back to Mali to teach at his university in the city of Timbuktu. Timbuktu became famous as a center for learning. The university swelled to 25,000 students and had a library of up to 700,000 manuscripts.

Amazing empires and civilizations of this time were not limited to Africa. Almost directly west, across the Atlantic ocean from Mali, another major civilization, the Aztecs, were building their capital.

The Aztec city of Tenochtitlán was spectacular. It sat in the middle of Lake Texcoco, at the site of present-day Mexico City. Tenochtitlán was connected to the mainland by walkways built up from the bottom of the lake. Each one had gaps allowing boats to pass through. Over those gaps, the Aztecs built bridges that they could take down in times of war to stop invaders from getting in. It was like having a city surrounded by a giant moat.

A huge 200-foot- (60-m-) high Templo Mayor, or Great Pyramid, was built at the heart of the city in honor of Tlaloc, god of rain and fertility, and Huitzilopochtli, god of war and the Sun. Special

This Aztec art shows prisoners of war being sacrificed to the god Tlaloc at the Templo Mayor in the the city of Tenochtitlán.

Drawn by an Aztec artist in the 1500s, this shows some animals from the zoo in Tenochtitlán, along with one of the zookeepers.

opening ceremonies are said to have involved human sacrifices. The hope was that these precious gifts would persuade the gods to send good luck and lots of rain so the Aztecs' crops would grow.

The Aztecs spread out and conquered most of what is now south-central Mexico, creating an empire that made the capital richer and richer. At its height, it had aqueducts bringing water in for its citizens, busy city markets, and a zoo full of animals. The zoo was so big that it took 300 zookeepers to care for all the animals, some of which came from as far as 1,000 miles (1,600 km) away.

When the Aztecs were building Tenochtitlán and Mansa Musa was on his pilgrimage, something mysterious was happening about 1,400 miles (2,200 km) northeast of the Aztec Empire. The city of Cahokia was in trouble.

The Mississippian people lived across the whole Midwest and Southeast of what is now the United States, and Cahokia was their largest city, situated near what is now St. Louis, Missouri.

The Cahokians were brilliant city planners. Cahokia was laid out in straight lines, with streets running east to west and north to south. And even before they built the city, the Cahokians moved dirt from hilly areas to low-lying areas to create a flat space.

The city had 120 large mounds of earth, the biggest one ten stories tall. Cahokia also had a circle of wooden posts that lined up with the movements of the Sun throughout the year, another structure very much like Nabta Playa or Stonehenge. Cahokia lasted from 600 to 1350 CE. At its height in the 1200s, between 10,000 and 40,000 people lived there. But by 1400, the city had been abandoned. Was climate change the cause? Maybe. There is evidence of droughts in the area at the time. Were there conflicts with other nations? Maybe. The Cahokians built a wall around the center of the city in its later years. Did the troubles start in the early 1300s or was it a sudden change at the end of the century? We don't know.

Some of the mounds in Cahokia were platforms for temples or houses of important people, and some were burial mounds.

By 1315, when the Zimbabweans, Malians, Aztecs, and Mississippians were thriving, a series of three wet, cold summers had brought most of Europe north of the Alps and the Pyrenees to its knees. Crops would not grow. There was no food to feed the animals. And salt, vital for preserving food, was almost impossible to find.

> "THERE WAS A BELIEF [IN CAHOKIA] THAT WHAT WENT ON ON EARTH ALSO WENT ON IN THE SPIRIT WORLD, AND VICE VERSA. SO ... EVERYTHING HAD TO BE VERY PRECISE."
>
> James Brown, archaeologist

In that time and place, salt had to be made by evaporating sea water. And when it's raining or very humid, water doesn't evaporate well. Without salt for food preservation, no one but the richest landlords could afford to eat.

Even the English king, Edward II, was unable to find enough bread to feed his court while touring the country that summer. Survival meant killing farm animals and eating seeds saved for next year's crops. Terrible things followed.

All over Europe, children were abandoned and left to find food for themselves. The German fairy story of Hansel and Gretel being sent away by their parents is thought to date from this time. Some elderly people even starved themselves to death on purpose for the sake of the rest of their families.

Disease spread quickly through the hungry, weakened people. In 1276 the length of life for the average European was 35 years. By 1325 it had fallen to not much more than 20.

What happened next was an even greater catastrophe. The plague that had caused so many deaths in the 500s was back, with its armpit swellings, black skin spots, nosebleeds, and often death.

Rats are usually blamed for spreading the appalling Black Death that struck Europe between 1347 and 1351. But humans were just as much to blame. As we saw before, this awful disease is caused by bacteria that live inside tiny insects called fleas. The fleas mostly prefer to live on small, furry creatures like rats. But if a human comes along, they'll hop right on.

And, of course, anyone, human or animal, with an infected flea on them carries the bacteria anywhere they go. This time the pandemic probably started in eastern Asia in the 1330s and spread from there along the Silk Route.

There is a legend of how it spread to Europe. As the story goes, in 1346 the Mongol ruler Jani Beg and his troops had the trading port of Kaffa on the north coast of the Black Sea surrounded. They were trying to force the city to surrender by keeping anyone from going in or out. This is called a siege. But so many of Beg's troops got sick and died from the plague that he knew he would have to abandon his plans.

In this painting from the 1300s, plague victims are blessed by a priest. Without the benefit of modern medicine, prayer was their only hope.

In a desperate last stand, Beg's few surviving troops loaded the bodies of the many dead soldiers onto catapults, and hurled them over Kaffa's walls. At the time, a group of traders from Genoa, Italy, were in Kaffa. Once they understood what was happening, they got on a ship bound for home. But they had unintentionally brought some infected fleas with them. Most of the Genoese died on the ship, but the few who reached Italy passed on the killer disease. Genoa was a major trading hub at the time, so the plague spread as people got on their horses and boats and headed to other parts of Europe to trade.

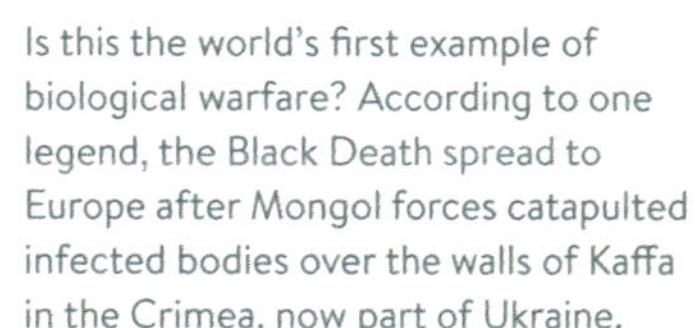

Is this the world's first example of biological warfare? According to one legend, the Black Death spread to Europe after Mongol forces catapulted infected bodies over the walls of Kaffa in the Crimea, now part of Ukraine.

This story might be true and it might not be. No one really knows. But what we do know is that over the next three years, more than 40 million Europeans died. That was more than half the continent's population. Between 1348 and 1375, the average European lived to be just over 17 years old, the youngest ever.

Feudalism eventually broke down because there simply weren't enough peasants left to become soldiers or to work for the lords. English kings like Henry V were forced to pay soldiers to fight for them. To get the money to do that meant more taxes on the people. But the people had the upper hand this time. Because there were so

The thunderbird symbolizes power over nature.

few of them to do the work, they could demand more power, freedom, and fair pay in return for their labor.

By now you can see that history is great at telling the stories of people who left behind writing or huge buildings full of stuff. But the world of the 1300s (and of most other times, too) was also full of people who are more difficult to learn about. We can guess how these people lived from the smaller number of objects or structures they left behind, from accounts of other people who met them, and from the histories and traditions of their modern descendants.

The Haida, Tlingit, and other communities on the Pacific coast of what are now Canada and Alaska built giant totem poles from cedar trees to honor their gods. Some of their descendants still carve poles and participate in other traditions that probably date back to well before the 1300s.

The Hohokam, of what is now the southwestern

The grizzly bear protecting the human represents strength, family, courage, and health.

The Indigenous nations of the Pacific coast of what are now Oregon, Washington, and Alaska, as well as British Columbia in Canada, carved totem poles from large cedar trees, and some still do. Traditionally, each clan, or extended family, placed its pole at the front of its family house. The symbols carved into the pole and their order on it tell of a mythical or real event. This is an illustration of the Thunderbird house post that stands in Stanley Park in Vancouver, British Columbia, Canada.

Scarlet macaws

United States, had the largest system of irrigation canals in North America in the 1300s. With this method of bringing water to their dry fields, they could grow corn, beans, and squash in the desert and support a big enough community to build multi-story houses. In addition, they traded with cultures as far as 2,000 miles (3,000 km) away. One of the things they traded was scarlet macaws, a type of parrot. The Hohokam bought them from the Maya in what is now eastern Mexico and traded them all around North America.

The Calusa of what is now Florida ate so many shellfish that they could build their houses on the top of giant mounds made of the shells. Archaeologists have discovered one shell mound that people lived on as early as 2,000 years ago. Plus the Spanish who tried to defeat the Calusa in the 1500s described the mounds, too. So it's a good bet they lived that way in the 1300s.

The Roma (traveler) people arrived in Europe from what is now northern India at the beginning of the 1300s, bringing their skill with horses and music and their distinctive culture. The music they brought to Spain developed into flamenco.

Historians believe the Ainu culture of northern Japan started

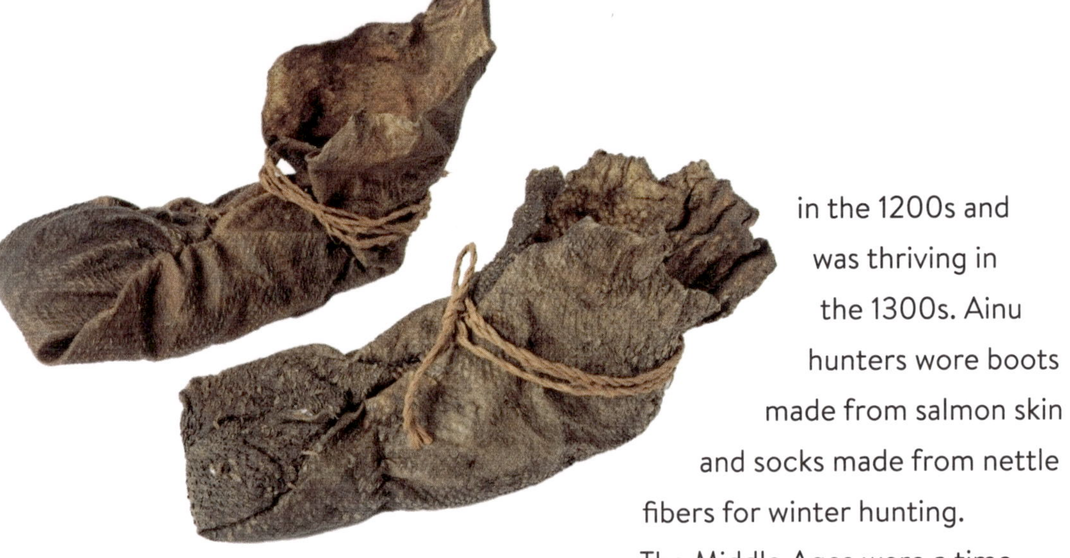

The Ainu people of what is now Japan went barefoot most of the year. But in winter, when hunting in snow and ice could cause frostbite, they wore salmon skin shoes like these.

in the 1200s and was thriving in the 1300s. Ainu hunters wore boots made from salmon skin and socks made from nettle fibers for winter hunting.

The Middle Ages were a time of tremendous variety of cultures and lifestyles. Though some left behind few weapons and seem to have lived mostly in peace, others, including the Calusa, were frequently at war with their neighbors. But to find people who were turning war into a science, we need to travel back to Europe and the Middle East, where Christians and Muslims were still competing for power.

Remember gunpowder, that world-changing invention of the Chinese? It took quite a long time for knowledge of it to get to Europe and even longer for Europeans to start using it in war. The first European mention of the explosive substance was in 1267. That's when a recipe for it appeared in a book called *Opus Majus*. Though Roger Bacon, an Englishman, had written the book, no European army tried out cannons until the 1300s.

The first in Europe might have been in 1342 at the siege of the Spanish city of Algeciras. There, Muslims defending the city fired

> THE BESIEGED DID GREAT HARM AMONG THE CHRISTIANS WITH IRON BULLETS THEY SHOT.
>
> Juan de Marianas, historian

simple cannons that shot pieces of iron over the city walls to drive off attacking Christian forces. The siege lasted almost two years. But in the end the Muslims surrendered. Gunpowder hadn't been enough to hold the city.

Four years later, in 1346, a gunpowder cannon was rolled out by the English against their arch-enemies, the French, at the Battle of Crécy. Though the English won, the cannons didn't work so well. In fact, it was probably safer to be targeted by one of those cannons than to be operating it. But within 100 years, guns were an army's first-choice weapon. Cannon fire could sometimes reduce a stone castle to rubble in just minutes. Guns turned unskilled peasant fighters into lethal soldiers who could kill at a distance.

A Hungarian cannon engineer named Urban may have been the world's first arms dealer. It was 1452, and he had designed a huge cannon. Looking for someone to pay him to make it, he went to the Byzantine emperor, Constantine XI. Constantine turned him down. So Urban went to Constantine's enemy, Sultan Mehmed II, leader of the Ottoman Empire. Mehmed said yes. Urban's giant gun ended up on the Ottoman side of an incredibly important battle.

And when I say giant, I really mean it. Each cannon was 25 feet

English forces used Europe's first cannon against their arch-enemies, the French, at the Battle of Crécy in 1346. The guns didn't work very well, but over time the technology improved, transforming warfare.

(8 m) long and made of copper and tin. Some said it took 50 oxen to pull one and 700 men to fire it. Nearly 750 years had passed since the last time Muslim forces had tried to take Constantinople, capital of the Byzantine Empire and guardian of rich trade routes. In the meantime, the Islamic world had gone through a lot of changes. New empires had replaced the older ones. One of them, based in Turkey, was the Ottoman Empire, Urban's new employer.

By the spring of 1453, a giant force of 80,000 Ottoman soldiers had gathered just outside the massive walls of Constantinople. Urban's cannons slowly rolled across the plains to just outside the city. Giant balls of stone and marble pounded Constantinople's walls. They landed with such force that it was said they smashed 6 feet (2 m) into the ground. On May 28, 1453, the Ottomans broke through the city walls, and troops flooded inside.

Europe was absolutely not prepared for such a defeat. Remember that merchant Leonard of Pisa, also known as Fibonacci? Well, after he introduced Arabic numerals from North Africa to his home country in what is now Italy, a huge change began taking place in the world of high finance. City-states such as Florence, Milan, Genoa, and Venice turned into epic centers of trade between East and West, with a new banking system that used Arabic numerals to track credits and loans. Banking families such as the Medici, Bardi, and Peruzzi spurred on what is known as the Italian Renaissance—meaning rebirth—where dizzyingly rich patrons commissioned architects, writers, painters, scholars, sculptors, musicians, and others to create dazzling buildings, books, and works of art.

Muslim attackers face off against Christian defenders at the Siege of Constantinople in 1453.

11. *The* Global Middle Ages

1220 – 1521

This painting of the angel Gabriel telling the Virgin Mary that she will be the mother of Jesus was painted by Renaissance artist Fra Angelico in 1450. One of the big inventions of the Renaissance was realistic perspective, where distant objects are smaller and seem farther away than close ones.

When news of the fall of Constantinople reached Europe, it stunned the Christian world. With Constantinople went the remaining territory of the Byzantine Empire. That included the silver mines of Serbia and Greece, which were very important to Europe's economy, including those very rich bankers. And some people living in the former Byzantine empire were converting to Islam, which scared Christians.

Ottoman Sultan Selim I closed in even more. He invaded Egypt, cutting off historic trading links between Europe and east Asia.

Selim I's successor, Suleiman the Magnificent, was also called "the Lawgiver" because he fixed the Empire's legal system. He started a cultural golden age by building public works such as aqueducts and by encouraging the arts. The Ottoman Empire was especially known for calligraphy, miniature paintings, paper marbling, and bookbinding.

Suleiman also continued his father's empire building. His army invaded Hungary in 1521. After winning the Battle of Mohács there, Muslim armies gathered outside the walls of Vienna, in what is now Austria. It was only the harshest of winters that forced Suleiman

This illustration shows the city of Vienna surrounded by the armies of Suleiman the Magnificent in 1529.

to call his troops home, saving Vienna from falling. He would try again in 1532, with the same result.

Very cold winters had become more common by the late 1400s, a trend that continued for hundreds of years. But if the cold weather provided temporary relief for the people of Vienna, it proved fatal to the adventurous Vikings of Greenland. Plummeting temperatures were just too cold to handle. The sea ice closed in, and nobody could get to or from the frozen land. The Europeans there disappeared completely. They may have starved or frozen to death. (The Indigenous Thule people, ancestors of today's Inuit, were perfectly fine in the cold. They had the culture and technology to thrive in an environment of snow and ice.)

Christian Europe was now surrounded. To the north lay ice, to the west an ocean that seemed too vast to navigate. The east and south were firmly in the hands of enemy Muslim traders and rulers. It's fair to say that Europe was badly in need of a miracle.

12

COLONIALISM TAKES OFF

1469 – 1621

One person's miracle is another's disaster

This monument in Lisbon, Portugal, celebrates Prince Henry the Navigator, who funded much of Portuguese exploration in the 1400s, as well as other explorers of the period. Gil Eanes, the ship's captain who worked out how to sail past Cape Bojador on the western shore of Africa, is fifth in line here.

1443
The Portuguese find a sea route to African gold.

1488
Portuguese explorer Bartolomeu Dias is the first European to see the southern tip of Africa.

1492
Ferdinand and Isabella defeat the last Muslim stronghold in Spain and force all Muslims and Jews to convert or leave the country.

1492
Christopher Columbus arrives in the Caribbean, which he thinks is Asia.

1517
Martin Luther protests against the Church, sparking the Protestant Reformation.

1522
Spain conquers the Aztec Empire.

1620
English Protestants settle in New England.

She was an eighteen-year-old princess and the heir to a throne. He was a prince, one year younger, and first in line to be king in another land. They met and a week later they were married. Her family was furious.

Sound familiar? No, this isn't the trailer from a Hollywood movie. Nor is it the blurb from a Shakespeare play. It's the true story of two monarchs who lived in what is now Spain – Isabella of Castile and Ferdinand of Aragon. And this story is not about love and romance. It's about power and politics.

When Isabella's brother, the king of Castile, died, a war broke out over who should lead the country: Isabella or her niece Joanna. But Isabella was ready for a fight. She had chosen to marry Ferdinand, a man whose father had a big army. She won the war with help from Aragon and became Queen of Castile in 1474, aged twenty-three. Five years later, Ferdinand's father died. So he became King of Aragon. Isabella and Ferdinand's marriage made them immensely powerful, ensured peace between Castile and Aragon, and eventually led to the modern country of Spain.

And what did Isabella and Ferdinand do with all their power? First of all, in 1492, they defeated the Muslim rulers of the southern state of Granada and forced all the Jews and Muslims who had been peacefully practising their religions in the area to convert to Christianity or leave. The Pope was very pleased with them and called them The Catholic Monarchs. Their other goal was to challenge the rising power of Portugal, their rival to the west.

By combining their two countries, Ferdinand and Isabella became two of the most powerful monarchs in Europe.

Portugal had a huge head start. That's because over fifty years before, they'd had a prince who was a treasure hunter. In 1415, when Prince Henry was twenty-one, he helped the Portuguese navy capture a north African town called Ceuta. Pirates based there had been kidnapping Portuguese villagers to sell into slavery in Africa. Henry's father, King John I of Portugal, wanted that to stop. Henry wanted to catch the pirates, too, but he also had his eyes on Ceuta for another reason – gold.

Muslim traders came into the town's market, their camels laden with treasure. They had travelled for forty days across the vast Sahara to the fantastically rich Songhai Empire, which now controlled most of West Africa. On the way to Songhai, the camel caravan carried blocks of salt mined in the desert.

The Songhai had huge gold mines, but they didn't have enough salt to preserve their meat. So they were happy to trade their gold for the precious salt.

The Sahara desert was a daunting barrier between North Africa and the rest of the continent. Traders who crossed it found their way partly by following the stars at night, just as sailors did at sea.

Gold might have been plentiful in Songhai, but it was expensive in Ceuta. That's because its price included not just the cost of the salt that was used to pay for it but also the expense of carrying the gold hundreds of kilometres across the Sahara and big profits for the Muslim merchants. If only, thought Henry, a way could be found to get to that gold without having to cross the desert or pay those merchants!

Henry's plan was to reach the source of the gold by sea – sailing south along the West African coastline. He sent out expedition after expedition of intrepid sailors. When they came back, he had his map-makers update their charts so that they could be used for future expeditions.

Henry's first challenge was to navigate past Cape Bojador, just south of modern-day Morocco. This was the most southerly point Europeans had reached. Because of its fearsome currents and strong winds, it was known as the place where sea monsters dwelt. Some thought it was the end of the Earth.

You have to hand it

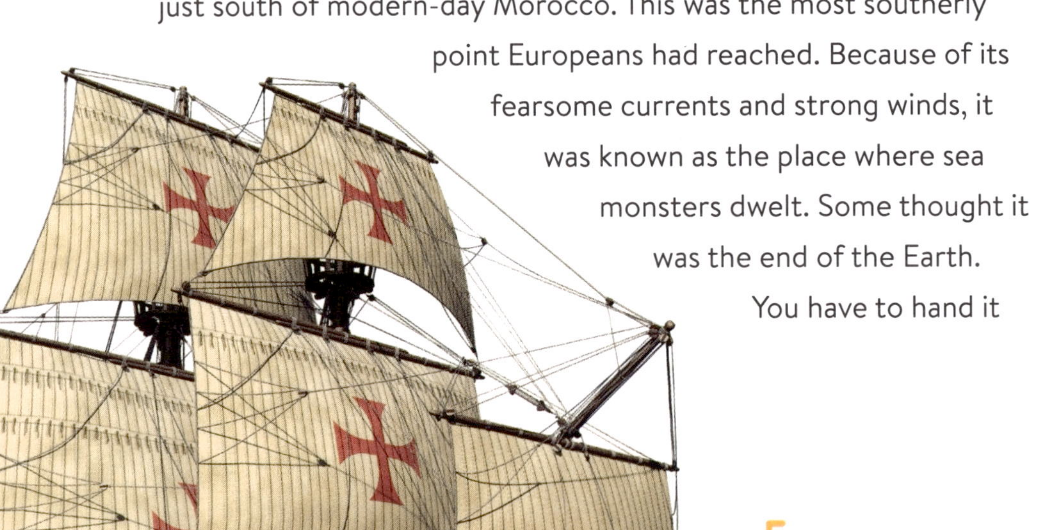

Portuguese explorers sailed in caravels – small, easy-to-manoeuvre sailing ships.

to Henry. He had perseverance. He sent out fifteen expeditions over ten years but they all failed to sail further south. Finally, in 1434, one of Henry's captains, Gil Eanes, found that by sailing far out to sea, he could catch winds that would push his boats further down the coast. Ten years later, Portuguese sailors reached the Bay of Arguin, on the coast of what is now Mauritania. There they built a fort.

Now Henry was able to buy gold south of the desert and cut out the Muslim middlemen. But he had also found he could get super-rich another way – by buying and selling human beings. At first, the Portuguese kidnapped African sailors. But it didn't take long for the Africans to start fighting back and winning. So the Portuguese then bought people who had already been captured by African slave traders. Things went so well for the Portuguese (but not for the people they were buying and selling) that in 1452, Portugal celebrated by making its first ever gold coins.

The Portuguese made cruzado coins out of gold transported by sea from south of the Sahara.

Prince Henry died in 1460, but his successes inspired a generation of European explorers. If gold and people to enslave could be found just down the coast of West Africa, what other riches lay out there in the unknown world?

New expeditions produced astonishing results. In May 1488, Portuguese explorer Bartolomeu Dias and his crew were the first

Europeans to see the southern tip of Africa. Maybe this was a new sea route to the spice-rich lands of East Asia? King John II of Portugal named Africa's southern tip the Cape of Good Hope.

Exciting progress like this possibly explains why John II rejected the proposal of an ambitious Italian sailor named Cristoforo Colombo, whom we know as Christopher Columbus. Columbus had sailed the whole coast of Europe and traded along the West African coast. He relished the excitement of the unknown.

Christopher Columbus is the English version of Columbus's Latin name, Christophorus Columbus. He was called Cristòffa Cónbo in Ligurian (the language of Genoa, where he was probably born), Cristoforo Colombo in Italian, and Cristóbal Colón in Spanish.

Columbus was gripped by a big idea. Like all educated Europeans of his day, he knew the world was round. He had also read a lot of books, including stories of the riches of the Mongol emperor Kublai Khan written by a famous traveller called Marco Polo. Polo's book *Il Milione* told of his travels through Asia between 1271 and 1295. The book was one of the bestsellers of its day and for hundreds of years after.

Columbus decided that Indonesia, China and Japan (the area the Europeans called the Indies) were actually closer to Europe if you went west across the Atlantic Ocean than if you went east across the land. If that were true, whoever found a westward sea route to the Indies would become very rich indeed. The country that paid for the trip would, too.

Columbus went to King John II of Portugal twice to ask for the money to fund his exploration. But the king was having none of it. Perhaps he knew Columbus was making a big mistake thinking it was so quick to reach China by sailing west. After all, he already had a lot of explorers and map-makers hard at work. Columbus's request for funding was also rejected by the rulers of Genoa, Venice and England. So, thought Columbus, why not try Portugal's chief rivals – Ferdinand and Isabella?

Marco Polo (shown here leaving Venice, in what is now Italy, in 1271) was from a trading and exploring family. The Polos travelled all over Asia at a time when few Europeans knew anything about faraway places. Marco Polo's bestselling book about his travels inspired many other explorers.

By January 1492, Granada had surrendered to The Catholic Monarchs, and more than 750 years of Muslim rule in Europe were over. Now that Ferdinand and Isabella were set on driving out the Muslims and Jews, they couldn't demand gold from them anymore. And because of a deal made at the end of a war with Portugal, they couldn't get gold directly from Africa either. Therefore they needed to find a new source of the precious metal. They also wanted to stop Portuguese merchants grabbing the whole world for themselves. And so they placed a bet on Columbus, who set out with three ships and their crews into the unknown.

Columbus is often described as the discoverer of North and South America. But of course he wasn't. Many diverse cultures and civilisations were already living in the Americas when he got there, as we've seen. He just stumbled into their world. Plus, the first Europeans in the Americas had been the Vikings, though they hadn't stayed long.

> "ALL THESE ISLANDS ARE DENSELY POPULATED WITH THE BEST PEOPLE UNDER THE SUN; THEY HAVE NEITHER ILL-WILL NOR TREACHERY."
>
> Christopher Columbus, describing the Caribbean islands

Columbus himself never claimed he had discovered a continent. In fact, he never stopped believing he had reached Asia, even after pretty much everyone else knew that he hadn't. He had landed in the Bahamas, now an island nation in the Caribbean. The Lucayan people lived there, and

Columbus's map-maker, Juan de la Cosa, drew this map of the world as he understood it in 1500. The right-hand side shows Europe, Africa and Asia pretty accurately. The left-hand side shows the Caribbean Sea with its islands, surrounded by the American coastlines that had already been explored by Europeans. To the north is probably the coast of North America from about what is now North Carolina in the US to what is now Newfoundland in Canada. To the south is the coast of South America to the most eastern point of what is now Brazil.

he promptly started calling them 'Indians', which meant 'Asians' to Columbus.

But Columbus's voyages were important for three reasons. First, he finished solving the puzzle of the Atlantic winds, a process started by Portuguese explorers of West Africa. Now any Europeans could follow his route west. Second, he began an epic rivalry between Spain and Portugal that got almost the entire globe mapped. Third, the colony he founded on the Caribbean island of Hispaniola (now Haiti and the Dominican Republic) became the springboard for Spanish explorers and colonists preparing to conquer the rest of the Americas. Columbus had opened the floodgates. The Americas would never be the same again.

In 1494 Spain and Portugal signed a pact called the Treaty of Tordesillas. Incredible as it sounds today, this agreement divided the entire world into just two parts along a line drawn down the middle of the Atlantic Ocean. Everything 'discovered' to the east would belong to Portugal, everything to the west to Spain. Portugal got all of Africa. And when it came to the Americas, that meant that

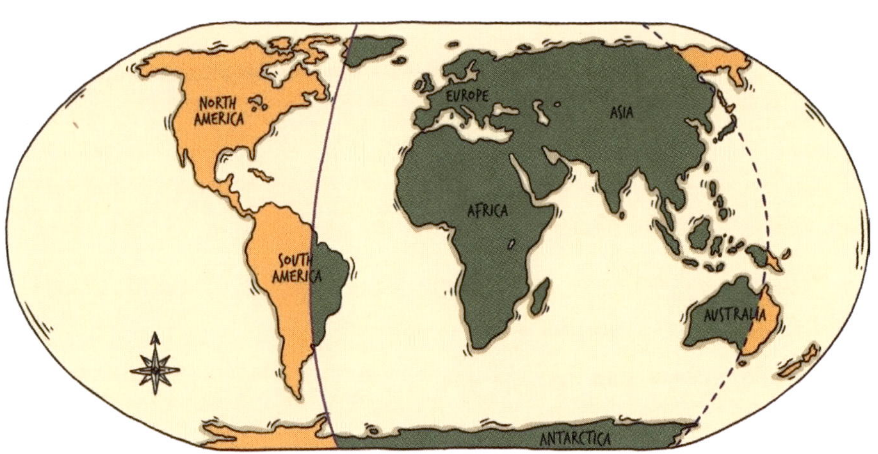

Treaty of Tordesillas (1494)

Treaty of Zaragoza (1529)

Spanish territories

Portuguese territories

In 1494 Spain and Portugal ignored hundreds of independent civilisations around the world and divided the right to rule newly 'discovered' places along a line drawn down the middle of the Atlantic Ocean. In 1529 they agreed to another line along the Pacific coast of Asia. Together, these two treaties gave Africa and Asia to Portugal and most of the Americas to Spain.

Portugal got the area that would be Brazil, which sticks out further east than the rest. Spain got everywhere else. Of course, nobody asked the people who already lived in Africa, Asia or the Americas what they thought of this plan.

This was the beginning of something called western colonialism. That's the time period when European countries went about taking control of faraway places and exploiting their people and natural resources to make themselves rich. We have seen a lot of empires come and go in this book already. But this global approach was a whole new way to build an empire. As with other empires, it was no fun for the people being conquered, controlled, and often killed.

Many Europeans of the period were just fine with all of this. They believed that they were bringing Christianity and a future in heaven to the whole world. The idea was that if you were a Christian, you could go to heaven. If you were not a Christian, you would go to hell. So they believed that by converting native people to Christianity they were doing them a big favour, even if it meant the loss of everything the new converts cared about and a life of slavery. Looking at it from centuries later, this whole idea seems appalling, but it really is what many Europeans thought at the time.

Portuguese sailor Vasco da Gama, the first European to sail east around the Cape of Good Hope (he arrived in India on 14 May 1498) hated Muslims. Before he would have trade negotiations with a city, he made its leader kick out all of the Muslims living there. Once he even captured a ship full of Muslim pilgrims on their way to Mecca, locked the pilgrims into the storage area of the ship, and set it on fire, killing all of them.

Not every Portuguese settler was a bad as da Gama, but for the people along the coast of the Persian Gulf and in India, Indonesia, and finally Japan, the arrival of the Portuguese was far from easy. Meanwhile, Pedro Álvares Cabral, also from Portugal, sailed west, arriving in what is now Brazil in April 1500.

By the 1530s, the African slave trade was booming. Europeans were buying people in Africa and transporting them across the ocean to Brazil and the Caribbean. This wasn't the colonisers' first choice. They had tried to enslave the Indigenous people of the area, but they had mostly died or run away.

The enslaved Africans were forced to work harder than anyone should ever have to. One of the most notorious jobs was farming sugar cane and processing it into sugar. This work was so dangerous that most enslaved workers died in less than five years if they didn't manage to escape first. The sugar they made was shipped across the ocean and sold in Europe for high prices. The sugar growers were making so much money that they could afford to buy more people to work to death. Thanks to this ugly business, European nations got richer and richer.

Sugar cane plantations included both the fields that grew the cane and the factories where the juice was squeezed out and made into sugar, molasses and sometimes rum. That meant enslaved people were forced to work long hours all year round, with no break even when the fields didn't need working.

So what was going on here? Why were the European colonisers so brutal? And how were they able to overrun so much of the rest of the world? One thing to understand is that not every European felt the same way. There was a lot of disagreement in Europe itself about the way the colonisers treated the local people. But those in charge (kings, queens and rich companies) were after more riches, and they chose brutal leaders on purpose because they brought back more stolen goods.

The biggest prize for a coloniser was gold. This shiny yellow metal was so valuable that the hope of finding it made Europeans willing to face any kind of danger. Spanish cousins Hernán Cortés and Francisco Pizarro were after gold when they set out on separate expeditions. Each of them was responsible for the destruction of a huge, powerful empire. Cortés brought down the Aztecs, Pizarro the Inca. They, and other Spaniards like them, were known as conquistadors – or conquerors. Quite how they made these conquests counts as one of the most extraordinary – and distressing – stories in all history.

Gold was prized by cultures throughout the Americas and stolen in enormous quantities by European colonisers. This small figure was created by a craftsperson of the Tairona people of northern Columbia.

Hernán Cortés was able to communicate with native people through Gerónimo de Aguilar, a Spanish sailor, and Malintzin, a Nahua woman who had been sold into slavery and given to Cortés as a gift.

When Cortés arrived off the coast of Mexico in the spring of 1519, he had eleven ships, 110 sailors, 530 soldiers and very little understanding of the people he was to meet. He then chanced upon a Spanish sailor who had been shipwrecked on a previous expedition. Gerónimo de Aguilar had been captured by the Maya and had lived among them as a slave for eight years. During that time, he had learned their language, so he spoke both Spanish and Mayan.

Then a group of Mayan people gave Cortés twenty enslaved people as a gift. One of them was a Nahua woman named Malintzin, who spoke both Mayan and Nahuatl (the language of the Aztecs). Now Cortés could speak Spanish to Aguilar, who would translate his words into Mayan. Then Malintzin translated them from Mayan to Nahuatl. With these two, Cortés found he could make himself understood by just about anyone he might meet on his hunt for gold.

Cortés made a military alliance with two local peoples, the Totonac and the Tlaxcalans. This wasn't so hard when he explained he wanted to defeat the Aztecs. The Aztecs demanded that the surrounding communities pay them taxes. So of course those communities were happy for a chance to conquer them.

Now Cortés and his small band of warriors had the allies they needed to advance to Tenochtitlán, the glorious capital of the Aztec Empire. You know, the one built in the middle of a lake.

The Aztec king was called Moctezuma II. After welcoming Cortés and his army as guests, the ruler soon found himself a prisoner in his own palace. Cortés demanded an enormous ransom in gold as the price of the king's freedom. As more and more treasure was given over to the Spanish, the Aztec people got angrier and angrier at Cortés, his warriors and the huge ransom demand.

But within a few days, Moctezuma lay dead. No one quite knows how he died. Did Cortés or one of his men kill him? Or perhaps a disgruntled Aztec official did the

The last Aztec emperor was Moctezuma II. During his reign the Aztec Empire reached its peak. But all was lost soon after he was murdered in 1520.

dastardly deed? Anyway, by the beginning of July 1520, furious Aztec citizens forced the Spanish to flee the city.

When the Spanish returned a few months

This drawing of the 1521 final Siege of Tenochtitlán is from a visual history by artists in or near Aztec territory. They created it only about thirty years after the fall of the Empire.

later, they came with a huge new army, mostly made up of people sick of being under the thumb of the Aztecs. But worse killers than any army were the diseases the Europeans carried with them. They didn't know why the smallpox that they were used to in Europe was killing whole villages in the Americas. The Americans didn't know why either. It seemed like a horrible supernatural plague.

We now understand what was happening. Like the bubonic plague that struck medieval Europe, smallpox is a highly infectious disease. Unlike bubonic plague, though, smallpox in Europe was what's called endemic. That means it was always around. It killed some people, but others survived. Over time, lots of people had already been exposed to the disease, so they were immune.

In the Americas, it was different. The smallpox virus had never been there before, so nobody had ever had it. It ripped through the native people of both North and South America. About forty per cent of the Aztec population died within a year of their first contact with the Spanish. Weakened by these deaths and besieged by Cortés's army, Tenochtitlán fell into Spanish hands. More than 240,000 Aztecs died in the final eighty-day siege, some in the fighting and some from smallpox.

The way was now clear for a Spanish conquest of the whole region of what is now Mexico, and beyond. The area was renamed New Spain, and a governor was appointed as overlord in 1524. When news of the discovery of Aztec silver mines began to filter back to Spain, more European adventurers set sail, hoping to get rich quick in the Americas.

The Inca city of Machu Picchu was built in the 1400s and 1500s, 2,430 metres high in the Andes mountains of Peru. It includes more than 150 buildings and more than 100 flights of stairs, many carved from single slabs of stone.

In 1529, Cortés's second cousin, Francisco Pizarro, received royal Spanish approval for a conquest of the Inca in South America. Pizarro's tactics were inspired by those of his cousin Cortés. On 16 November 1532, he arranged for some of his men to meet the Inca emperor, Atahualpa, in the central square of a hilltop town called Cajamarca.

The Inca of what is now Peru were a major power in South America. About a hundred years before Europeans arrived, they had united the whole Andes mountain region through a combination of warfare and cooperation. When Pizarro marched into town, this great empire was the largest in the Americas, and possibly the largest in the world.

One of the Incas' biggest achievements was a 30,000-kilometre network of footpaths and trails, some of them crossing mountains more than 5,000 metres high. Many of these trails are still in use today. In Inca times, there were stations about every twenty-five kilometres along the major trails. Runners stood ready at each station to carry messages as in a relay race. That way, Inca rulers and officials could communicate as fast as possible along the whole length of the empire. With each runner having to cover only a short distance, the system could keep up top speed.

Instead of paper, parchment or clay, the runners carried quipu, those pieces of string that contained messages written in rows of knots. Like the pharaohs of ancient Egypt, the Inca emperor was believed to be divine. He was regarded as the son of Inti, the Sun god. The Inca revered Inti so highly they believed that precious shiny gold itself was his sweat.

None of that prepared Atahualpa for the trickery of Francisco Pizarro. The emperor approached the town square in a ceremonial procession with a large group of followers. When the Inca wanted to take over territory, Atahualpa always met with the ruler first to discuss his plan and to try to come to an agreement. So he expected Pizarro to have the same sort of conversation with him. What actually happened next was a huge and unpleasant surprise.

According to accounts written by the Spanish, the emperor was ordered to abandon his native religion and accept the word of Jesus

Christ. A Spanish priest probably read *The Spanish Requirement of 1513*, a document that the Pope required conquistadors to read aloud (in Spanish) to any people they wanted to conquer, whether their audience could understand it or not. If the people did not agree that the Pope and Spain were in charge, the conquistadors were allowed to make war on them.

> "[IF YOU DON'T ACCEPT SPANISH RULE], WE SHALL POWERFULLY ENTER INTO YOUR COUNTRY, AND SHALL MAKE WAR AGAINST YOU ... AND WE PROTEST THAT THE DEATHS AND LOSSES WHICH SHALL ACCRUE FROM THIS ARE YOUR FAULT..."
>
> *The Spanish Requirement of 1513*

When Atahualpa refused to accept the priest's demands, Pizarro's men charged on horseback and opened fire. Horses had been extinct in the Americas for more than 10,000 years, so the surprise attack from men riding these unknown beasts created mass panic. Huge numbers of Inca were killed in the confusion.

From there the story is very similar to Moctezuma's. The emperor was captured and imprisoned in a small room. A 'ransom room' was piled high with treasure to try to make the Spanish take money instead of executing Atahualpa, but the Spanish took the money and executed him anyway.

A bitter six-year war ensued, but even with a much larger army, Inca battle axes,

When the third Inca emperor – Inca Huayna Capac – died, he left his older son Huáscar to rule half his kingdom and his younger son Atahualpa (left) to rule the other. A civil war broke out between the brothers, which Atahualpa won, becoming the last ruler of the Inca empire.

spears and arrows were no match for Spanish guns and armour. Soon huge ships called galleons were arriving in Spanish ports filled to the brim with Inca and Aztec gold and silver.

Other European nations were also on the move. As early as 1497, merchants in Bristol, England, had paid John Cabot to explore the coast of North America. Jacques Cartier, a French navigator, sailed to what is now Canada on a series of expeditions for the French king. In 1522, Portuguese explorer Ferdinand Magellan's expedition became the first to travel all the way around the world.

So far, most colonisers were trying to get rich quick. But in northern Europe, a massive shift in the way people thought about themselves and their God was about to change that. It is called the Protestant Reformation.

You see, while rulers and merchants were making fortunes by exploiting the people and places they had 'discovered', everyday people were no better off than before. And the Church wasn't helping. Imagine going to church on a Sunday morning only to be told by the priest that you are so sinful that what awaits you in the next life is eternal damnation in the fires of hell. Understandably, you'd feel terrified.

"Luckily," says the priest, "there is a solution. Confess your sins to me and they will be forgiven by God!" Sometimes you would have to do a good deed to achieve forgiveness.

But sometimes there was a catch. If your priest was corrupt, he might demand money in exchange for forgiveness. As a result, priests and the Church became fabulously rich, whilst ordinary people still struggled to put food on their tables.

There was plenty of grumbling about the problem of corrupt priests, but the big moment came when a German monk called Martin Luther decided that selling forgiveness was completely wrong. In fact he went one step further. Luther argued that the only way to be forgiven for your sins was to have complete faith in Jesus Christ.

Martin Luther fastened his list of ninety-five protests on the doors of Wittenburg Cathedral in 1517.

In 1517, Luther nailed a list of ninety-five complaints against the Catholic Church, known as 'The Ninety-five Theses', on the door of a cathedral in Wittenburg, Germany. He also encouraged everyone to read the Bible instead of just letting priests tell them what it said. Of course not everyone could read. But an easy-to-use printing press had been invented by Johannes Gutenberg in 1450. That made the Bible in Latin, and later in other languages, available to anyone who could read it. And there's nowhere in the Bible where it says you have to pay money to have your sins forgiven. You can see why many people felt abused and angry.

Luther's protest gave its name to a new form of Christianity, called Protestantism, which grew throughout Europe in the years that followed.

It wasn't just ordinary people who welcomed

After German goldsmith Johannes Gutenberg invented the moveable-type printing press, books became much cheaper to buy. The most popular was a Latin translation of the Bible.

Luther's message. Rulers keen to break free of the Catholic Church also leaped on to the protesters' bandwagon, not necessarily for religious reasons. When the Pope refused to allow Henry VIII of England to divorce his Spanish wife Catherine of Aragon, Henry declared that he, not the Pope, was head of the Church of England.

Protestantism spread elsewhere, too. Bitter enemies of Catholic Spain, such as the Netherlands, Denmark and Sweden, became Protestant. Others, like France and Britain, went back and forth between the old and new faiths. In these countries, whatever religion you followed, you were in danger if the other side was in power. Neither Catholics nor Protestants were safe for long. And Protestantism itself splintered into many branches, or denominations, which frequently fought one another.

What would you have done if you had lived in Europe at that time? Would you have chosen a side and joined in the fighting? Or would you have tried to mind your own business, hoping to be left alone? Both seem rather risky.

Of course, there was one other option. Escape. Some people who got fed up with all the wars and arguments and danger did exactly that. In the autumn of 1620, a group of just over one hundred English people (adults and children) set off on a dangerous one-way voyage on board one of the most famous ships in history. It was called the *Mayflower*.

There was already one main British colony in North America – Virginia. Jamestown, its first permanent settlement, had been founded in 1607. The Virginia Colony was a huge place, stretching up the coast to where New York City is now. The *Mayflower* passengers had permission to settle in the northern part of Virginia, but partly because of stormy weather at sea, they wound up about 160 kilometres north, in an area the British called New England.

The leaders of the expedition were a group of about thirty-five Protestants known as Puritans or Separatists. They were looking for a place where they could practise their religion and preserve their culture. The rest were servants or farmers hoping to find a better life than they could have back home. They arrived in December of 1620 and settled in a town they called Plymouth, in what is now Massachusetts, USA. This motley crew was later known as the Pilgrim Fathers.

The Plymouth colonists had some very good luck. Early on, they found corn in graves and storage areas of the local Indigenous people, the Wampanoag. They stole it, hoping it would sustain them through the winter and give them seeds to plant in the spring. They found an area of cleared land

Before they decided to start a colony in America, the religious congregation known as the Pilgrim Fathers lived for about twelve years in Leiden, the Netherlands. This painting shows them getting ready to leave the Netherlands and sail first to England and then, on the Mayflower, to America. It was painted in 1620, just after they left.

ready to build and plant on. They thought God had left it there for them, so they began building houses.

The settlers found out later that Plymouth was on the site of a village called Patuxet that had been abandoned because the local people had died in a disease outbreak. The English called the disease 'Indian fever'. But it was probably smallpox brought over by European explorers, part of the same pandemic that helped Cortés defeat the Aztecs.

Soon after the Pilgrim Fathers arrived, visitors began to appear. First came an Abenaki man named Samoset, who spoke a little English. Then came a Patuxet man named Tisquantum. He had been kidnapped and enslaved by earlier English explorers, had lived in England and spoke the language. Despite his miserable experience, he offered to help the new settlers get to know the local people and learn to live off the land. What a miracle it must have seemed to the settlers to have Indigenous Americans walk out of the woods speaking their language.

Even with all this good luck, they had arrived too late in the year to grow food, and it was a horrible winter. More than half of the original group died of either starvation or disease. But by September 1621, those who survived had grown enough food for the next winter and had a peaceful relationship with their neighbours, the Wampanoag. The two groups celebrated the harvest together. Much later, the US holiday of Thanksgiving was created to commemorate that moment.

Indigenous Americans mark that same holiday with mourning for the people killed by Europeans and their diseases and for the loss of their lands and freedom. Because, of course, the peace didn't last. It couldn't. With tens of thousands of colonists flooding into the Americas, things were getting crowded. The Europeans continued to believe that anything they found was theirs to take. But, as you can imagine, the Indigenous people, whose ancestors had been in the Americas for over 30,000 years, didn't like that idea one bit.

Metacom (known to the British as King Philip) was the sachem, or leader, of a group of Native Nations in New England, including the Wampanoag. In 1675, he led his people in a war to reclaim the rights the British had taken from them. After a year of fighting, the colonists won and executed Metacom. His head was displayed on a stake in Plymouth for twenty-five years.

The next 250 years were a time of continual war and misery for the native people of the Americas. Almost everywhere they lost the power to govern themselves. In some places they were forced to move from their traditional lands to smaller areas called reservations. Often, they were not considered citizens of the countries that had been taken from them. Even today, Indigenous people from the Inuit of the Arctic to the Tehuelche of Patagonia on the southern tip of Argentina are treated as second-class citizens throughout the continents that were once all theirs.

In the French Revolution of 1789, the people of France overthrew their rich king and queen and challenged the very idea of some people being born with more rights, privileges, and power than others.

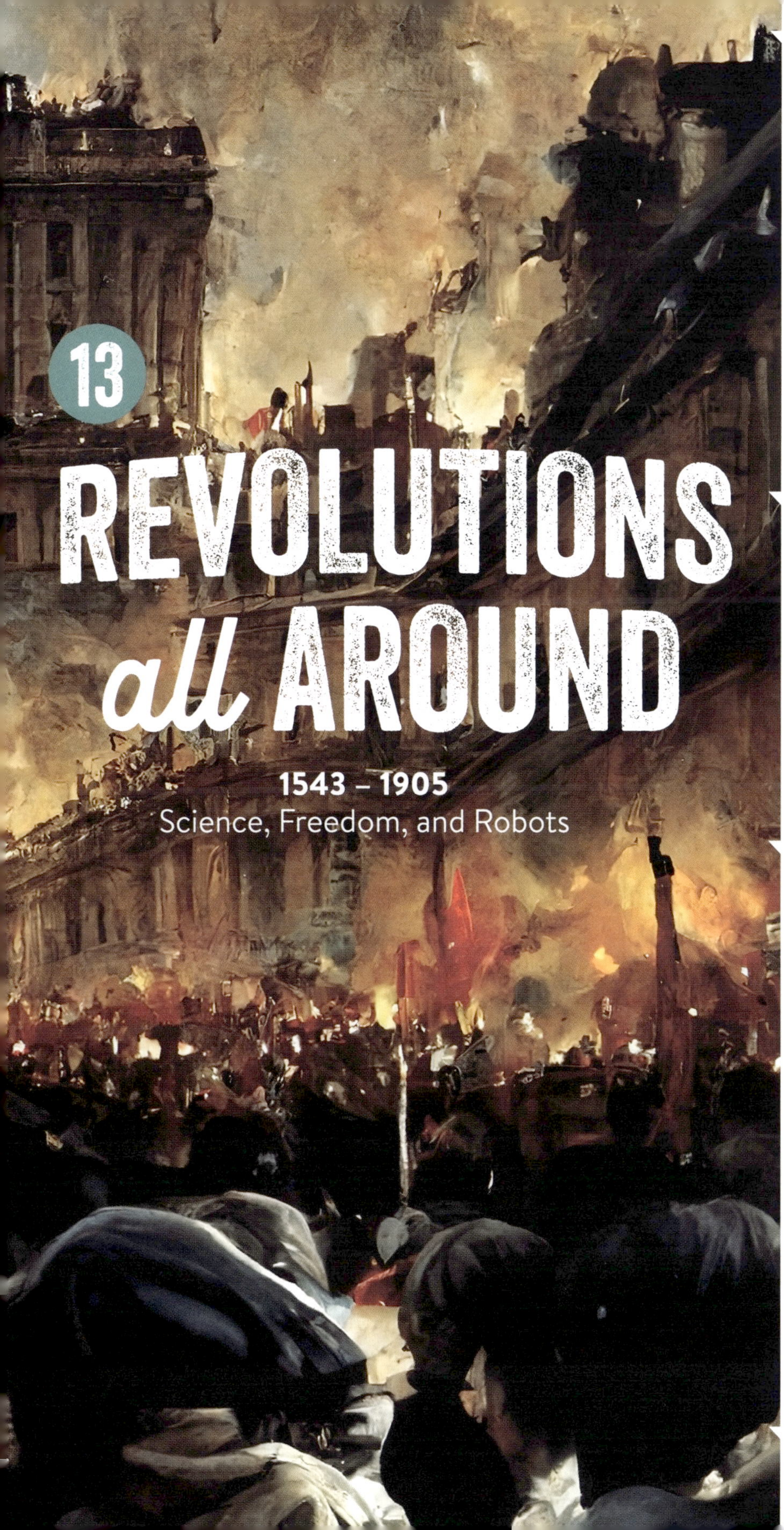

13

REVOLUTIONS *all* AROUND

1543 – 1905

Science, Freedom, and Robots

1543
Copernicus publishes his theory that the Sun is in the center of the Universe.

1776
The United States declares its independence from Great Britain.

1789
French revolutionaries storm the Bastille in Paris.

1804
Haiti wins its independence from France.

1833
Britain outlaws slavery throughout its empire.

1829
George Stephenson's steam locomotive, Rocket, wins the Rainhill trials.

1876
Bell invents the telephone; Benz invents the gasoline-powered car.

1905
Albert Einstein figures out that $E=mc^2$.

Jacques de Vaucanson was an 18th-century French inventor who made clockwork robots. His constructions included a flute player who could play 12 different tunes and a waiter who could serve drinks at a party. His most famous robot was the Digesting Duck. It could flap its wings, eat food—and even poop out of the other end!

The Digesting Duck—a clockwork creature that could eat, flap its wings, and even poop out of its mechanical backside!

De Vaucanson was part of a long history of people imagining and building lifelike machines. The Chinese had built a clock with gong-ringing mannequins as early as 1088. Ismail Al-Jazari, a Muslim inventor who lived from 1136 to 1206, had constructed several automatons, mechanical devices that moved like living things, including one where automated musicians floated on a lake. In 1292 Count Robert II of Artois, in what is now northern France, had filled a garden with robots, including waving monkeys. These machines were powered by steam, wind, water, or wound-up springs.

In the 1730s, when de Vaucanson made his automatons, robot-making was a sign of the times in Europe. That's because these lifelike machines seemed to show clearly that nature could be copied and controlled by brilliant human minds.

Muslim scholars had believed in the importance of reason and observation in understanding the world for hundreds of years. But Europeans were now in the midst of their own revolution in thinking.

Called the Enlightenment, this set of ideas offered individuals hope for both a rational way of thinking about the world and power over their own lives as well as over nature.

As we have just seen, the Protestant Reformation had already made people question the right of the pope and priests to tell them what to do. That was one of the first steps.

Another early step had been a radical book published in 1543 by Polish astronomer Nicolaus Copernicus. At the time, Europeans believed that Earth was at the center of the universe, with the Sun, the planets, and all the stars moving around it.

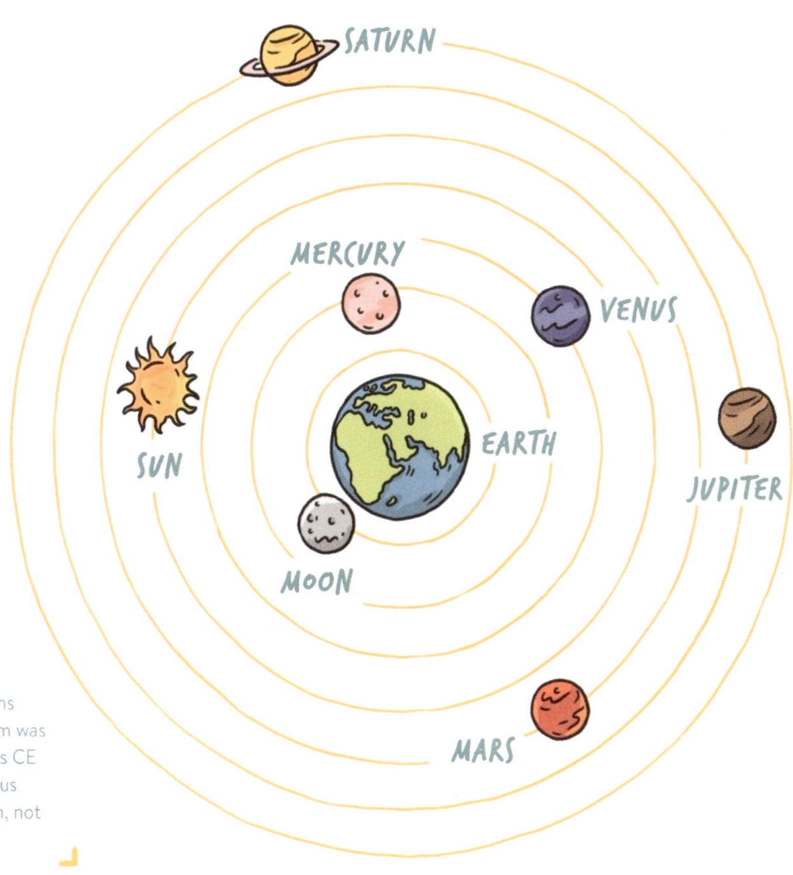

This is the way Europeans thought the solar system was organized from the 100s CE until Nicolaus Copernicus figured out that the Sun, not Earth, was at its center.

Copernicus had looked at the way the planets moved in the sky and realized the observations only made sense if Earth and the planets were all moving around the Sun. Copernicus's ideas were later proved correct by Italian astronomer Galileo Galilei. Here was another triumph of independent thinking over traditional beliefs.

Two great Enlightenment thinkers used reason and observation to develop other new ideas. French scientist and philosopher René Descartes said the universe and its laws of nature were like a giant clockwork machine. Only humans had minds, he said, which made us special. According to Descartes, if we could figure out how the machine of nature worked, we could make it work for us.

You may have heard of Isaac Newton. He was a big observer and experimenter. Sometimes he was even reckless with his own body. Once he stared at the Sun to see what would happen to his eyes. He went blind for four days and was lucky to get his sight back afterwards. (Do not try this!)

Sir Isaac Newton was a genius at connecting things in his mind. It is said he was inspired to think of the idea of the universal force of gravity after seeing an apple fall from a tree.

Newton is most famous for wondering what makes an apple fall from a tree. Some people might say, well, apples are supposed to fall from trees. That's just what apples do. Applying the philosophy of Descartes, Newton wanted to explain a falling apple using the laws of nature. He said that an invisible force—gravity—was responsible and that the size of this force was related to the size of the objects involved.

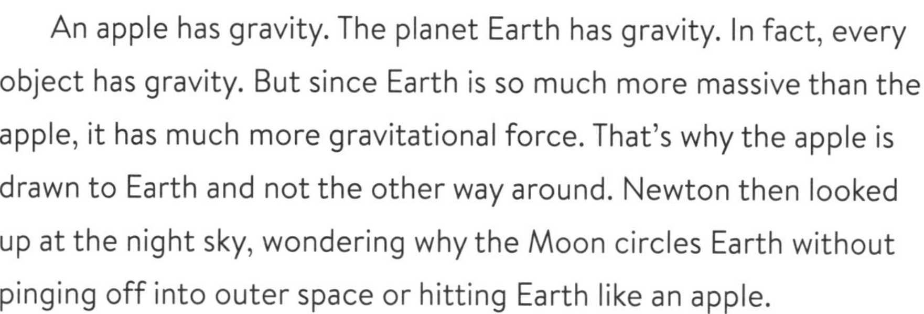

The Moon

An apple has gravity. The planet Earth has gravity. In fact, every object has gravity. But since Earth is so much more massive than the apple, it has much more gravitational force. That's why the apple is drawn to Earth and not the other way around. Newton then looked up at the night sky, wondering why the Moon circles Earth without pinging off into outer space or hitting Earth like an apple.

He figured out that because the Moon is less massive than the Earth, it must be drawn toward it by Earth's larger gravitational force. But he also realized that there must be another factor at work. That factor is speed. The Moon is moving so fast that when it falls, it misses Earth entirely and travels in a circle around it. This delicate balance between speed and gravity is called an orbit. You see—discover the laws of nature, and the secrets of the universe are revealed.

Other Enlightenment philosophers said that individuals should have the freedom to make their own choices. Different people have different ideas about freedom. There is the freedom to choose your own religion, the freedom to share your opinion about the government, and lots more. Remember the Totonac people of Mexico who allied with the Spanish to defeat the Aztecs? They did it to be freed from having to pay taxes they thought were unfair. (Of course, they had no idea that the Spanish would turn out to be worse than the Aztecs.) That same idea of freedom now sparked a brand new kind of revolution in North America.

In the mid 1700s, there was a terrible Seven Years War between a group of countries led by Britain and another group led by France. Some people think of the Seven Years War as the real first world war because it was fought all over the world, including in Europe, West Africa, India, and North America. In the United States, it is known as the French and Indian War, and it pitted the French colonies and their Indigenous allies against the British colonies and theirs.

In the more than 100 years since the Virginia and Plymouth colonies were founded, most of the East Coast of North America had filled up with British colonies. In the Seven Years War, Britain won even more land—including what would become Florida and much of eastern Canada. But these areas were mostly French or Spanish speaking, and it would be a while before they would have much in common with the rest of the British colonies in America.

The people of the English-speaking colonies had been arguing with the British government over taxes for a long time. There were taxes on goods imported from Britain (including tea), and taxes to

This political cartoon was created by Benjamin Franklin in 1754, at the start of the French and Indian War. With it, he was trying to convince his readers that the colonies should get together to fight the French and that if they didn't they would end up like this cut-up snake—dead. Experts think this is the first time anyone suggested that the separate colonies should unite. Franklin would go on to be a leader of the American Revolution and a founder of the new United States of America.

support British soldiers stationed in the colonies, and taxes on printed material such as newspapers. All these taxes made some colonists furious. They complained that they should not be taxed at all. Why? Because they didn't get to vote in British elections, so they hadn't had a part in deciding what should be taxed and by how much.

That's part of why, on December 16, 1773, a group of Massachusetts colonists disguised themselves as Indigenous people to avoid being identified, snuck onto a British merchant ship in Boston Harbor, and ruined the cargo of tea by throwing it into the water. The event became known as the Boston Tea Party.

Following the Boston Tea Party, 13 British colonies teamed up to declare their freedom from Britain. They formed a new nation called the United States of America. In the Declaration of Independence, a document that gave the reason for the revolution, the 13 colonies said that "the Laws of Nature and Nature's God" entitled them to be independent. Then they went on to list all the ways they felt the British had mistreated them.

Britain was having none of it. They fought hard to keep their colonies, and the newly minted Americans fought to be independent. The

There is no record of who made the first American flag, but in 1870 a man named John Claypoole claimed that his grandmother, Betsy Ross, had done it. Ross was a flag maker in Philadelphia, and was related to a revolutionary leader, so it's possible that the legend is true. This painting shows her presenting her design to general George Washington (sitting in blue), financier Robert Morris (in red), and her uncle, delegate George Ross (standing).

Revolutionary War raged from 1775 to 1783. In the end, the United States won, becoming the first European colony ever to secure its independence. It adopted a Constitution that gave citizens the right to elect representatives to govern them. The Bill of Rights, a set of ten amendments to the Constitution, protected the rights of individuals against the majority and the government. Back then, usually only white men who owned property could vote, though. So, like Ancient Greece, this was not a true democracy.

> “WE HOLD THESE TRUTHS TO BE SELF-EVIDENT, THAT ALL MEN ARE CREATED EQUAL, THAT THEY ARE ENDOWED BY THEIR CREATOR WITH CERTAIN UNALIENABLE RIGHTS, THAT AMONG THESE ARE LIFE, LIBERTY AND THE PURSUIT OF HAPPINESS.”
>
> Thomas Jefferson, United States Declaration of Independence

When the United States won its freedom from Britain, people all over the world sat up and took notice. If colonies could win their independence, maybe there was hope for other downtrodden people. French people were disgusted at how much money their king and his nobles spent feasting in enormous palaces while ordinary people starved.

French ideas of freedom were to do with fairness, equality, and getting fed. Leaders of the ordinary people negotiated to get equal voting power for everyone. But they couldn’t move fast enough. The people’s anger spilled out like lava from an erupting volcano, directed at the kings and nobles who used the country’s riches for themselves. Angry Parisians attacked a prison called the Bastille on the night of July 14, 1789, to take weapons and gunpowder and free some of the prisoners. This was the start of the French Revolution.

Before it was over, revolutionaries had used a new form of execution called the guillotine to chop off the heads of rich nobles, including King Louis XVI and his wife Marie Antoinette. (It was meant to be kinder than using a sword or axe.) Some non-humans were destroyed as well—including De Vaucanson's Digesting Duck, which he had given to Louis XVI as a gift.

You may have noticed that throughout this book most of the people mentioned have been men. This isn't because men are more brave, clever, or adventurous than women. It's because throughout history women's opportunities and contributions have been suppressed or hidden.

One person who was beheaded during the French Revolution was a playwright called

This illustration shows Olympe de Gouges presenting her pamphlet to King Louis XVI (seated with the scepter) and Queen Marie Antoinette (taking the pamphlet) to convince them to give women equal rights with men in French society.

Olympe de Gouges. Earlier in her life she had written a pamphlet called "The Declaration of the Rights of Woman," in which she called for equal rights for women to choose their own lives, to own property, and to be treated respectfully. This was one of the first times a woman had published a call to change the way women were treated. De Gouges also called for the end of slavery. She took a moderate position in the French Revolution, so the revolutionaries arrested and executed her.

The American Revolution inspired people closer to home as well. By 1800 the French colony of Saint-Domingue, on the Caribbean island of Hispaniola where Columbus had settled, was home to 450,000 enslaved Africans who produced almost half of the world's sugar. After a 13-year struggle, they freed themselves of French rule in 1804. Their new country, Haiti, was the second liberated colony in the world after the United States and the first independent Black-ruled democracy in modern history.

Similar freedom movements followed in Central and South America. On July 20, 1810, the people of Colombia (then called New Granada) declared their independence from Spain. Over the next few years, a series of other Spanish and Portuguese colonies followed.

A free Black man who had grown up enslaved, François-Dominique Toussaint Louverture was a leader of the Haitian revolution.

Newton's laws predict that when it comes to the physical world, for every action there is an equal and opposite reaction. Sometimes in history it is the same. In 1799, shortly after the French people had successfully overthrown their corrupt king, a new ruler seized absolute power over the country. His name was Napoleon Bonaparte.

Napoleon's plan was to conquer Europe to build himself an empire. Wars cost money, and Napoleon cared more about defeating new European empire than about American colonies. That's why in 1803, in the midst of losing the long battle to hold on to Haiti, Napoleon sold the colony of New France to the United States for $15 million. The land, known as the Louisiana Purchase, included what would become all or part of Arkansas, Missouri, Iowa, Oklahoma, Kansas, Nebraska, Minnesota, North Dakota, South Dakota, New Mexico, Texas, Montana, Wyoming, Colorado, and Louisiana, as well as parts of the Canadian provinces of Alberta and Saskatchewan.

President Thomas Jefferson was eager to know more about this vast stretch of land that had doubled the size of his country. He arranged for a group of explorers headed by Meriwether Lewis and William Clark to explore the new territory. They called themselves the Corps of Discovery and worked with Lemhi Shoshone guide

Though mostly remembered for trying to take over the world, Napoleon also made important changes in French government. He set up a system of public education and introduced the Napoleonic Codes, which guaranteed several civil rights, including freedom of religion.

Sacagawea, who led them across thousands of miles of uncharted territory—all while carrying her baby on her back.

Britain successfully fought off invasion by Napoleon, but these Napoleonic wars, on top of the loss of its American colonies, left it desperate for money. So Britain used the Roman Empire strategy of expanding abroad once more.

In the 1770s, British sea captain James Cook explored the South Pacific. His expeditions led to the establishment of a British prison colony in Australia. It became routine for British courts to sentence criminals and people who couldn't pay their bills to be transported there.

Meanwhile British forces were out capturing colonies elsewhere. By the mid 1820s, large parts of India and Burma (now Myanmar) were under British control and providing vital supplies to the ever-growing British Empire. Saltpeter, one of the ingredients for gunpowder, came from India. Precious hardwoods for making ships came from Burma.

In Britain, thoughts about freedom were being focused in some people's minds on the idea of banning slavery. William Wilberforce was a tireless campaigner whose efforts eventually resulted in the British parliament voting in 1807 to outlaw the buying and selling of human beings. In 1833 Britain went further, declaring slavery illegal throughout its empire. The British government managed this by paying slave owners the "value" of the people they had owned. The formerly enslaved people themselves didn't receive a penny.

When a barber from Bolton, U.K., named Richard Arkwright, invented the world's first water-powered cotton mill, it set off another type of revolution. This one is known as the Industrial Revolution. Arkwright's mill opened in 1771 in the village of Cromford in Derbyshire, U.K. It spun thin, strong threads that were then fed into a mechanical loom and woven into cloth. Never before had so few people been able to make so much fabric.

New machines changed lives for workers. A carpenter, for example, has to be skilled in many ways to make a fine piece of furniture. And they have to take the time to find the right tools for different stages of the job at hand. But a factory assembly-line worker waits for the arrival of the next partially made object as it passes down the line, ready to do a single task again and again and again.

The idea of mass production really took off in the United States. In 1801 an inventor named Eli Whitney demonstrated how he could assemble

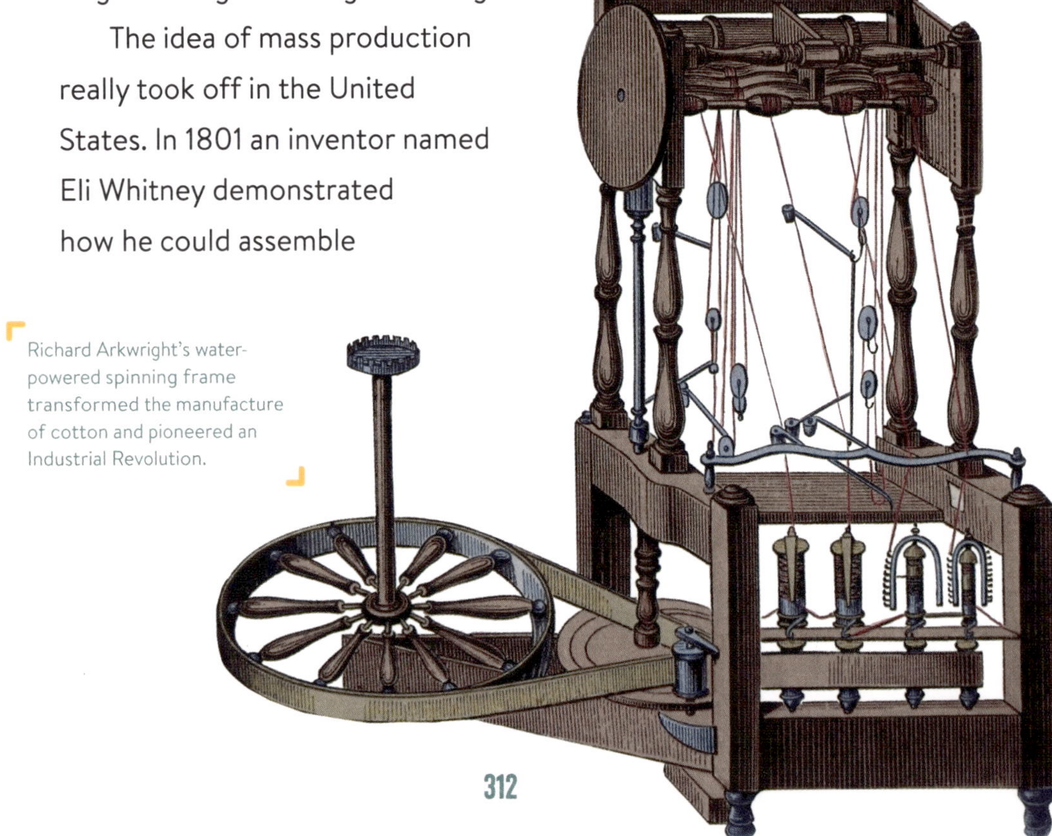

Richard Arkwright's water-powered spinning frame transformed the manufacture of cotton and pioneered an Industrial Revolution.

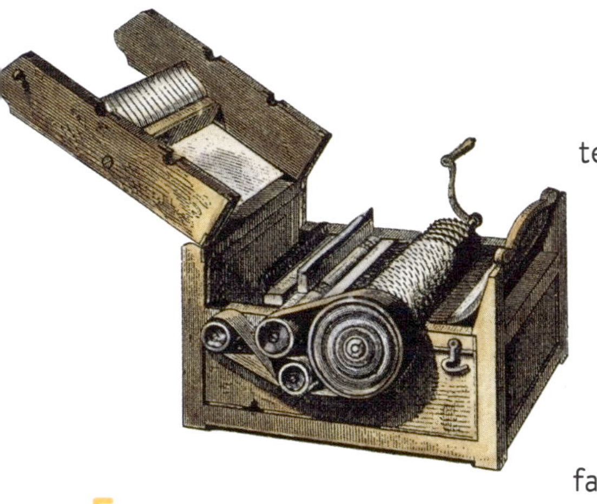

Eli Whitney's cotton gin was a mechanical solution to the problem of removing seeds from cotton fiber.

ten separate guns from a heap of interchangeable parts. Congress was so impressed that they awarded him a contract to produce 10,000 guns called muskets. Although it is now thought Whitney may have faked his presentation just to win business, the idea really did work. By the time of Whitney's death in 1825, American weapons factories were using the method to churn out thousands of guns each year.

Whitney is also famous for inventing a machine that could remove seeds from raw cotton—an extremely time-consuming job when done by hand. His mechanical cotton gin ("gin" is short for "engine") helped transform the economy of the southern United States. It made cotton farmers rich, greatly expanding the demand for enslaved people to farm cotton.

New machines were all very well, but there was still a problem. Until about 1825, factories and vehicles of all kinds still relied on getting power from animals, water, or the wind. Without a breeze, sailing ships can get stuck at sea for days. Water-powered looms work just fine in places with flowing water. But in times of drought, they stand idle. If humans wanted to continue their experiments with freedom, they needed another breakthrough.

Which is exactly what happened in 1801 when Richard Trevithick turned up the pressure on his *Puffing Devil* steam engine in Cornwall, England. Here was a machine that didn't rely on Earth's natural forces at all. No horses, no humans, no wind, no river or stream. All it needed were plentiful, portable raw materials—water in a tank and some wood or coal to make a fire. The heat turned the water to steam. The steam pushed through pipes to drive wheels. Here was the world's first fully independent source of mobile power.

Within 30 years, high pressure steam was connecting pieces of the world together. In 1829, a competition was held at Rainhill, in Lancashire, England, U.K., to find a steam locomotive that could pull a wagon along a new 35-mile- (56-km-) long railroad line being built to connect the cotton-manufacturing city of Manchester with the trading port of Liverpool. George Stephenson's *Rocket* won the day. The line opened to great fanfare on September 15, 1830.

Britain went railway crazy. New companies were set up and people invested money in

George Stephenson's *Rocket* was the most advanced locomotive of its day, bringing together the latest innovations.

building railroads, sometimes making fortunes, sometimes losing everything. By 1914 the landscape had been transformed by rail networks covering more than 20,000 miles (32,000 km) and run by 120 competing companies.

Before the arrival of the railroads, different parts of Britain had their own local time. For example, Bristol was 11 minutes behind London because the Sun rises 11 minutes later there. But railroad timetables could not work unless all clocks ran on the same standard time. So people started setting their clocks to the same time across the country. Eventually, the rest of the world joined in, and the time zones we know today were established.

Railroad mania also erupted across North America. One of the first American-built steam locomotives was the *Best Friend of Charleston*, which entered service the same year as Stephenson's *Rocket*. Unfortunately, it was also the first locomotive to suffer a boiler explosion, tragically killing one of its crew in June 1831.

On May 10, 1869, American engineers completed the Transcontinental Railroad, connecting the east coast of the United States to California in the west. Now the United States was united in a new mechanical way. Canada followed with its own Canadian Pacific Railway, from Ontario in the east to British Columbia in the west. So by 1885, North America had two transcontinental railroads, and railroads had spread all around the world, to France, Russia, India, Australia, Argentina, and many other countries. The famous Orient Express, which ran from Paris, France, to Constantinople (now Istanbul, Turkey, but then the capital of the Ottoman Empire), opened in 1883.

Newly arrived Chinese immigrants made up most of the labor force who built the western ends of the U.S. Transcontinental Railroad and the Canadian Pacific Railway. These heroes who made the new railroads possible were treated as inferior to white people and often underpaid and abused.

Steam power also allowed ships to sail without being troubled by windless seas. The *SS Great Britain*, built by railwayman Isambard Kingdom Brunel, was launched in 1845. At 322 feet (98 m) long, she was the first iron steamship to cross the Atlantic Ocean, taking just 14 days.

While much of the world was embracing the Industrial Revolution, some of the Far East, including China, Japan, and Korea, retreated into hiding. From about 1600 to 1860 Japan tried to cut itself off from the outside world completely. The same is true for Korea, which was so successful at keeping itself out of the way of European influence that it became known as the Hermit Kingdom.

On his voyages, Zheng He collected treasures of all kinds to bring back to the royal court in Nanjing, China. From his trip to Somalia in eastern Africa, he brought back giraffes, leopards, lions, and zebras, which he called "celestial horses."

China also had little interest in expansion. Almost 100 years before Columbus reached the Americas, a Chinese Muslim admiral called Zheng He had taken a fleet of hundreds of huge ships and tens of thousands of sailors and passengers overseas to explore faraway lands. On at least one of his seven epic voyages in the early 1400s, he reached the east coast of Africa. But he wasn't like European conquistadors, waging war and enslaving people. Rather, he wanted to tell everyone about the glorious Chinese emperor, who, thanks to God in heaven, was supreme ruler of the world. In return, he collected exotic gifts from foreign rulers. His expeditions also led to extensive Chinese trade routes throughout Asia and to Chinese colonies in Southeast Asia.

But by 1520, China had abandoned its giant fleet and the idea of overseas exploration. Instead, invasions by Mongols from the north forced it to put all its energy into upgrading the Great Wall of China, turning it into a spectacular 5,499-mile (8,850-km) barrier.

This extraordinary line of defense worked well for a while. Then China entered into a period of civil war leading to the end of the Ming dynasty, which had ruled since the time of the Mongols. By 1662 the Qing dynasty had taken charge. Like Japan and Korea, the Qing had little interest in dealing with Europeans. But starting in about 1850 Western powers were snooping off the shores of Japan and sniffing up the rivers of China in their new steam-powered warships.

“OUR CELESTIAL EMPIRE POSSESSES ALL THINGS IN PROLIFIC ABUNDANCE … THERE WAS THEREFORE NO NEED TO IMPORT THE MANUFACTURES OF OUTSIDE BARBARIANS IN EXCHANGE FOR OUR OWN PRODUCE.”

Qianlong, Emperor of China in the Qing dynasty

Thousands of years ago, ancient Greeks discovered that if they rubbed cloth against a mineral called amber it would produce a series of mysterious shocks or sparks. The word "electricity" is actually based on the Greek word elektron, meaning "amber."

In the 1820s, English scientist Michael Faraday gave a series of famous demonstrations at a science club called The Royal Institution in London, England. Faraday showed how it was possible to move an object using an invisible force, called electromagnetism, that is created by passing electricity through a wire. This was the world's first electric motor. Then, in 1831, he showed how to generate electricity by waving a wire through a magnetic field. This is the principle used to produce electricity in a power station.

Thomas Edison never gave up. It took him and his team of engineers more than five years to figure out how to make a light bulb work without it exploding when connected to an electric current.

Once American inventor Thomas Edison perfected his design for cheap, mass-produced light bulbs, it became possible to create the world's first electrical power grid. In 1882 a steam-powered generating station linked 59 customers in New York City with electric power for the first time.

Electricity also gave rise to the first telegraph system, which sent coded messages over wires. In 1837 inventor Samuel Morse showed that it was possible to communicate using his Morse code across a distance of

I SHOUTED ... THE FOLLOWING SENTENCE: "MR WATSON – COME HERE – I WANT TO SEE YOU." TO MY DELIGHT HE CAME AND DECLARED THAT HE HAD HEARD AND UNDERSTOOD WHAT I SAID.

Alexander Graham Bell, inventor

It's possible Alexander Graham Bell was not the first person to invent a telephone. Others were working on the idea at the same time. But he was the first to register the invention with the United States patent office, so got the rights to make and sell phones. In this picture from the *Detroit News*, an unknown man demonstrates Bell's telephone.

nearly 40 miles (65 km) from Washington, D.C., to Baltimore, Maryland. Within 20 years all of North America was connected by wires. By the 1860s, cables were even being laid under the Atlantic Ocean, allowing instant communication between North America and Europe. The first cable ran from Ireland to Newfoundland, Canada.

So when Scottish-born Canadian-American inventor Alexander Graham Bell came up with a way of sending voice signals over electrical wires, he got very excited. On March 10, 1876, Bell spoke the first ever words over a telephone line to his assistant Thomas Watson, who was in the next room.

Machines were now changing every walk of life. But if you had to choose one that made the biggest difference of all, my guess is that many people might vote for the automobile. Unless you live in a big city with good public transportation, it's hard to imagine life without cars. Many of us are used to the freedom of driving anywhere we like, whenever we like.

Surprisingly, in 1900 almost all the cars in New York were electric. Edison's new power transmission system led to a surge of interest in creating cars that could be charged up at home. But by 1915 electric cars were in steep decline as a result of our next revolutionary invention.

In 1888, Bertha Benz, wife of inventor Karl Benz, publicized her husband's experimental car—the first to run on gasoline—by driving it more than 60 miles (100 km) to visit her mother. She took her teenage sons along so they could push the car to get it started. When the car broke down on the way, she fixed it herself. This was the very first time anyone had driven a car for more than a few feet.

German scientists Nikolaus August Otto, Gottlieb Daimler, and Wilhelm Maybach developed a series of gasoline engines beginning in 1876. A few years later, German mechanic Karl Benz used one of them to build the world's first gasoline-powered car. Here was a far lighter, faster mobile machine than those powered by either electricity or steam. Of course automobiles rely on plentiful supplies of gasoline, which comes from petroleum, often called crude oil, found deep in the ground. The first modern oil wells were dug in the late 1850s to provide a source of fuel for lamps. Now, with the invention of gasoline-powered cars, demand for oil increased very quickly.

On January 10, 1901, prospectors at Spindletop in Texas struck oil that gushed out at a rate of 100,000 barrels a day. And it kept on gushing for the next nine days until someone could figure out how to stop the flow. Local farmers were furious that their crops were drowning in oil, but a new age of exploration had truly begun.

Henry Ford applied mass production techniques to cars. His factories built more than 16 million Ford Model Ts between 1908 and 1927.

The first spectacular oil geyser at Spindletop was just the beginning. In all, over seventy-five million barrels of oil were pumped out of the area before it went dry in 1936.

New roads were built by governments eager to support people's passion to travel wherever and whenever they chose.

In 1903 two brothers who owned a bicycle shop had the brilliant idea of seeing if they could fly by putting a pair of wings on a bicycle and then mounting a small gasoline engine on the back. On December 17, Orville and Wilbur Wright successfully flew the first controlled, powered flights on the beach near Kitty Hawk, North Carolina. Their flights lasted only between 12 and 59 seconds, but they proved that it was possible to build a gasoline-powered flying machine that could carry human beings.

Within 15 years, the idea had been developed into sophisticated airplanes. World War I (1914–1918) picked up the pace, with nations on both sides of the conflict using aircraft to spy on enemy forces and drop bombs. Mass production techniques were quickly applied to making aircraft. During World War II (1939–1945), almost 800,000 planes were built.

Imagine finding a brand new source of power nobody had ever thought of before. In 1905, German physicist Albert Einstein did just that—at least theoretically. Newton's theories of motion and gravity worked fine for large objects, he said, but not when you zoom right in to look at what's happening at the level of atoms.

Einstein figured out that atoms are held together by an almost unimaginably strong force, which might be possible to unlock, releasing a massive source of untapped power. The famous equation that shows this relationship is $E=mc^2$, where E = energy, m = mass

Albert Einstein figured out that the universe is not what it seems. In this picture, he is writing an equation to calculate how crowded (or empty) the Milky Way is.

(stuff), and c = the speed of light.

Einstein showed that there was enough trapped energy in a single grain of sand to boil a kettle 10 million times. The starting gun had now been fired on a nuclear race, as rival scientists tried to find ways of splitting atoms to release their energy.

Advances in science and engineering were reshaping the world, bringing us close to how we live today. But to get to the present we need to travel through the next period in history. Sadly, it is not an easy trip to take, as we are about to see.

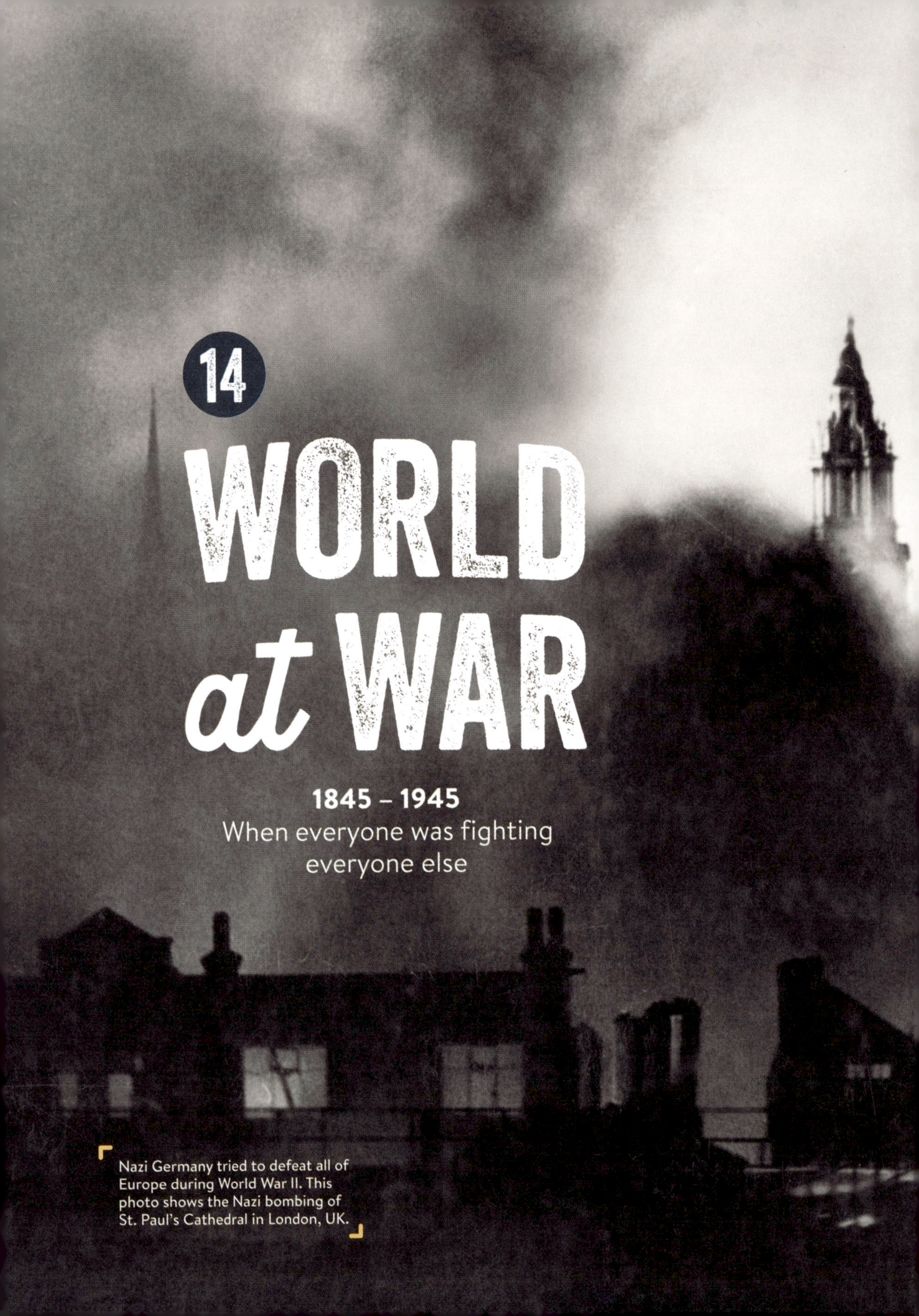

14

WORLD at WAR

1845 – 1945

When everyone was fighting everyone else

Nazi Germany tried to defeat all of Europe during World War II. This photo shows the Nazi bombing of St. Paul's Cathedral in London, UK.

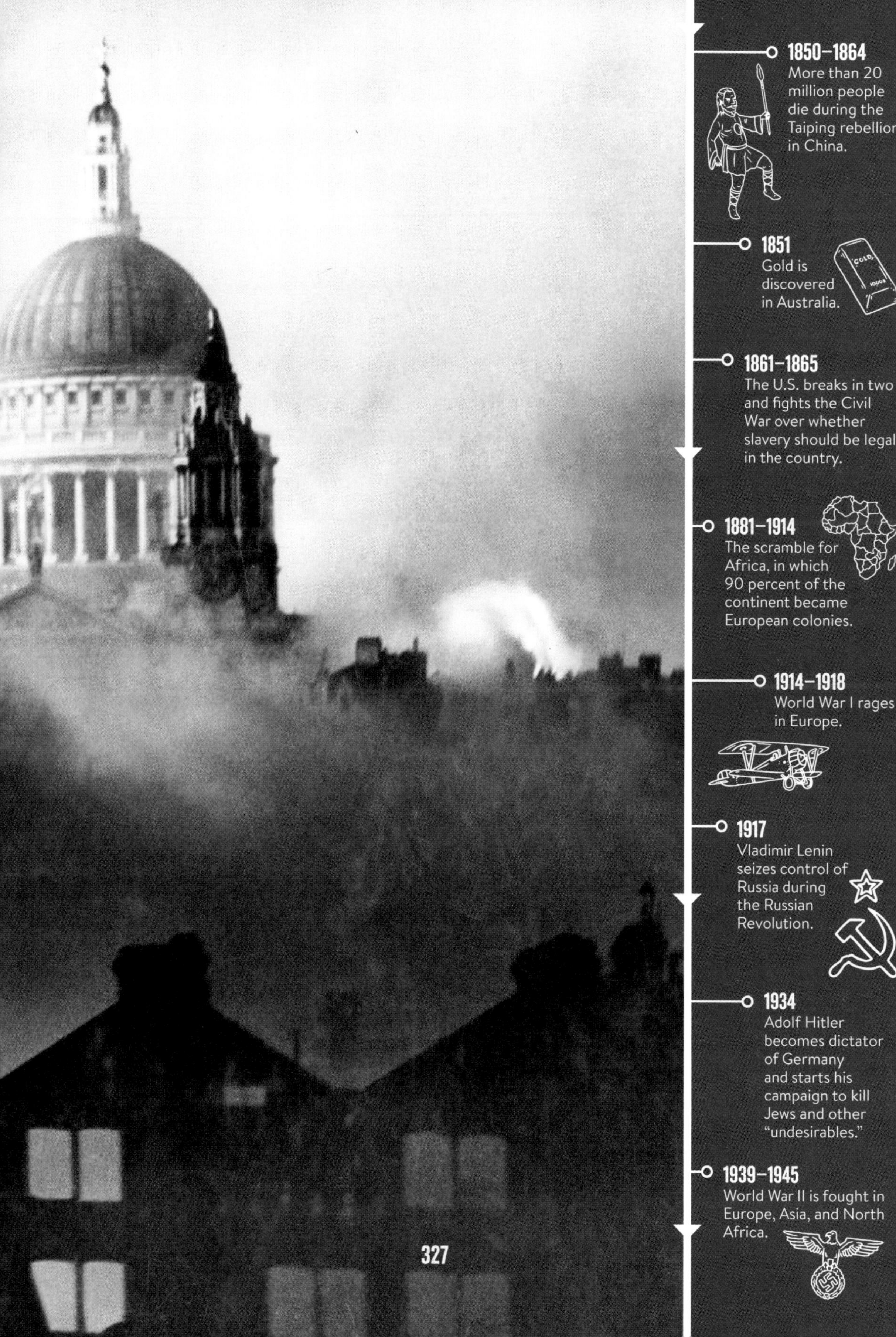

1850–1864
More than 20 million people die during the Taiping rebellion in China.

1851
Gold is discovered in Australia.

1861–1865
The U.S. breaks in two and fights the Civil War over whether slavery should be legal in the country.

1881–1914
The scramble for Africa, in which 90 percent of the continent became European colonies.

1914–1918
World War I rages in Europe.

1917
Vladimir Lenin seizes control of Russia during the Russian Revolution.

1934
Adolf Hitler becomes dictator of Germany and starts his campaign to kill Jews and other "undesirables."

1939–1945
World War II is fought in Europe, Asia, and North Africa.

Sad as it is to say, the time between 1845 and 1945 seems to me to have been one of the most brutal periods in the history of humankind. During this 100 years, and for reasons that I find hard to understand, appalling violence and fighting between humans erupted in almost every part of the world.

Maybe it was because the number of people in the world was increasing quickly thanks to advances in farming and technology. In 1804 the world's population passed 1 billion. By 1950 it had more than doubled to 2.5 billion. Having so many more people very possibly increased the chance of clashes between countries and cultures. Or maybe living in an increasingly connected world made some people feel jealous or deprived and others more greedy.

Many Europeans spent the beginning of this 100-year period busily trying to take over the whole world. Most of the Americas were now claimed. But Europeans saw the chance to gain more control over South Asia, the Middle East, and Africa.

Africa is a strikingly diverse continent, with as many as 3,000 ethnic groups speaking around 1,500 languages. When Europeans began carving it up, they paid no attention to ethnic boundaries or the needs or ways of life of the local people.

North Africa was the first to feel the effects of European settlement. In 1834 French troops invaded Algeria. There they built roads for transporting goods and materials to Europe. By 1848 more than 100,000 French people had settled in the territory. They farmed the land and exported cotton.

The Scramble for Africa, as it became known, kicked off in 1881. Twenty years later, European nations controlled more than

The Scramble for Africa

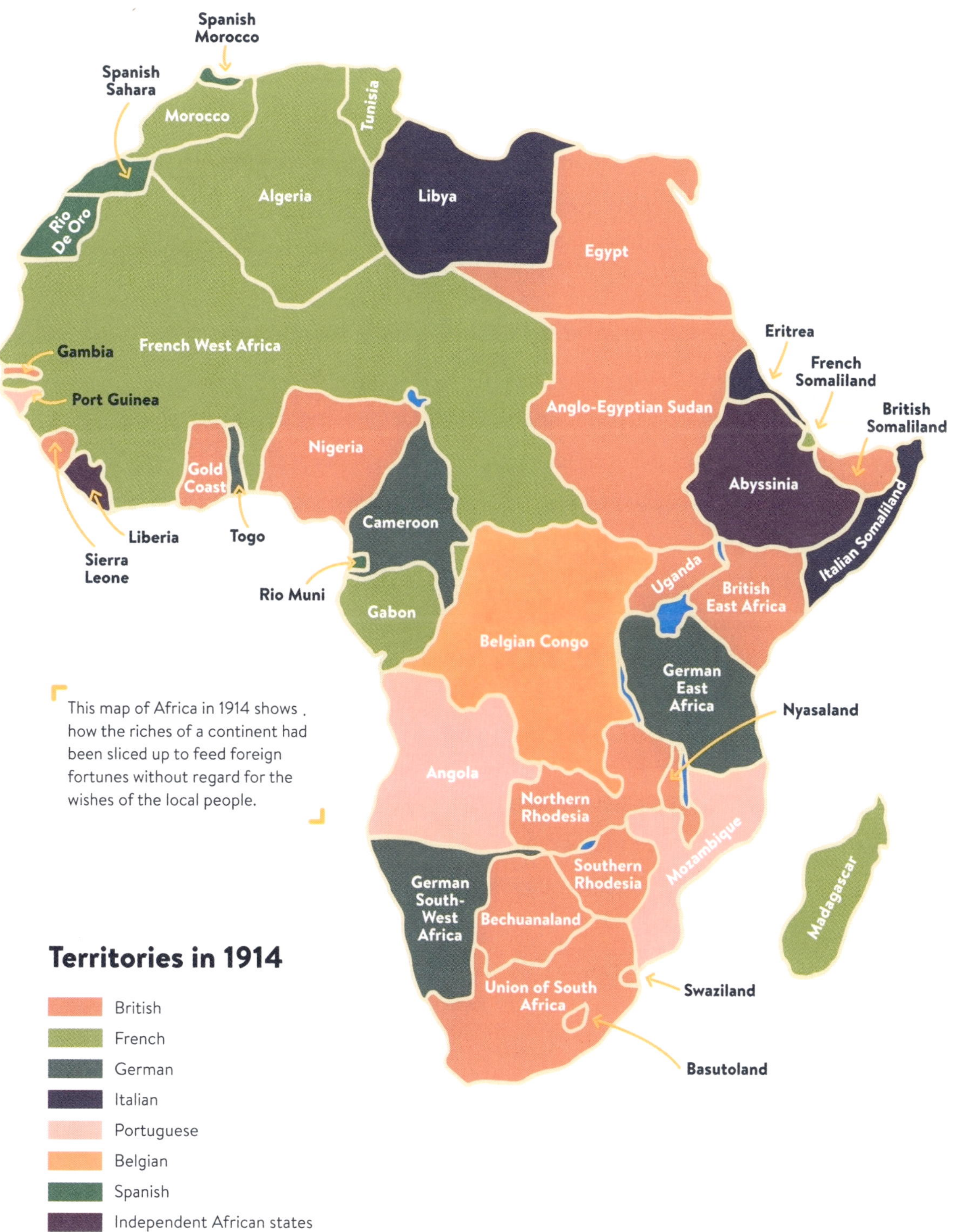

This map of Africa in 1914 shows how the riches of a continent had been sliced up to feed foreign fortunes without regard for the wishes of the local people.

Territories in 1914

- British
- French
- German
- Italian
- Portuguese
- Belgian
- Spanish
- Independent African states

90 percent of the continent. The people of colonized Africa were forced to raise crops such as coffee, cacao, rubber, cotton, and sugar for export. Others had to mine precious minerals such as copper, diamonds, and gold. Treasure flowed out of Africa, making Africans poorer and Europeans richer.

This behavior toward the people of Africa was part of a great lie known as racism. As we've seen, slavery has been around practically as long as humanity, and empire building has quite a long history, too. Plus, in some places lighter skin was considered higher class because it showed people you didn't have to work outdoors.

But in the mid 1700s, a new idea emerged: that people who looked different from one another were scientifically different, so much so that they were probably different species.

One of the first people to talk about this was Carl Linnaeus, a Swedish scientist who became famous for classifying the natural world into different species. In his most famous work, called *The Systems of Nature*, he divided humans into four varieties: *Europaeus albus* (European white), *Americanus rubescens*

In the middle of the 1800s, it was fashionable for white women in England to be as pale as possible, with pink cheeks. It was thought to make you look rich, sensitive, and intelligent. The disease tuberculosis caused this sort of paleness and was very common. The downside: it also killed you. Women who weren't sick tried to appear as if they were. They covered up when they went outdoors, and many used white makeup or took small amounts of the poison arsenic, which was known to whiten your skin.

> RACE IS A SOCIAL CONCEPT, NOT A SCIENTIFIC ONE.
>
> Craig Venter, geneticist and businessman who worked on decoding the full human genome

(American reddish), *Asiaticus fuscus* (Asian tan), and *Africanus niger* (African black).

In the mid 1800s, an American scientist named Samuel Morton published an experiment that took these ideas a step further. He measured the size of a small number of human skulls and claimed that his data proved there were five species of people (also known as races). He said white people had the largest skulls, followed by East Asians, South Asians, Indigenous Americans, and Africans.

He also believed that the bigger your skull, the higher your intelligence. So he thought white people must be super smart, and Black people must be so stupid that they were safer and happier enslaved. This thinking was used to justify slavery in the United States. It was also picked up by European leaders colonizing Africa. It was easier to steal from people you thought were inferior.

We now know that Linnaeus and Morton were 100 percent wrong and that Morton probably included a skull from a very large white man in his sample on purpose to try to show that whites were superior. When the human genome was decoded in 2000, it was proved beyond any doubt that there are no significant differences between what we call races. Humans are all one species, and there is absolutely nothing about the way we look that determines how intelligent we are or any other aspect of our talents or personalities. But hundreds of years of racism cannot be erased instantly. The arguments of the 1800s affect us today, with racism still common in many parts of the world.

The miners of the Australian gold rush were nicknamed "diggers." Here are three of them on a break at their temporary home in what had just become the state of Victoria.

Gold was discovered in Australia in 1851. As usual, Europeans rushed to get rich quick, and this time people from China also joined in. In just 20 years, Australia's population rose from 437,000 to 1.7 million. The new settlers did very well. But the First Australians, who had been there before the Europeans, didn't. From the very beginning of the British colonization of Australia in 1788, Europeans had stolen their land, brought new diseases, and massacred whole communities that refused to convert to Christianity or live like white people. Now this process accelerated. By 1900, the Aboriginal Australian population was less than a third, and possibly as little as a tenth, of what it had been when the first British settlers landed on their shores.

As you know, Europeans had been trading with China for hundreds of years at this point. In the mid-1800s, Europe was buying tremendous amounts of Chinese tea, silk, and porcelain.

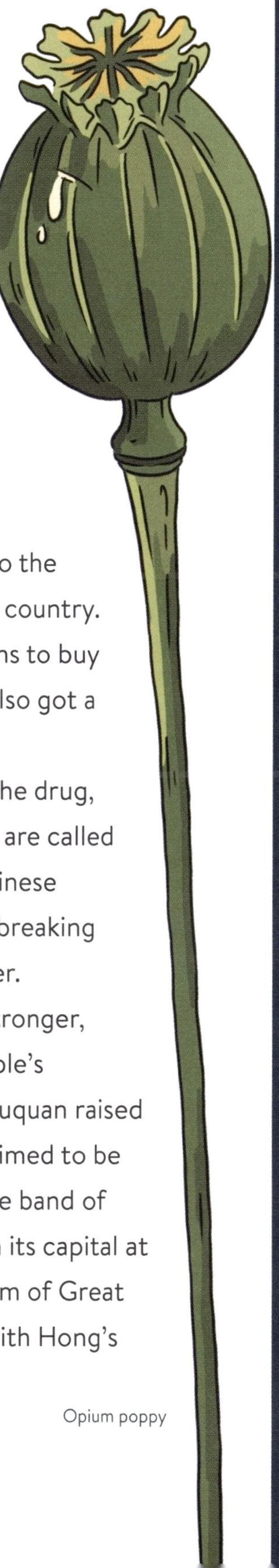

But there was a problem. At that time, the Chinese didn't really want to buy anything made in Europe. That meant European traders had to pay in silver for goods from China, but nobody in China was paying in silver for goods from Europe. This caused a silver shortage for European countries.

British traders eventually came up with something Chinese people would pay silver for—the drug opium. Opium is very addictive. The drug was illegal in China, so the British sold it to drug dealers, who smuggled it into the country. The silver they got in return made it easier for Europeans to buy more Chinese silk, tea, and porcelain. But of course it also got a lot of Chinese people addicted to opium.

The Chinese government tried to stop the flow of the drug, but the British went to war to keep bringing it in. These are called the Opium Wars. British traders didn't care that the Chinese people were suffering. They didn't care that they were breaking Chinese law. All they cared about was getting their silver.

As the Chinese people's addiction to opium grew stronger, the Chinese government grew weaker. Finally, the people's unhappiness boiled over. In 1850 a man named Hong Xiuquan raised a giant army to challenge the Qing government. He claimed to be the long-lost brother of Jesus Christ. Hong and his huge band of followers set up a rival kingdom in southern China, with its capital at Nanjing. They called their country the Heavenly Kingdom of Great Peace. And they replaced the teachings of Confucius with Hong's

Opium poppy

own translation of the Christian Bible.

A gigantic civil war, usually called the Taiping Rebellion, broke out between these two rival parts of China. No one was safe. The war lasted 14 years, from 1850 to 1864. It is not clear exactly how many people died. Estimates range from 20 million to 70 million. It remains the most deadly civil war in the history of the world.

Ellen Craft in disguise as a rich white man

Ellen and William Craft escaped slavery in Georgia in 1848. Ellen, who had light skin, disguised herself as a man and posed as a rich white plantation owner. Like almost all enslaved people, she couldn't read or write, so she wore her arm in a sling to avoid having to sign papers. With her husband, William, pretending to be her servant, she bought train tickets, and the two of them rode to freedom in the North. It was a very dangerous four-day journey. If they had been caught, they would have been returned to their owners and punished severely or even killed.

The Taiping Rebellion happened in one of the oldest countries in the world. But at the same time something similar was taking place in one of the newest countries, the United States of America. By then, the northern states had mostly outlawed slavery. Those against slavery—called abolitionists—said if all people are created equal as the Declaration of Independence said, then surely nobody should be enslaved.

Southern slave owners disagreed. Enslaved people were so valuable that they couldn't imagine life without them. Enslaved workers grew cotton, tobacco, sugar cane, and other crops. They did skilled jobs such as carpentry. And they also worked in their owners' houses, cooking, cleaning, and caring for children.

> FOUR SCORE AND SEVEN YEARS AGO OUR FATHERS BROUGHT FORTH, ON THIS CONTINENT, A NEW NATION, CONCEIVED IN LIBERTY, AND DEDICATED TO THE PROPOSITION THAT ALL MEN ARE CREATED EQUAL.
>
> Abraham Lincoln, Gettysburg Address

For a while the country agreed to disagree. Each state decided for itself whether to allow slavery. But when new states were joining the United States, fights broke out over whether they would allow or ban the practice.

Then Abraham Lincoln, who had spoken out against slavery, became president in 1861. Eleven southern states decided enough was enough. They declared themselves no longer part of the U.S. and formed their own country, called the Confederate States of America. There, slavery would stay legal.

Between April 1861 and the spring of 1865, more than 600,000 people died in a brutal civil war. The northern states eventually won, forcing the breakaway states back into the union. Four million people were released from slavery. Amendments were adopted into the U.S. Constitution that outlawed slavery and gave Black men the right to vote. However, white women couldn't vote, so neither could Black women. And there was still a very long road ahead to true equality.

I am sorry to say that our 100 years of terrible warfare are only just warming up. In Europe things were spinning out of control. The creation of two new European countries had made things a lot more competitive. The Italian city-states merged to become the modern country of Italy in 1861. Ten years later, German Chancellor

Otto von Bismarck united 25 German states into a single mighty nation. This new Germany was headed by Emperor Wilhelm I. He was very aware that Germany had been left out as other European nations had built up mighty empires. So Germany took over parts of Africa, including present-day Namibia, Rwanda, Ghana, and Tanzania. All of this made France and Britain very nervous.

This political cartoon shows Otto von Bismarck sweeping up smaller German states into a new super-nation.

Gradually, two alliances emerged. Britain, France, and Russia were on one side. On the other were Germany, Italy, and Austria-Hungary (made up of what are now Austria, Hungary, Czechia, Slovakia, Slovenia, Croatia, Bosnia and Herzegovina, and parts of Poland, Serbia, Ukraine, and Romania).

France was eager to win back lands lost to Germany in 1870. Italy and France were arguing over colonies in Africa. Russia was battling with Austria-Hungary for control of lands near the Black Sea. And Britain was terrified of Germany's craving to build a rival empire. By 1914 Europe was like a box of fireworks just waiting for someone to strike a match.

That match was struck by Serbian student Gavrilo Princip in Sarajevo, Bosnia. It was June 28, 1914. Princip was angry because he thought Bosnia should be free from the Austro-Hungarian Empire. So he shot and killed Archduke Franz Ferdinand, heir to the throne of Austria-Hungary, as he rode by in his car.

Archduke Franz Ferdinand of Austria-Hungary and his wife, Sophie, Duchess of Hohenberg, were attacked twice on June 28, 1914. The first time, a grenade missed and exploded under the car behind them. The second time, Gavrilo Princip shot them both from about 5 feet (1.5 m) away. They died within an hour.

Because Princip was Serbian, Austria-Hungary blamed the Serbian government for the assassination and invaded Serbia in revenge. But then everything got completely out of hand. Serbia's allies—Britain, France, and Russia—lined up on one side. Austria-Hungary's ally Germany lined up with it on the other. One assassination had turned into a war that involved almost all of Europe. It was so confusing that many of the soldiers didn't even know why they were fighting.

This war, later named World War I, was fought mostly in Europe between 1914 and 1918. The United States entered the war on the side of the British and their allies in 1917. Before it was all over, about 20 million people were dead, either in the fighting itself or of a horrible flu that broke out toward the end of the war.

"POOR FELLOWS SHOT DEAD ARE LYING IN ALL DIRECTIONS...EVERYWHERE THE SAME HARD, GRIM, PITILESS SIGN OF BATTLE AND WAR. I HAVE HAD A BELLY FULL OF IT."

Captain James Patterson, a British soldier fighting in France during WWI. He was killed in battle on November 1, 1914.

Russia hasn't featured much in our story so far, but now it comes center stage. From prehistoric times, this vast country was home to a wide range of ethnic groups. Then, as we saw earlier, the Viking Rus settled in Russia around 840 CE and a wave of settlement by the Mongols followed.

From 1547, Russia was ruled by kings and queens known as tsars and tsarinas. Like most rulers, they had their good sides and their bad sides. The first tsar was Ivan the Terrible, who built a huge empire, mostly by taking over territory that had been part of the Mongol empire created by Genghis Khan and his family. Peter the Great, who ruled from 1682 to 1725, modernized the country by supporting science and technology and starting Russia's first newspaper. Catherine the Great, who ruled from 1762 to 1796, was planning to free Russia's serfs, who, like enslaved people, were the property of nobles. But in the end she needed the nobles on her side, so she changed her mind and took away the few rights the serfs had.

In 1917, three years after the outbreak of World War I, Russia collapsed into chaos. The war had weakened the country, and the people blamed Tsar Nicholas II. Food shortages made people miserable, hungry, and angry. And nobody trusted Grigori Rasputin, a royal adviser who called himself a holy man.

Women in the city of Petrograd (now St. Petersburg) revolted over the shortage of bread in February 1917. Across the country, others joined the protest. In March, Tsar Nicholas was forced to resign the throne. After a power struggle, Vladimir Lenin and Leon Trotsky seized control of the government, in what is known as the Russian Revolution. In May 1918, the Tsar and his family were executed.

Lenin and Trotsky were eager to try out

Revolutionary posters like this one inspired people to throw off the chains of the Tsar and support Lenin's Russian Revolution, which he promised would result in better lives for workers.

под Ленинским знаменем
Коминтерна – вперед!
Дени 29г.
ДА ЗДРАВСТВУЕТ ПЕРВОЕ МАЯ

an experimental form of government called communism. The basic idea had been developed by a German philosopher named Karl Marx, who proposed that the world would be a better place if governments were run by the workers. He also believed that workers should own the companies they work for.

Civil war now broke out between two sides—Lenin's communist army (Reds) and those who didn't like the idea of communism (Whites). Britain, France, the United States, and Japan supported the Whites. In June 1923, Lenin's Red Army won the war. They changed the name of Russia to the Union of Soviet Socialist Republics (USSR), or Soviet Union.

But what started off as a great idea got hijacked by someone who cared only about power. Joseph Stalin ruled with an iron fist from 1924 to 1953. Anyone who disobeyed him was either executed or sent to labor camps, known as gulags, in bitterly cold Siberia. During his reign, Stalin is believed to have caused the deaths of up to 20 million of his own people.

Some people thought World War I had been so awful that Europeans would never want to go to war again. It was even called "the war to end all wars." But sadly, that's not how it turned out. In fact, its end sowed the seeds of an even more devastating conflict.

The Treaty of Versailles, the peace agreement that ended the war, blamed Germany. As punishment, the German people had to give up all their weapons and pay 106,000 tons (96,000 tonnes) of gold, which would be worth $2.2 trillion today. Even though they could pay over time, the penalty left them very poor and very angry.

One man who took part in World War I felt deeply let down. His name was Adolf Hitler. In his view, Germany's leaders had dragged the country into a war and then lost it. Hitler wanted to go back to the ideas of ancient Sparta. He would make sure that Germany had only the strongest people. This, he said in his book *Mein Kampf*, would make Germany great again.

The downtrodden people of Germany liked what they heard. So on January 30, 1933, Hitler was voted in as head of the German government, a position known as Chancellor. Almost immediately Hitler's real plans became clear. He believed his country needed to get rid of people who he didn't think were "real" Germans. He also decided that the best way to improve the German economy was to give people jobs building weapons. Tanks and airplanes could scare Germany's neighbors into giving it more land. If that failed, they could be used to take the land by force.

Hitler used emergency powers to make himself dictator. He then banned all political parties except his Nazi party. Finally, he introduced a secret police force to make sure anyone saying anything against Hitler was spotted and punished.

When Adolf Hitler came to power in 1933, he set about making sure everyone in Germany obeyed him. His dreams of conquering Europe were shattered by the Nazi defeat in 1945.

Supermarine Spitfire

In 1938 Hitler's armies rolled eastward into Czechoslovakia, a country that is now Czechia and Slovakia. (Austria-Hungary had broken up after World War I.) Britain, France, and the Soviet Union were still hoping that they could persuade Hitler to stop without actually having to go to war. But the next year Hitler invaded Poland, and Europe collapsed into a second dreadful conflict that lasted until 1945. Hitler's forces advanced rapidly through Europe, invading Belgium then France. Nobody could stop them. By May 1941. it looked like Hitler's dream of European conquest might come true.

This was Europe's darkest hour. Between 1941 and 1945, Hitler's Nazis ran a group of prisons known as concentration camps. In some, prisoners were worked to death. In others, they were executed. In all, about 11 million innocent people were killed. The victims included about 3 million prisoners of war, 6 million Jews and 2 million other people the Nazis thought were inferior. In this last group were Roma, LGBTQ+ people, people with disabilities, political opponents, and others. This atrocious crime is known as the Holocaust.

The German Heinkel He 111 bomber was so sturdy it could take a lot of damage without crashing. But the British fighter plane Supermarine Spitfire was lighter and easier to steer and was one of Britain's best tools in its fight to keep the Nazis from taking over the UK.

Heinkel He III

World War II wasn't just fought in Europe the way World War I had been. It truly included most of the world. That's because in the 1930s, Japan had started to do

Over a million people, most of them Jews, were murdered at Auschwitz, a complex of Nazi concentration camps in Poland. The words above the gate say *Arbeit macht frei*, meaning "work will set you free." But the prisoners knew they would never be set free no matter how hard they worked.

what European countries had been doing for 400 years—build a mighty empire.

In 1931, even before Hitler came to power, Japan invaded the northeastern Chinese province of Manchuria. A few years later, the Japanese launched a full-scale invasion of China with 350,000 soldiers. They used airplanes to bomb cities all over the country.

Japan and Germany both wanted to defeat the Soviet Union (Japan had its eye on the Asian part and Germany wanted the European part), and each wanted to dominate its part of the world. So Japan signed the Tripartite Pact with Germany and Italy in 1940. That made it officially an enemy of the Soviet Union and also of Britain, France, and the United States.

China fought back against Japan, and Britain and the United States helped by preventing the Japanese from getting the fuel they needed. Without oil, Japan could not power its army, navy, or airforce. No oil, no victory. The best plan for Japan would be to take over oil-rich Dutch and British territories in Asia.

That's why Japan launched a surprise attack on the U.S. Naval base in Pearl Harbor, Hawaii, on December 7, 1941. It needed to destroy the U.S.'s battle ships there so they couldn't interfere with the Japanese takeover of the oil territories.

Japan hoped that the United States wouldn't want to get into a war in Asia and would quickly negotiate a peace deal once it was clear that Japan had successfully built their empire. But Japan was wrong. Attacking Pearl Harbor proved a terrible mistake. The United States had been selling weapons to Britain and France. But now U.S. president Franklin D. Roosevelt had the reason he needed to convince his country they had to fight. The United States entered the war in December 1941, both in Europe and in Asia.

The fighting was brutal. It ended in Europe first. On April 30, 1945, Hitler's army was surrounded on all sides by British, American, and Soviet forces. He knew he was about to lose the war, so Hitler shot himself in his underground hideout near the German capital of Berlin. Without its leader, Germany surrendered.

But that wasn't the end of the war. Remember $E=mc^2$? In 1933 Albert Einstein had been touring America. As a Jew, he was so worried about the rise of Hitler that he decided to stay in the U.S. instead of returning to Germany. When war broke out, Einstein and another scientist, Leo Szilard, wrote a letter to President Roosevelt. They warned that Nazi Germany might find a way to unlock all that energy trapped inside atoms. They feared that a new generation

This monument in Hiroshima, Japan, features 12-year-old Sadako Sasaki, who died from cancer caused by the atom bomb's radiation. When she was in the hospital, Sadako folded origami cranes as fast as she could, finishing 644 cranes before she died. After her death, children from around the world folded cranes in her honor. Here she holds a giant crane above her head.

of superbombs would surely help the Germans win. Once the United States entered the war, the government started a top-secret project. Its goal? To make sure the U.S., with support from Britain and Canada, developed nuclear bombs before the Nazis did.

The program, known as the Manhattan Project, invented the atom bomb before Germany did. But in the end, Germany wasn't the target. On August 6, 1945, the people of two Japanese cities, Hiroshima and Nagasaki, were the first to feel the power of this terrible force. Only one bomb was dropped on each city. But each of those bombs killed as many as 70,000 people in an instant. Thousands more died later in a flood of invisible but deadly radioactive energy that lingered for years.

Einstein felt bad that his letter to President Roosevelt had led to such a horrible weapon. "Had I known that the Germans would not succeed in producing an atomic bomb," he said, "I would have never lifted a finger."

But the bomb did end the war. By August 15, Japan had surrendered and World War II was over. Estimates of the death toll range from 50 to 80 million people, making this the most devastating conflict in human history.

The August 1994 launch of the Space Shuttle Atlantis. During the Cold War of the mid-1900s, the Soviet Union and the United States competed to have the best space program. After the break-up of the Soviet Union, many countries around the world began collaborating to send missions to space.

15

MARCHING TOWARDS *the* MILLENNIUM

1945 – 2001
The Cold War, Human Rights, and the Dawn of the Digital Age

1945
The world's population reaches 2.5 billion.

1945
The United Nations is established to prevent another world war.

1947
India wins its independence from the UK.

1955
Rosa Parks sparks the Montgomery Bus Boycott.

1957
The Soviet Union sends Sputnik, the first artificial satellite, to space.

1975
The Vietnam War comes to an end after taking the lives of well over half a million people.

1981
IBM introduces the first personal computer.

1991
The Berlin Wall comes down, marking the end of the Cold War.

2001
September 11 terrorist attacks.

After all that war, I am relieved to say the period between 1945 and 2001 was probably the most peaceful period in all human history. That's not to say there weren't wars or famines or that poverty and suffering had come to an end—far from it. But there has been no World War III—and for that we can all be grateful.

A new power balance emerged from the rubble of a world devastated by war. The United States offered an umbrella of military security and protection for any countries that joined its network of free trading nations. In addition to the U.S., this group included the western European countries, almost all of North and South America, Japan, Australia, and several others. They practiced capitalism, a system where individuals own companies and can get rich from their profits. Capitalists believe this is the best way to give everyone an equal chance to do well in life.

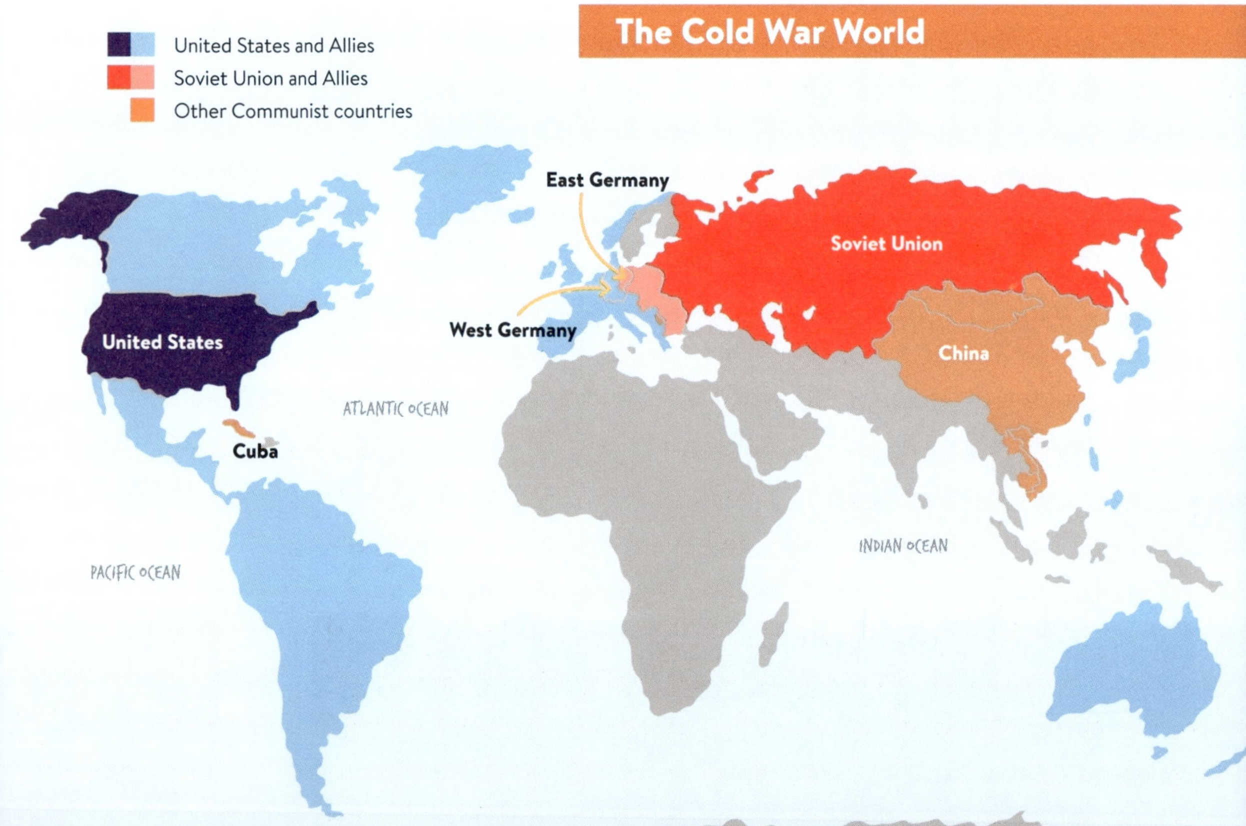

There was one binding condition about belonging to this club of nations, however. Everyone had to line up against the other emerging superpower from that dreadful war. Though the Soviet Union, dominated by Russia, had been an ally of Britain, France, and the U.S. in World War II, it wanted to dominate Europe so it became enemy number one to the United States and its allies after the war. The North Atlantic Treaty Organization (NATO) was officially formed in 1949 with the purpose of using the United States's military might to resist any expansion of the Soviet Union. Its central doctrine was that an attack on any one NATO member country would be considered an attack on them all.

The Soviet Union embraced communism, Karl Marx's idea of the government owning all businesses. They believed that would make it possible for profits to benefit all people, not just those who are lucky or smart enough to start a successful company or get a high-paying job. The Soviet Union had been communist since World War II—following the Russian Revolution of 1918. China became communist after another civil war. This one took place right after global hostilities ended in 1945. So the Soviet Union and China formed the core of the communist side of the world after WWII.

Germany, whose Nazi party had started World War II, was divided in two after the war. Half became capitalist West Germany. The other half became communist East Germany.

Capitalists and communists each wanted other countries to join them in their way of life. And neither of these groups wanted the other to grow too

Most (but not all) of the countries in the world allied themselves with either the U.S. or the Soviet Union.

After Germany lost WWII, it was divided in half. East Germany was communist and West Germany was capitalist. The German capital, Berlin, was divided, too, even though it was located inside East Germany. East Germany built a wall—known as the Berlin Wall (above)—in August 1961 to keep people from moving between the two parts of the city. The wall was torn down in 1989, and the two Germanies reunited the next year.

powerful. So the two groups built thousands and thousands of nuclear bombs. They put them in missiles that could be shot up into space and across oceans, and pointed them at one another. And so the world entered a new phase. Two giant superpowers armed to the teeth with nuclear missiles pointed at each other, ready to fire but never actually going to war. This time is known as the Cold War. It was called "cold" because fortunately it never heated up into fighting with nuclear weapons.

The threat of nuclear war made people feel so chilled to the bone that it scared them into not attacking first. This idea became known as MAD—Mutually Assured Destruction. Some people believe MAD has been good for keeping the peace, because each group knows that if they start a nuclear war, the other side will fire back, and everyone will die.

But there were some close calls. In 1962, the Soviets put some nuclear weapons in Cuba, a communist country located in the Caribbean Sea only 90 miles (150 km) from Key West, Florida. The U.S. threatened to attack if they didn't remove them. A war was only averted when the two superpowers struck a deal. The Soviet Union would remove its weapons from Cuba. In exchange, the U.S. would secretly remove the nuclear weapons it had in Turkey, close to the Soviet Union. The event is known as the Cuban Missile Crisis.

> “[I] CONSIDER AN ATTACK TO BE ALMOST IMMINENT—WITHIN THE NEXT 24 TO 72 HOURS.”
>
> Cuban Prime Minister Fidel Castro, during the Cuban Missile Crisis

More than 60 non-nuclear wars took place during the Cold War. In most of them, the communists supported one side and the capitalists the other. In Asia, American attempts at stopping the Soviets and China from taking Korea under their control led to a three-year war from 1950 to 1953. The country was (and still is) divided between north and south. North Korea is communist, and South Korea is capitalist.

Another conflict broke out in Vietnam between communist North Vietnam (supported by China and the Soviet Union) and capitalist South Vietnam (supported by the U.S.). This war raged from 1954 to 1975 and ended with the whole country becoming communist. It cost the lives of as many as 250,000 Vietnamese soldiers, nearly 60,000 U.S. soldiers, and about 250,000

> THAT'S ONE SMALL STEP FOR A MAN, ONE GIANT LEAP FOR MANKIND.
>
> Neil Armstrong, astronaut

Vietnamese civilians—people who are not soldiers at all but just trying to live their lives in the middle of a war. So even the Cold War had its hot moments.

The Space Race is considered another element of the Cold War. In 1957 the Soviet Union launched the world's first ever artificial satellite, Sputnik, which could orbit Earth in space. The Americans found the idea of their enemies spying from space too much to stomach. From that moment, the U.S. committed itself to putting a man on the Moon by the end of the 1960s. And they did it! Neil Armstrong was the first, followed by 11 others. (It was a sign of the times that women weren't even considered.)

Today all kinds of new spacecraft are being developed in the United States, Europe, China, and Russia. One rocket, called Falcon Heavy, was launched for the first time in 2018. Built by a private company called SpaceX, the Falcon Heavy was designed to take people to Mars and back again. Its rockets are fully reusable.

The Cold War officially ended in 1991 when the Soviet Union broke apart into 15 republics. The wall that divided Berlin, Germany, was

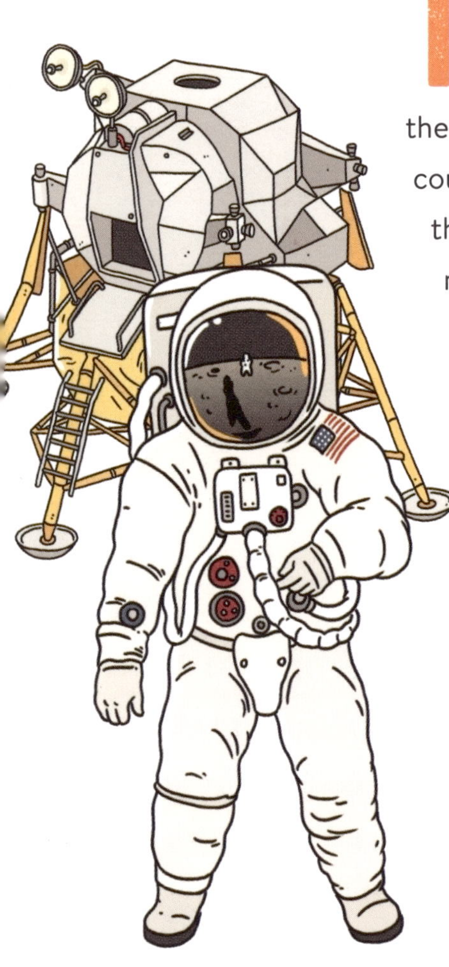

Neil Armstrong was the first person ever to set foot on the Moon. Twelve astronauts walked on the Moon between 1969 and 1972.

demolished and Germany reunited. During the 1990s Russia and China embraced some parts of capitalism. And in 2004, nine of the former Soviet republics joined a new community of nations known as the European Union.

For a while the prospects for World War III seemed to fade away. It even looked as if the world might just unite and consign the prospect of global war to the pages of history books that told stories of the 20th century. All this was backed up by a series of treaties designed to reduce the number of nuclear weapons.

Another kind of war became a new threat in the 1980s, as the Soviet Union struggled internally and the Cold War began to wind down. This one doesn't need a big army. The goal is to frighten your enemy and bring attention to your cause. It's called terrorism.

Remember how World War I was started by someone who wanted freedom for his country? Well, the biggest mass murder in Canadian history had the same motivation. It was the bombing of an airplane in 1985. Air India Flight 182 was on its way from Canada to India, carrying a suitcase with a bomb in it. When the bomb exploded, the plane broke into pieces and crashed into the sea, killing everyone on board.

The bombers were members of an Indian-Canadian group. They wanted an independent country for Sikhs, one of India's religious minorities. They were furious at the Indian government for killing more than 1,000 Sikhs in a raid on a temple where rebels were hiding. The 329 people on Flight 182—most of them Indian-

Terrorists almost always attack ordinary people going about their ordinary business. To mourn those innocent victims, people across the world create public shrines with flowers and messages and hold candlelight vigils like this one, held in London, in response to the 2014 attack on a school in Peshawar, Pakistan.

Canadians—were innocent victims. They were killed to draw attention to the terrorists' cause.

Terrorists can be anyone. The Oklahoma City bombing in 1995 killed 168 people. The bombers were white Americans angry at the U.S. government for attacking a religious cult whose members refused to let them in to search for illegal weapons. The September 11, 2001, attacks, which destroyed the Twin Towers of the World Trade Center in New York City and killed about 3,000 people in New York, Washington D.C., and Pennsylvania, were the work of a militant Islamist group known as al-Qaeda. They were angry because they believed that the United States was unfair to Muslim countries and overgenerous to the mostly Jewish country of Israel.

It seems impossible to make wars extinct. But people did try—and still do. Right after World War II, in October 1945, a group of countries got together to form a new international organization called the United Nations (UN). The idea was to unite all countries and prevent another world war. The UN also helps countries suffering from famine or war. It tries to get the whole world to agree to obey a set of international laws. Not everyone always sticks to the rules, but having them in place has made a difference.

> "THE WEAK CAN NEVER FORGIVE. FORGIVENESS IS THE ATTRIBUTE OF THE STRONG."
>
> Mahatma Gandhi, independence activist and civil rights leader

Following the founding of the UN and NATO, the world-war-exhausted countries of Western Europe began to loosen their grip on their colonies. In India, Mahatma Gandhi had spent 30 years organizing protests against colonial rule. Gandhi was an unusual revolutionary leader. What made him so special was that he insisted his followers never use violence. Pictures of British soldiers attacking Indian people who refused to fight back were seen all over the world. Such images had a profound effect on opinion in Britain itself and around the world. In 1947 India finally won its independence.

Many people who lived in European colonies in Asia and Africa had fought for Europe's freedom in World War II. Returning home, they began to think of their own freedom and that of their countries. Many independence movements arose during this time, and most of the countries of the world were independent by the end of the century.

Ideas of freedom are not just about countries. They are also about individuals and how we treat one another every day. On December 10, 1948, three years after the founding of the United Nations, its members adopted a Universal Declaration of Human Rights that includes 30 articles, each a right that should be protected. Among many other things, it says all forms of slavery must be banned. It says people should be allowed to move freely around the world. It says everyone should be able to practice whatever religion they choose or no religion at all. It says governments are responsible for their people having enough food to eat and access to healthcare.

These rules are not legally binding. Few countries in the world guarantee their citizens all of the rights listed. But the Declaration has been very important because many countries have used it as a basis for their own laws and because it has encouraged human rights movements. The second half of the 20th century turned out to be a big one for human rights struggles around the world.

In the United States, activists of the Civil Rights Movement of the 1950s and 1960s

“COURAGE IS MORE EXHILARATING THAN FEAR AND IN THE LONG RUN IT IS EASIER. WE DO NOT HAVE TO BECOME HEROES OVERNIGHT. JUST ONE STEP AT A TIME, MEETING EACH THING THAT COMES UP, SEEING IT IS NOT AS DREADFUL AS IT APPEARED, DISCOVERING WE HAVE THE STRENGTH TO STARE IT DOWN.”

Eleanor Roosevelt,
chairperson of the United Nations
Commission on Human Rights

risked their lives to change the treatment of Black Americans. Since just after the Civil War in the mid 1800s, laws across the southern United States had kept Black people separated from white people. Trains and buses had special sections reserved for whites only. White children and Black children went to separate schools, and I bet you can guess which ones got the new books and the indoor toilets. And unfair voting rules kept Black people from voting even though the Constitution said it was their right.

When Rosa Parks took an illegal seat on her bus in 1955, she knew how the driver would react. She had already been thrown off that bus before, and by the same driver. She also knew jails were dangerous places for African American women. But she and other activists had agreed that this was the right time to stand firm. (By the way, there were no cameras on the bus. This picture was staged later.)

Many activists in the Civil Rights Movement embraced Mahatma Gandhi's nonviolent methods. One such activist leader was Rosa Parks. In 1955 she refused to give up her seat on a bus for a white man. This sparked the Montgomery Bus Boycott, where thousands

> "I HAVE A DREAM THAT MY FOUR LITTLE CHILDREN WILL ONE DAY LIVE IN A NATION WHERE THEY WILL NOT BE JUDGED BY THE COLOR OF THEIR SKIN, BUT BY THE CONTENT OF THEIR CHARACTER."
>
> Martin Luther King Jr., minister and activist

of Black people refused to ride buses in Montgomery, Alabama, for over a year. Finally, a judge ruled that buses had to let anyone sit anywhere, regardless of skin color.

One of the other leaders of that boycott was the Reverend Dr. Martin Luther King, Jr., who became the most recognized figure of the Civil Rights Movement. Little by little, the combination of well-organized non-violent protests and judges willing to overrule southern laws shifted public opinion in the country.

In 1964, Congress passed a series of new laws called the Civil Rights Act. These laws protected equality for people of color. Now, more than 50 years later, conditions for Black people are much better but still not fully equal. Racial prejudice has not gone away, parts of the Civil Rights Act are no longer in effect, and new efforts to keep Black people from voting have popped up. A movement known as Black Lives Matter has picked up the struggle for equal treatment.

While the Civil Rights Movement was at its height, protests broke out in South Africa, a majority Black country that at the time was ruled by white people, colonialists who had originally come from the Netherlands and Britain. The government made laws separating people based on the color of their skin and preventing Black people from having any power. That system was called apartheid. In 1962 one of the anti-apartheid movement's leaders, Nelson Mandela, was jailed for life. He was eventually freed after serving 27 years in prison. In an extraordinary turn of events, Mandela was elected president of South Africa in the country's first free election after apartheid ended, in 1994.

As president, Nelson Mandela set an example to people of all backgrounds by creating a Truth and Reconciliation Commission. Hundreds of people, including government officials, told the truth to the public about their part in the horrible system of apartheid. Mandela's vision was based on forgiveness. He did not seek revenge for what had happened in his country's past but looked forward and worked to create a peaceful future. He and the last white president of South Africa, F. W. de Klerk, shared the Nobel Peace Prize for managing such a peaceful end to apartheid after so many years of misery and violence.

Nelson Mandela

It's not just skin color differences that lead to unfair treatment. Women have struggled for equality with men since well before World War II. It wasn't until 1893 that any country in the world gave women the right to vote. New Zealand was first, followed by Australia, Finland, Norway, Denmark, and Iceland. Then, in 1918, many of the European countries that had been involved in World War I followed, including Russia, the UK, and Germany. In 1920, so did the United States. The most recent country to give women the right to vote was Saudi Arabia, in 2015.

But getting equality in other areas of life—such as women and men being paid the same amount for the same job—has continued to be a struggle. Even worse, there are countries where girls still don't have the right to an education or to choose whom to marry. And women own less than 20 percent of the world's land.

The good news is that many groups of people who have traditionally been discriminated against are successfully fighting for their rights. Some do that through direct action and others by telling the wider world what is happening. A few do both.

Rigoberta Menchú Tum comes from a Mayan community in Guatemala, in Central America. Her family worked on coffee plantations. When she was a young woman, Guatemala was ruled by a military government that treated Indigenous people as less than human, and she became an activist for fair treatment for all.

When a civil war broke out and the rest of her family were killed, Menchú fled to Mexico. There she continued to work for her people and collaborated on a moving book and documentary movie about her life and the cruelty inflicted on Indigenous Guatemalans. She wanted to make sure the whole world knew what was going on.

Rigoberta Menchú Tum won a Nobel Peace Prize in 1992. That year was the 500th anniversary of the year Columbus stumbled upon the Americas,

Rigoberta Menchú Tum

beginning the takeover of the two continents and the destruction of Indigenous peoples. She won the prize for working to gain respect for her people. In 1996, four years after her award, a peace agreement was signed in Guatemala, and Menchú was made a United Nations Goodwill Ambassador, speaking out for the world's Indigenous peoples.

> "THERE IS NO DOUBT WHATSOEVER THAT [MY NOBEL PRIZE] CONSTITUTES A SIGN OF HOPE IN THE STRUGGLE OF THE INDIGENOUS PEOPLE IN THE ENTIRE CONTINENT."
>
> Rigoberta Menchú Tum

Little by little, other mistreated groups have followed Gandhi's and Parks's, Mandela's and Menchú's leads. People with disabilities have fought in many countries for changes that give them equal access to education and jobs. LGBTQ+ people have recently won the right in some places to live and work openly and legally to marry the person they love. There is much more work to do, but seeing this progress gives me hope.

War and peace, politics, and the struggle for human rights are only part of what shaped the world between the end of World War II and the beginning of the 2000s. Huge advances in science and technology literally changed lives everywhere.

Have you heard about the transistor? This little marvel was invented in 1947 by a team of three American physicists: John Bardeen, Walter Brattain, and William Shockley. They shared the Nobel Prize for Physics in 1956 thanks to this incredible invention. It's a kind of electrical switch usually made from silicon, and it spawned the digital age.

IBM introduced the first personal computers in 1981. It could never have happened without the transistor. Since then, computers, mobile phones, and the Internet have completely transformed the world. These days, it's hard for most people in the developed world to imagine life without them.

We use computers and smartphones for gaming, reading, shopping, making friends, and taking pictures. We use them for sending messages, writing, doing research, and watching movies. We use them to find people with similar interests and concerns. And we use them to share news and videos of the things that make us laugh and things that make us cry.

Steve Jobs co-founded Apple, a US computer company, in 1976. He launched the iPhone, the world's bestselling smartphone, in June 2007.

But like all advances, the benefits of the digital age aren't shared evenly. Poorer people (even poorer people in rich countries) have been shut out of many of its benefits, making it even harder than it used to be for them to live their lives. Plus, polluting and dangerous factories and power plants are usually built in areas where poor people live, so when accidents happen, it is the poor who suffer the most. One of the most tragic was the Union Carbide disaster in Bhopal, India, where a leak from a chemical factory in 1984 exposed more than half a million people to a highly poisonous gas. One estimate puts the total deaths at about 16,000—but no one really knows and countless others are still suffering today.

You will probably have heard of Chernobyl, the world's worst ever nuclear disaster. The Chernobyl nuclear reactor, on the border of Ukraine and Russia, exploded in April 1986 with a radioactive cloud that is thought to have led to at least 4,000 deaths.

The Chernobyl nuclear disaster contaminated an area about 20 miles (32 km) wide. About 335,000 people lost their homes, and cities and towns were abandoned. This photo shows the bumper car ride in a theme park in the city of Pripyat, which nature is slowly taking back.

Remember when the world was one giant supercontinent called Pangaea? Well, just to remind you, that was some 250 million years ago. In many ways it feels like that now, thanks to what's called globalization.

Since 1945, the world's landmasses have been connected by giant container ships that transport raw materials from one country to another, where they are turned into consumer products and then shipped to yet another country to be sold in shops. And it wasn't really until after 1945 that people began taking to the skies to travel from one side of the world to another for vacations, to visit relatives, and on business. Many goods, such as perishable food and flowers, are also sent this way—not to mention countless tons of other freight—just stuff being sent by air from one place to another to get it there quickly.

It's also worth taking a good look around—in your home, at school, or when you go to the store. What's everything made of? That's something that has changed hugely since 1945. Most things today are made of glass, steel, plastic, or concrete. Cars are mostly plastic and steel. Buildings are usually concrete and glass. Some

traditional materials such as wood are still being used, but not nearly as much as they were 100 years ago. Until World War II, entire Japanese cities were made of wood. When Tokyo was bombed by Allied forces in 1945, the city simply burned down. Tokyo has been rebuilt, and now it's a giant jungle of concrete and glass.

Why do we need so many new buildings? One reason is that in the years following World War II billions of people have moved from living in the countryside to living in towns and cities. In China alone, it is estimated 800 million people have made the move into city living. For the first time in history, more than half of the world's population lives in cities and suburbs. That's an enormous change from fewer than 10 percent at the beginning of the Industrial Revolution. But why?

Night view of Chongqing, China, one of the largest cities in the world. Some 30 million people live here, almost as many as in all of Canada.

Los Angeles, California, is home to almost 4 million people. Many of them pass through the Harry Pregerson Interchange (right), which connects two major highways, the east-west Interstate 105 and the north-south Interstate 110. Many movies are made in the area, and the interchange has appeared in some of them, including 2015's *La La Land*.

Mostly it's about jobs. Tractors, combine harvesters, and other farm equipment in richer countries allow a small number of people on giant farms to grow and harvest enough food for everyone. So, there aren't many jobs in the countryside, and people move into cities and towns to find work. At the same time, industries of all kinds have sprung up in cities—from manufacturing plants to restaurants and from shopping malls to hospitals, universities, and high-rise financial centers.

It's also a lot easier, these days, to get from the countryside to the town and back again. Roads go almost everywhere, and highways, first built in the 1960s, now criss-cross the richer parts of the globe, allowing people to move even more easily from place to place. And the total number of cars in the world has shot up from about 126 million in 1960 to nearly 1.5 billion today!

We should probably look back on the period from 1945 to 2001 with mixed feelings. Most people grew richer—although, as in all history, much of how you personally fared depended on where you lived and into what level of society you were born. And unfortunately, the same forces that shaped the modern world—with its improved lifespans, bountiful food supplies, ingenious medicines, slick transportation, and high-tech gadgets—may also end up destroying it. The final stop on our whistle-stop tour is to find out why and also what, if anything, can be done.

15. Marching towards *the* millennium

1945 – 2001

In 2023 researchers announced that they had figured out how to produce oil from the easy-to-grow swamp plant duckweed (shown here surrounding the frog). So growing duckweed could turn out to be an inexpensive way to produce biodiesel, a renewable energy source.

16

To be CONTINUED

2002 – present

Where we are now and what might come next

2004
SARS virus jumps to humans.

2014
Boko Haram kidnaps girls to keep them from going to school.

2014-PRESENT
Russia invades Ukraine.

2014
Malala Yousafzai wins the Nobel Peace Prize.

2019
The Covid-19 pandemic begins.

2020
Plastic-eating bacteria discovered.

2021
The first energy-producing nuclear fusion reaction on Earth.

2022
The population of the world hits 8 billion.

2023
Artificial intelligence is solving real-world problems.

Are you feeling a little dizzy? I certainly am. We've been whizzing at tremendous speed through history and around the world. Now we arrive at the last one-hundredth of a second before midnight on our 24-hour clock. Even though we are almost at the end of a book about history, there are some stories that will have to stay unfinished.

Take plastic. In 1863, John Wesley Hyatt from New York State decided to enter a contest to create a new material for billiard balls. At the time, the balls were made from ivory, which came from elephant tusks. Elephants were in grave danger of going extinct. It took him six years of work, but Hyatt eventually came up with the very first plastic made from petroleum, the same oil that fuels our cars. He called his invention celluloid. It did replace most ivory and saved an untold number of elephants.

Nowadays, most of the plastic we use comes from petroleum. And plastic has become a huge part of our lives. Plastic is in our toys. Plastic fibers (called synthetics) are in our clothes. We carry things in bags made of plastic. We use plastic furniture. We wrap food in plastic to keep it fresh. We make artificial legs and arms and heart valves from it. We even make cars and planes out of it. Plastic vehicles are lighter than metal ones, so they use less fuel and cause less pollution.

But like all stories, it's not that simple. It took a while for anyone to see the problem with all the plastic, but there is one. Because it's so easy to make things from plastic, and because plastic is so cheap to buy, we throw a lot of it away.

Tupperware, plastic containers that give people an inexpensive and convenient way to store food, have been on sale since 1948.

A lot of waste plastic ends up either buried

Guaranteed by Good Housekeeping

TUPPERWARE

The Miracle on your pantry shelf

AS ADVERTISED IN GOOD HOUSEKEEPING

Tupperware Home Parties

in the ground or, worse, floating in the seas. Here it can do huge damage to fish and seabirds who can't help eating tiny plastic particles or getting caught in floating plastic trash. When that happens, they can get sick or even die. In 2022, microplastics were even discovered in the blood of humans.

And ocean currents gather floating plastic into areas called gyres. The biggest is called the Great Pacific Garbage Patch. It's hard to measure its size, but experts say it's at least as big as Texas.

Once we realized that all of this plastic was a problem, humans began trying to work out what to do. So far, we haven't been very successful. Some plastic is recycled

Waste plastic moves through the ocean, carried by currents and collecting in gyres. The largest gyre is the Eastern (or Great Pacific) Garbage Patch. You might have heard that this one can be seen from space, but that's not true. The plastics in it are mostly small pieces, sort of like specks of pepper in soup.

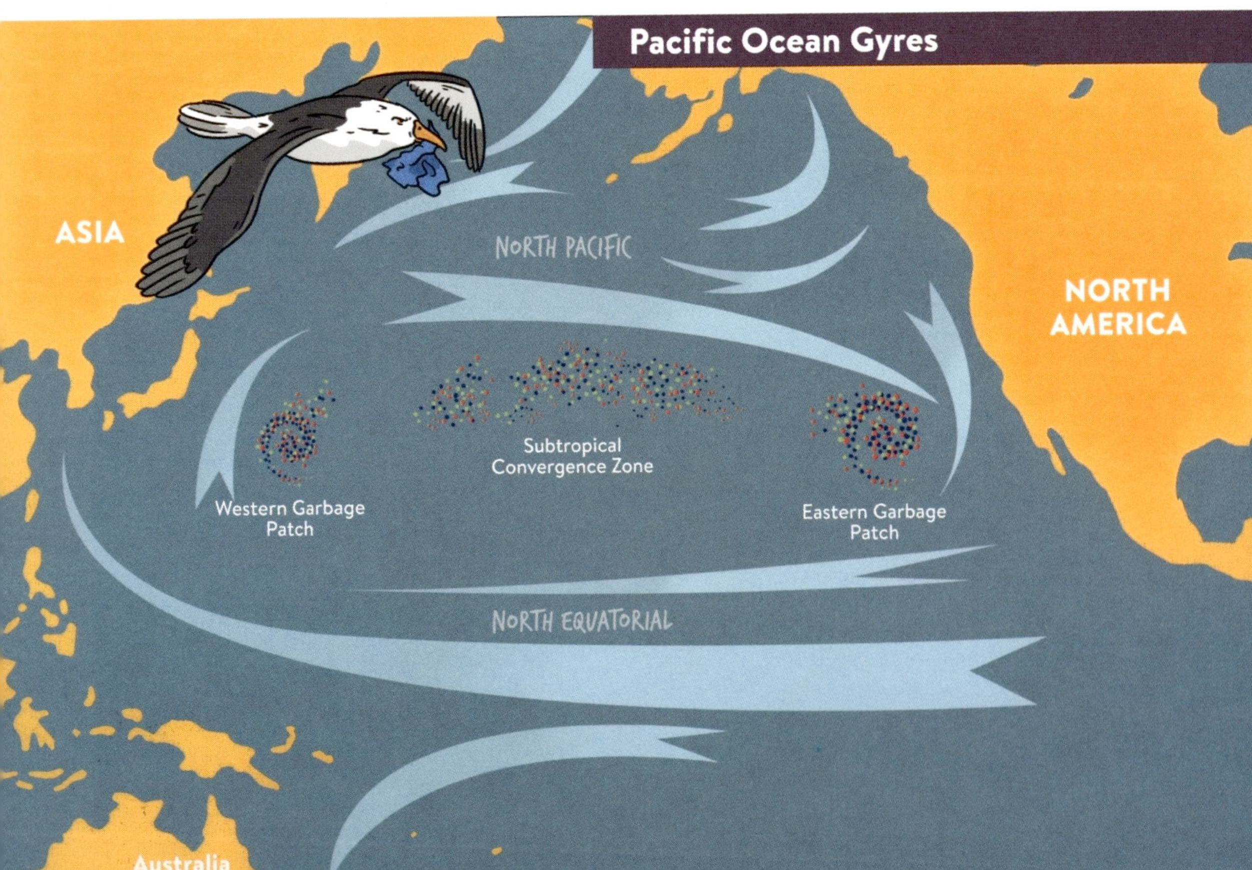

and made into new plastic. But there are problems with plastics recycling. One is that there are lots of different plastics and it takes a lot of work to separate them for recycling. The other is that the usual way of recycling is just chopping up the plastic, melting it, and forming it into poor quality plastic. The chopped-up stuff can be used to make carpets and a few other things, but there isn't enough need for low-quality plastic to use up all the waste we put in our recycling bins. So even when we think we're recycling, a lot of the plastic in the recycling bin just gets thrown away, adding to the problem.

But what if there were a way to recycle plastic differently? What if rather than just chopping it up, we could break it down into its most basic chemicals so they could be easily reused? Well, that would be a whole different story.

Actually, this sort of recycling happens all of the time in nature. Microbes in the environment break down fallen leaves and dead creatures, turning them into basic chemicals that can be reused by plants. Microbes in our guts do the same with our food. But most plastic doesn't go through this process. That's because it's a fairly new material, so there hasn't been enough time for a lot of microbes to evolve to eat it.

But "not a lot" doesn't mean "none." Recently, scientists around the world have discovered plastic-munching microbes that probably evolved to live off all that lovely new food that nobody else was eating. Today there aren't enough of them to solve the problem of so much plastic waste. But teams of engineers are working to create new versions that will eat more plastic faster. If they succeed, we

A group of scientists in Scotland is working with bacteria that make vanilla flavoring from recycled plastic. Yum!

could set up recycling plants where millions of hungry microbes happily break down plastic into chemicals that could then be used to make new things.

Did you know that babies are being born around the world right now at the rate of more than four a second? That's about 383,000 babies every day! And did you know that only about 161,000 people are dying each day? So that means on average the world's population increases by more than 200,000 people each day. That is why Earth is now home to 8 billion people, three times as many as there were at the end of World War II.

The big reason we have so many more people is science. New drugs, vaccines, operations, and life-support machines can prevent and cure disease, helping people live longer. We have new chemicals and technologies to grow more food in less space. Cars and planes are safer, and so are factories. So, fewer people die in accidents. Many countries have systems to make sure citizens have enough to eat and a place to live even if they can't provide those things for themselves. The average person in the world now lives to the age of 73—that's more than 40 years longer than in 1900.

With so many more people on the planet, that means we need colossal amounts of energy to support them. In rich countries people consume far more energy than in poor countries—that's because they have more cars, go on more vacations in airplanes and own more appliances like stoves and refrigerators. They buy more stuff—and making things requires huge amounts of energy. So does growing food, which requires farmers to spread fertilizer on their land and use diesel fuel for tractors and other farm machinery.

The four most common and essential materials used in making today's human-dominated world are glass, steel, cement, and

One place medical technology matters is in the lives of people with disabilities. These finger prosthetics from the company Naked Prosthetics can be specially designed to suit each person's specific needs.

artificial fertilizer. The problem is that to make them requires heating furnaces to several thousand degrees, using vast quantities of fossil fuels—energy that has been trapped underground as coal, petroleum, and natural gas.

Burning all this fuel has triggered another problem. Remember that giant meteorite that killed off the non-flying dinosaurs 65 million years ago? It triggered a mass extinction, the death of many life forms all at once. Today many scientists think we are in the middle of another mass extinction. This time the meteorite has come in the form of a profound change to the climate that is likely to make planet Earth a very uncomfortable place for humans (and lots of other living things) to live in the future.

In 1896 Swedish climate scientist Svante Arrhenius was the first to suggest

Climate change is causing worsening draughts and wildfires in some parts of the world. Australia's most severe fire season ever lasted from July 2019 to March 2020. More than a fifth of Australia's temperate forests burned that season.

> "HUMANITY STANDS ... BEFORE A GREAT PROBLEM OF FINDING NEW RAW MATERIALS AND NEW SOURCES OF ENERGY THAT SHALL NEVER BECOME EXHAUSTED. IN THE MEANTIME WE MUST NOT WASTE WHAT WE HAVE, BUT MUST LEAVE AS MUCH AS POSSIBLE FOR COMING GENERATIONS."
>
> Svante Arrhenius, climate scientist

a link between the amount of carbon dioxide (CO_2) in the air and the temperature of Earth. You can think of CO_2 as a blanket. Too little and the world freezes, as it did in the ice ages, and as you would if you had no blankets on a cold night. But too much CO_2 and the world gets hotter. Imagine how uncomfortable you would be if you had ten blankets! In recent decades, all our burning of oil and gas has released blankets and blankets of extra CO_2 into the atmosphere.

Fortunately, nature has its own way of getting rid of CO_2—trees suck it from the air and use it to make their food. But unfortunately, at the very same time humans have been burning fossil fuels, we've also been cutting down trees to make way for cities and farms and huge networks of roads and railroads, all to support our growing population. Experts estimate that as many as 40,000 square miles (100,000 km^2) of forest are destroyed each year—that's an area bigger than Indiana!

This double whammy—adding CO_2 by burning fossil fuels and harming nature's ability to remove it by cutting down forests—has more than doubled CO_2 levels since 1832. And all that blanketing gas has made the world a whole lot warmer than it has been at any point in the last 125,000 years.

Plus, CO_2 isn't the only gas blanketing our Earth. Another dangerous one is methane. Though there is a lot less methane in

The Amazon rain forest is 2.1 million square miles (5.5 million sq km), covering almost a third of South America. Most of it is in the country of Brazil, which struggles to balance two different needs: its people need food and housing, and all living things need a stable climate. This photograph shows forest being cut down in northern Brazil.

the environment than there is CO_2, and though it doesn't last in the atmosphere as long as CO_2 does, methane has 80 times more warming power. The methane in our environment comes mostly from natural gas leaks plus burps and toots from cows and other cud-chewing animals we raise for food.

A warmer world makes the ice caps and glaciers melt. As this happens, sea levels rise. Remember when we talked about the time before there was an ice cap at the North Pole and the sea was 42 soccer players deeper than it is now? Well, if we stay on our current path, we'll have that deeper ocean back. When all the ice at the poles has melted, do you have any idea any how many feet the seas will rise? Why not ask the adults in your life and see if they know? I bet they don't!

Well, you can tell them the answer—it's 216 feet (66 m)! That means if you were to visit London, UK, you would have to be in a boat and the only part of Big Ben you would clearly see would be the clockface, popping out above the waterline. London, New York, Montreal, Tokyo, Shanghai, and most other low-lying communities would be totally submerged. The warming climate is already changing habitats. Some animals will be able to migrate and adapt. Others will go extinct.

No one really knows how long it might be before all the ice melts—anywhere from 5,000 years to 5 million years, perhaps. What happens next? As you can see, this story is far from over.

Another unfinished story is the age-old tale of war and peace. In April 2014, a terrorist organization from Nigeria called Boko Haram kidnapped 276 teenage girls from their schools. The message? Girls shouldn't go to school. This group believes that girls should marry very young instead of being educated, so they were trying to scare families into keeping their daughters at home.

That same belief—that girls shouldn't be educated—lay behind another terrorist atrocity. Malala Yousafzai, a 12-year-old Pakistani student, was passionate about learning and loved going to school. But, on October 9, 2012, she was shot in the head by a terrorist who came from a tradition where females are not supposed to be

Malala Yousafzai

educated. Amazingly, she did not die. Instead, she was airlifted to the UK and received emergency treatment that saved her life. Since then she has become a leader in the struggle for the right of women and girls all over the world to receive a good education. In 2014 she was the recipient of the Nobel Peace prize, just like Nelson Mandela and Rigoberta Menchú Tum before her.

Terrorist attacks continue, with about 1,000 people killed each year around the world. Some attackers believe they are acting for God. Others think they are fixing a broken political system. But they all use the fear of pain and death and disruption to try to make people change their ways.

Then there is the worry that when a country that has nuclear weapons goes to war, it might choose to use them. These scary moments often happen over border disputes. Some of the largest, most powerful countries in the world have disagreements with other countries about which land belongs to whom. China, for example, believes Taiwan is part of China. But Taiwan has been operating as an independent country since just after World War II and doesn't want to be part of China. Kashmir, the northernmost part of South Asia, is fought over by India, Pakistan, and China. Could any of these regions spark a nuclear war? Let's hope not.

Some terrorists disrupt people's lives by shutting off a whole region's electricity. In the last three months of 2022 alone, terrorists who think white people should be in charge of everything disabled electricity substations in the U.S. (including the one above in North Carolina, which is shown being repaired).

Russian President Vladimir Putin grew up in the Soviet Union, that enormous country that led the communist side of the Cold War. When the Soviet Union broke apart in 1988 and many of the countries that had been part of the giant nation became independent, he was angry. He (and plenty of other Russians) thought Russia should still be in charge of all of those other countries.

Ever since he rose to power in Russia in 1999, Putin has been trying to put the Soviet Union back together. He started by going to war inside Russia itself to stop the Chechen region of Russia from becoming a separate country. In 2008, he went to war with Georgia, a former part of the Soviet Union, to gain control of two parts of that country, South Ossetia and Abkhazia. In 2014, he invaded neighboring Ukraine, also formerly a part of the Soviet Union, and took over the Crimean Peninsula, the southern part of the country. Then, in 2022, Putin launched a full-scale invasion of the heart of Ukraine, including its capital, Kyiv.

Putin has won all of his previous wars, but this one is more in doubt. Ukraine has fought back much harder than expected, and Europe and the U.S. have helped by providing weapons and other aid. Russia has responded to those helping Ukraine by refusing to sell fuel to Europe. That refusal drove up fuel prices around the world and made it extremely expensive for Europeans to keep their houses warm in winter, leaving poor people at risk of freezing and governments scrambling to find solutions.

Remember the perilous Cuban Missile Crisis in 1962? Since then people have

Ukrainian women and children escaping Russian attacks on their home cities find a place to rest in a room on the third floor of the Lviv train station. As of March 2023, about 14 million Ukrainians had abandoned their homes. That's about a third of all the people in the country.

thought the idea of a nuclear war must surely be impossible. Who would be crazy enough to unleash waves of devasting nuclear bombs on millions of innocent people? But today there is talk of Russia using nuclear weapons against Ukraine. And if it did, what would NATO—that alliance of much of Europe and the U.S.—do? The possibility of a war between nuclear powers cannot be completely discounted, with consequences for the whole world too terrible for anyone to imagine. This is another story to be continued...

One thing we have learned from the recent past is that humans face the very real threat of global pandemics. Viruses are tiny particles that infect living cells. When they reproduce, they sometimes cause terrible diseases that can change human history. Think back to the story of how a virus called smallpox devastated the Indigenous people of the Americas. Over 90 percent of them died in the years after Europeans first arrived.

Another big virus outbreak happened in 1918, just at the end of World War I. It came to be known as Spanish flu. Historians think this epidemic killed even more people than World War I itself.

Viruses infect all types of living things, from tiny bacteria to plants, trees, fungi, and animals. When any new species gets infected, the virus can rip through its population very quickly. Luckily, thanks to nature's diversity, some individuals recover from the virus and are immune to it after that. The next time that same virus comes along, individuals with immunity make up a big part of the population, so fewer individuals of that species get sick.

Very occasionally, a virus changes so that it can skip over and infect other species. When this happens to humans, we have no immunity and the virus can wreak havoc, causing widespread illness and death. In today's world, a virus like that can spread more easily than ever. Many of us live close together in cities and suburbs, travel together on trains, buses, and airplanes, and mingle in crowded spaces.

This is what is thought to have happened in 2002 when a virus, possibly from a bat, skipped over to humans. It set off a new disease. First identified in southern China, it came to be called severe acute respiratory syndrome, or SARS for short. This illness affected people's breathing, so when more than 8,000 people got sick across 26 different countries, many died.

Smallpox virus

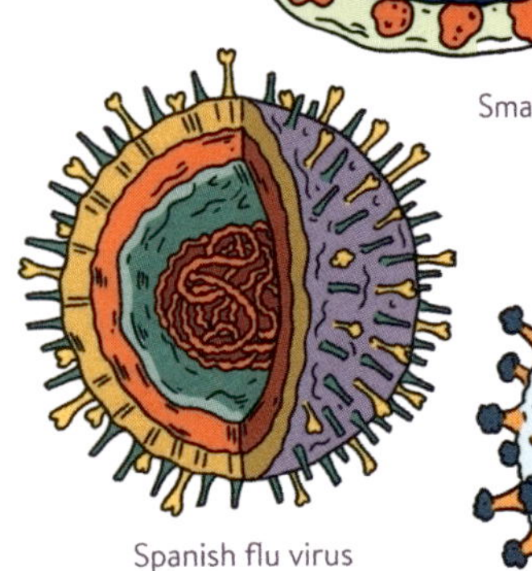

Spanish flu virus

Covid-19 virus

Viruses aren't officially living things because they can't reproduce on their own. They inject their genetic material into their host's cells, forcing the cells to produce more virus. When a cell fills up, it bursts, releasing fresh virus into the host, where it can infect even more cells.

Isolating people at home and setting up separate areas in hospitals to treat them is a good way of stopping a virus from infecting too many people, and eventually the SARS outbreak was controlled.

Then in December 2019, a virus from the same family as SARS started infecting people in Wuhan, China, about 600 miles (1,000 km) north of where the 2002 SARS virus first appeared. The new strain might have moved over into the human species from another animal. Or it could have gotten out of a lab where scientists were studying it. We still don't know for sure. What we do know is that within months, COVID-19, the disease caused by the new virus, had spread to more than 100 countries, infecting hundreds of thousands of people, with tens of thousands of deaths. And the numbers were going up fast.

In a desperate effort to contain the disease, countries closed borders, schools, shops, restaurants, airports, and train stations. They stopped people from socializing in groups and told them to stay home. Governments even demanded that everyone with symptoms isolate themselves from their families at home or in special quarantine rooms.

As soon as it was clear this virus was going to be a major killer, we knew we would need vaccines and anti-viral medicines, which take a long time to develop. There was no time to lose, though. People were dying. That's why hundreds of scientific laboratories all over the world got to work and kept at it as the number of cases rose into the millions.

Now, with vaccines available in most of the world and anti-viral drugs developed to treat the worst cases, millions of people are still coming down with COVID-19, but many fewer are dying of it.

If the virus that causes Covid-19 jumped from another animal to humans, one possible source is the raccoon dog—a fox relative that looks like a raccoon.

During the Covid-19 pandemic, healthcare workers risked their own lives caring for infected people during lockdowns. In appreciation for their dedication, communities around the world (including the residents of this apartment building in Mumbai, India) got together to applaud and cheer for their local healthcare workers.

All of which makes me realize this: though developments in science have caused many of our current problems, perhaps they will also help solve them. This is the biggest challenge we currently face and something you might want to discuss with your friends as well as the adults in your life. For example, if we can find a way of creating energy without harming the environment, then surely there is a chance we can stabilize the world's rising temperature. Solar panels, wind farms, safe nuclear power stations, oil made by plants—these are all part of the solution.

Then there is the prospect of using the same power the Sun uses by developing a technology known as nuclear fusion (as opposed to nuclear

When Covid-19 hit, countries had to act fast. China built new hospitals at incredible speed at the beginning of the pandemic in 2019. They built more in 2022, when loosened restrictions caused a major outbreak. Below, workers build a hospital in Chongqing in November 2022.

fission, which is used in today's nuclear power stations). The snag is that it takes a vast amount of energy to create and control a nuclear fusion reaction, and so far only one group of scientists has been able to produce more energy than it takes to create the reaction in the first place. But advances are being made every week.

Inside the National Ignition Facility in California, where it was proven that nuclear fusion can give off more energy than it takes to drive it. In fusion, two light atoms smash together to form one heavier one. The reaction releases tons of power and could turn out to be a new source of clean energy.

Another issue science is trying to solve is how we can live in a world with an upside-down age profile. In many countries there are now far more older people than younger people—and this creates a real problem. Older people need support, and a guaranteed income for retirement. If there are too few young people in the workplace, then how can a society afford to support its elderly?

Remember the hilarious mechanical Digesting Duck? That was

a toy, but working robots have been helping in factories for a long time. Robots also do jobs that require going places people can't, such as inside the human body. And with artificial intelligence (AI) in them, they can call the doctor's office to make you an appointment and figure out how protein molecules are structured. An AI called ChatGPT, launched in 2023, can hold a text conversation and write poetry and articles and computer code. Future artificial intelligence might be so lifelike that we won't be able to tell if we're speaking with a robot or a person.

> "IF WE WANT COMPUTERS TO DISCOVER NEW KNOWLEDGE, THEN WE MUST GIVE THEM THE ABILITY TO TRULY LEARN FOR THEMSELVES."
>
> Demis Hassabis, founder of AI company DeepMind

In a world without enough young people to do all the tasks we need, robots could be the answer. And they will certainly come in handy when we set out to colonize space. Even before humans visited the Moon, people longed to travel to other worlds. It's been a long wait, but new generations of rockets will at least offer a taste. It's even possible that in the next 50 years, we'll be building cities on the Moon and Mars. Maybe then even ordinary people will be able to visit!

Another big question is how on earth are we going to feed so many humans in the future when we can't afford

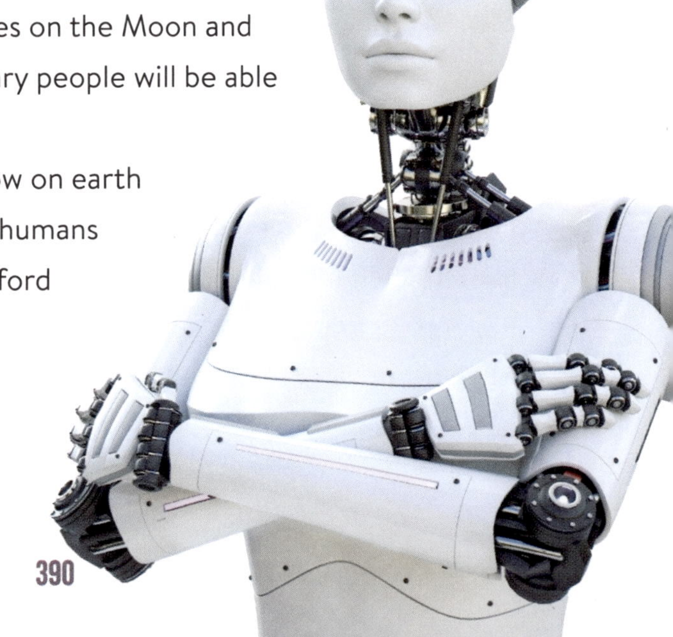

In 2022, the Chinese gaming company NetDragon Websoft appointed a robot with artificial intelligence (right) to run the company. They call her "Ms. Tang Yu."

Researchers live at the Mars Desert Research Station in Utah under the same conditions they would face on Mars. They wear special gear when they go outside and do scientific studies on the rocks of the area. This helps them develop the equipment humans would need to live on the Red Planet.

to keep on damaging the environment through farming the way we are used to? Amazingly, scientists are working on ways of growing meat and producing cow milk protein in laboratories using stem cells and microbes. This means one day we may be able to eat animal products without raising or killing any animals, and all without harming the climate!

But can we rely on science alone to solve all the issues we face as a species? Perhaps paying attention to those with traditional lifestyles can help, too? Surely there are lessons the rest of us can learn that could be the key to our survival in the future.

The Penan tribe lives in Sarawak, Malaysia. Their traditional way of life is nomadic, moving from place to place hunting for food, and gathering fruit and vegetation as they need from the forest. It is a key requirement in their culture always to share resources wisely. They have a word for it—*molong*, which means "never take more than is necessary."

When they gather fruit from trees, they always make sure to leave enough for others. After taking enough (but not too much) they mark the tree with a knife so others can see it has already been harvested and is not to be touched until it has fully recovered. For the Penan people, one of the biggest crimes is called *se hun.* Can you guess what that means? It means you have not shared properly.

Sharing is central to Penan culture. This man in Sarawak, Malaysia, is pouring a cup of tea for a visitor.

How can we adapt these ideas of consuming less so there will be enough for everyone without harming Earth? A few ideas may involve putting limits on how much people can fly in airplanes. Or

perhaps we could create ways of encouraging people to eat more vegetables and less meat. Perhaps employers could only hire people who live close to their places of work or who could work from home.

> THE BEST WAY TO PREDICT THE FUTURE IS TO INVENT IT.
>
> Alan Kay, one of the inventors of the personal computer

Maybe governments could help with installing solar panels on houses with suitable roofs and sharing the energy with those whose roofs aren't right for solar panels. Some places are already charging people money for throwing away excessive trash and punishing companies that use plastic packaging. All these approaches can help, and all of them can be done without waiting for new technologies to be invented and developed. We just have to make sharing our top priority.

Looking to people like the Penan as an inspiration allows us to lift up our chins and our imaginations to realize that we have the strength and power and creativity we need to save the planet. What do you see when you look around? And how about when you think back on history for ideas? When we stand back to see the big picture, there is always something new to be noticed, something fascinating to wonder about, something amazing to lift our spirits.

Here is something I see looking back over our journey. *Absolutely Everything!* teaches us that the story of nature, including humans, doesn't progress in a straight line. Rather, it is constantly changing and adapting depending on the conditions. When eyesight evolved in trilobites during the Cambrian Period, other creatures had to adapt or die. Humans do something similar. We adapt to new situations. After all, that's how our species thrived in the ice ages,

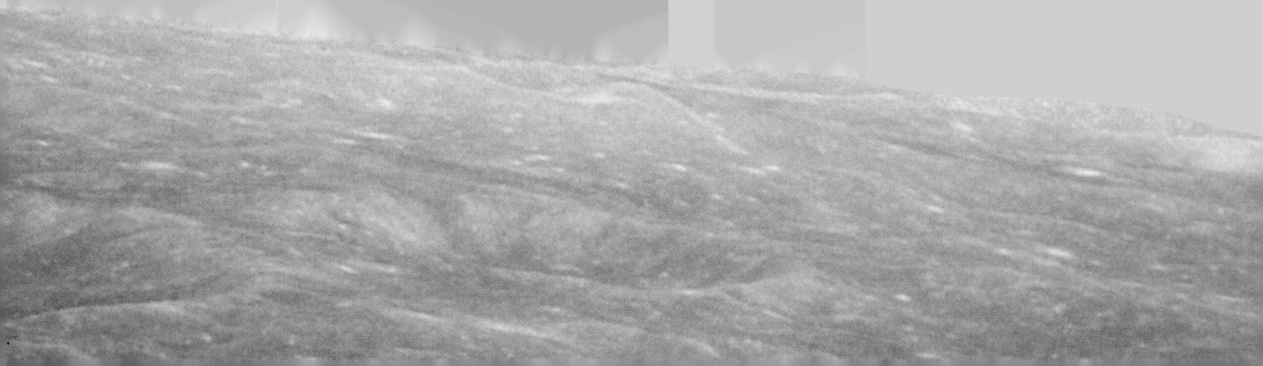

by moving around and changing our lifestyles as the giant glaciers came and went.

In fact, humans are superadapters. That is good news and a reason to have real hope for the future. Throughout all history, even when things have looked very grim, humans have adapted and survived.

Now, at last, as we zoom out and look with wonder at the story of Earth's history, the 24-hour clock is striking midnight. Whatever happens next, one thing is certain—the first one-thousandth of a second in a brand-new day is bound to be an exhilarating, incredible moment—far more amazing than anything you can make up.

When astronauts visited the Moon, they saw the first ever Earthrise. Seeing pictures of the whole planet as a fragile blue jewel surrounded by the black void of space helped launch a new environmental age. What will become of our precious planet in the future? It's up to us all.

A B C D E F G H

World map

1 We've included this map of the world today to help you locate
the places mentioned in the book. You'll see it has letters
running along the top of the page and numbers running along
the side. Every square on the map can be located using those
2 numbers. So, for example, Mali, where Mansa Musa ruled, is in
square J7. To find it, run one finger down from the J at the top
of the page and the other finger over from the 7 on the side.
To find any other country, turn the page to the map index, look
3 up the place you want to find, and use the letter and number
code to locate it. Try finding your own country first. The whole
world is here for you to explore.

Europe (left) and the Caribbean (opposite page, bottom left) are two places where many countries are too small to see well on the map of the whole world. When you look up one of those countries on the next page, you might find two codes—one for the country's place on the world map and the other for its place on one of the enlarged maps in the circles. If the name couldn't fit on the world map, you will find just the code for its place on the enlarged map.

Map index

N

OP

QR

S

T

U

WXYZ

Glossary

Aboriginal Australians
The native peoples of Australia, who arrived on the continent about 40,000 years ago.

Algae
Organisms that use photosynthesis to make energy and are the ancestors of plants.

Amphibians
Group of animals that live partly in the water and partly on land. Examples include frogs and toads.

Anthropologist
Someone who studies how humans live together and behave in societies.

Apartheid
System used in South Africa from 1948 until 1994 that separated people by skin color.

Archaeologist
Someone who studies what humans leave behind, including tools and ancient ruins.

Arthropods
Animals with hard external shells and at least six legs, like beetles and crabs.

Astronomer
Someone who studies space objects and phenomena, such as stars and gamma rays.

Astronaut
Someone who travels into space.

Astrophysicist
Someone who studies the forces, matter, and energy that make up the universe, from collapsing stars to speeding comets.

Atom
A combination of neutrons, protons, and electrons that is the smallest unit of a particular substance.

Automaton
A machine built to repeatedly perform the same task.

Biologist
Someone who investigates the mechanisms and varieties of life, including its origins.

Buddhism
Religion based around the teachings of Siddhartha Gautama, often known as the Buddha.

Capitalism
System where farms, factories, and stores are owned by individuals and companies, not the government, and owners compete to make a profit.

Catholicism
Christian religious group with a single leader, the Pope.

Christianity
One of the religions that believes in only one God, founded on the teachings of Jesus of Nazareth. Its primary sacred text is the New Testament.

Civil rights leader
Someone who leads others in the effort to improve equality in society.

Civil war
Conflict in which two groups within a single country or society fight against each other.

Climate change
Process in which environmental conditions on Earth change over long periods of time. These shifts can be natural or caused by humans.

Colony (biology)
Group of individual organisms of a single species living together and supporting one another.

Colony (history, politics)
Settlement established by a group, usually a nation, in foreign territory.

Communism
System in which farms, factories, and stores are owned by everyone and wealth is shared.

Confucianism
System of influential teachings developed by the ancient Chinese thinker Confucius.

Conquistadors
Spanish explorers and soldiers who conquered and colonized much of the Americas in the 1500s.

Constitution
Document outlining the basic laws and systems of government in a particular country.

Cosmochemist
Someone who studies the chemical make-up of the universe through extra-terrestrial objects such as meteorites and asteroids.

Crusades
Series of medieval religious wars fought by Christian Europeans, mostly against Muslims.

Cuneiform
One of the earliest writing systems, developed in the 3000s BCE in Sumeria.

Cyanobacteria
Tiny organisms, each only a single cell, that produce energy by photosynthesis.

Dendrochronologist
Someone who studies the make-up of tree rings for information about Earth's past atmosphere.

Democracy
Political system in which the people have power over their leaders, often choosing them by voting in elections.

Dictator
A ruler who governs with total power, making their own decisions without the approval of the people.

DNA
A chemical in the nucleus of cells that carries the instructions for how a living thing develops and functions.

Domestication
Process of breeding species to be more useful to humans than in their wild form.

Dreamtime
According to Australian Aboriginal belief, a period in the distant past when heroes created the universe.

Dynasty
A series of rulers or leaders from a single family.

$E=mc^2$
Equation in physics showing that matter can be converted into huge amounts of energy.

Egyptologist
Someone who studies ancient Egypt, including searching for and exploring ruins.

Electricity
The movement of electrons, particles that carry electrical charge. Used by humans to power machines.

Entomologist
Someone who studies insects, the most diverse and numerous group of animals on the planet.

Eukaryotes
Organisms with cells containing a nucleus and other structures that allow it to process energy.

Explorer
A person who travels to places unknown to their culture, with the purpose of reporting back with their findings.

Evolution
The process by which living things change over many generations.

Extinction
The end of a species, when all individuals have died out.

Fertile Crescent
Area in the Middle East and Egypt where farming developed around 10,000 years ago.

Feudalism
Medieval system in which people swear oaths of military service in return for the right to farm land.

Fish
Group of animals with backbones that live in water. Examples include sharks and goldfish.

Five Pillars of Islam
The five fundamental requirements of followers of Sunni Islam.

Fossil
Preserved remains or traces of a living organism from a long time ago.

Fungi
Group of organisms that feed on living or once-living things and reproduce using spores.

Galleon
Large wooden ship developed in the 1400s, mainly used in war.

Glacier
Mass of compacted snow and ice that lasts all year round.

Globalization
System that links people across the globe through trade and industry.

Global warming
The steady increase of average world temperature over time.

Golden Age
A period in history when major advances in technology, art, or other areas are made.

Gravity
Fundamental force of the universe. All objects have gravity, pulling other objects toward them.

Guillotine
An execution machine with a very sharp, heavy blade that drops down from a height. The force of gravity gives the blade enough strength to cut through a person's neck in one hit, making the guillotine a faster method of execution than a sword or an axe, which sometimes requires more than one hit.

Gyre
System of ocean currents that circles a central point and can cover thousands of miles.

Hajj
Pilgrimage to the Muslim holy city of Mecca, a religious requirement for every Muslim.

Hieroglyphics
Writing system of Ancient Egypt that used pictures to represent sounds or entire words.

Hinduism
Religion based around gods, religious texts, and cultural traditions, which originated in India.

Historian
Someone who studies the human past, from the invention of writing to the present day.

Holocaust
Mass killing of 11 million people, including 6 million Jews and 2 million other "undesirables," by the Nazis during World War II.

Human rights
Belief that humans have fundamental rights to certain things, such as freedom of religion, the right to an education, and the right to marry whomever they choose.

Indigenous
People or organisms native to a particular region, often used when comparing to a more recently arrived group.

Industrial Revolution
Period of rapid industrial development. In particular, Europe and the United States in the 1700s and 1800s.

Insects
Arthropods with six legs, three body parts, and usually wings as well, such as beetles.

Inventor
Someone who designs machines and other gadgets to solve problems and improve lives.

Irrigation
A system for transporting water to fields. This is especially useful when fields don't receive enough rain to grow crops.

Islam
One of the religions that believes in just one God, based on the visions and teachings of the Prophet Muhammad. Its sacred text is the Koran.

Judaism
The first religion to believe in just one God. Its sacred text is the Hebrew Bible.

Liberated
Freed.

Mammals
The group of animals with backbones that produce milk and mostly give birth to live young.

Mesoamerica
Region of Mexico and Central America where several major ancient civilizations developed.

Mesopotamia
Area in what is now Iraq where several ancient empires developed.

Microbe
A living thing too small to see.

Migration
The movement of large groups of people or animals from one place to another, seasonally, annually, or once.

Monotheism
Belief that only one God exists.

Mummy
Dead body of a human or animal that has been preserved either accidentally or on purpose.

Musket
A long gun that was used, particularly in war, before rifles were invented.

Muslim
A follower of Islam.

Nazism
German political movement beginning in the 1920s and led by Adolf Hitler.

Necropolis
A large cemetery, especially an ancient one. Means "city of the dead" in Ancient Greek.

Neurons
Cells that form the nervous systems of most animals and transmit information signals around the body.

Neuroscientist
Someone who studies the nervous system, in particular the brain.

New World
North and South America, continents unknown to Europeans, Africans, and Asians until the 1400s. Of course, the New World is not actually any newer than the Old World.

Nomad
Person who moves around regularly rather than settling in a single place permanently.

Nuclear (physics)
Relating to the nucleus at the centre of atoms.

Offerings
Gifts offered to the gods or a god when making a request or giving thanks.

Olympians
The 12 principal gods in the Ancient Greek religion, believed to live on Mount Olympus.

Orthodox Christianity
Christian religion, today followed primarily in Russia, Eastern Europe, and Greece.

Paleontologist
Examines the remains of ancient organisms, from dinosaurs to giant fungi, to learn about prehistoric Earth.

Pandemic
An outbreak of a disease across a huge area (usually including several countries) that makes a large part of the people in that area sick.

Pangaea
Supercontinent made up of all Earth's continents pushed together; it existed 250–150 million years ago.

Pantheon
The particular gods and goddesses worshipped in a religion.

Perishable
Able to rot. Fresh food is perishable.

Philosophy
The study of fundamental questions about human experience and the way we think about and respond to the world.

Physicist
Studies the science of matter, energy, and the forces that connect them.

Pilgrim
Someone who travels to a holy place to worship, or someone who travels to faraway places for another purpose.

Plate tectonics
Movement of the giant plates making up Earth's crust.

Pollen
Reproductive cells produced by flowers and some other plants, essential to the development of seeds.

Primates
Group of large-brained mammals that includes lemurs, monkeys, and apes. Humans are apes, so are therefore primates.

Prophesy
Prediction of the future, often by someone believed to be in communication with gods or ancestors.

Protestant
A Christian who rejects the authority of the Pope and believes faith is key to religious practice.

Quipu
A method of keeping records by tying knots in a group of strings.

Racism
The incorrect idea that differences in the way we look make some people more intelligent or wiser than others.

Reincarnation
Belief that the souls of the dead return to Earth in new bodies.

Reptiles
The group of animals with skin covered in scales that lay waterproof eggs. Includes lizards and snakes.

Revolutionary (n.)
A person who rebels against a political system as part of a movement to bring change.

Revolutionary (adj.)
Relating to a radical change in a political system or the violent overthrow of a government.

Robot
A machine that resembles a human or other living creature.

Sauropods
A group of long-necked, plant-eating dinosaurs.

Science writer
Someone who investigates scientific stories and writes about them in newspapers, magazines, and books, and on websites.

Shaman
A religious leader who uses magic to cure sick people, perceive the supernatural, and predict or control the future.

Silk Route
Network of trade routes reaching from China to western Europe and based around silk trading. Also called the Silk Road.

Smallpox
Highly infectious disease that causes spots to erupt across the skin and can cause death.

Telegraph
Early electrical communication system used to quickly send codes that can be translated into messages.

Terrorism
Strategy that relies upon fear to achieve a particular goal, usually through violence.

Theropods
A group of two-legged dinosaurs, most of which ate meat and had feathers.

Trilobites
Extinct water-dwelling arthropods with three body segments. Once widespread throughout the oceans.

United Nations
International organization established in 1945 after World War II to promote peace and dialogue between nations and defend human rights across the globe.

Vascular plant
Plant with a system of tubes inside it for transporting water and nutrients.

Index

D

E

F

N

R

T

U

V

W

Y

Z

Image credits

We would like to thank the following for their kind permission to use their photographs:
Key: t=top, b=bottom, c=center, l=left, r=right

pp.10–11 NASA, ESA, CSA, STScI. **pp.12–13** Mark Garlick/Science Photo Library/Getty Images. **p.19** Department of Biodiversity, Conservation and Attractions Western Australia. **p.23** lumaso/123RF. **pp.28–29** Alexis Rosenfeld/UNESCO/Fondation 1 Ocean. **p.30** fusaromike/iStockphoto. **pp.34–35** Maximbg/Dreamstime. **p.37** Richard Bizley/Science Photo Library. **p.38** olikim/iStockphoto. **p.39** igor.kramar.shots/Shutterstock. **p.43** Windchu/CC BY 4.0/Wikicommons. **pp.50–51** Sergey Krasovskiy/Getty Images. **p.57** Jonathan Lesage/iStockphoto. **p.58** Martin Shields/Alamy Stock Photo. **p.61** Sergey Krasovskiy/Stocktrek Images/Getty Images. **pp.62–63** Amy Toensing/Getty Images. **pp.68–69** NRP/CC BY 4.0/Wikicommons. **p.74 t** JackF/iStockphoto, **b** Muhammad Mahdi Karim. **p.75** undefined undefined/iStockphoto. **pp.76–77** Ettore Mazza/ethnocynology. **p.79** pum_eva/iStockphoto. **pp.80–81** javarman3/iStockphoto. **p.82 l** Sabena Jane Blackbird/Alamy, **r** leonelloo/iStockphoto. **p.84** Didier Descouens/CC BY-SA 4.0/Wikicommons. **p.90** Nikola Solic/Reuters/Alamy Stock Photo. **p.93** Luka Mjeda. **pp.98–99** The Natural History Museum/Alamy Stock Photo. **pp.102–103** Adél Békefi/Getty Images. **p.110** Biodiversity Heritage Library. **p.111** Metropolitan Museum of Art, New York/Anonymous Gift, 2013. **p.113** Zev Radovan/Alamy Stock Photo. **p.114** World History Archive/Alamy Stock Photo. **p.117** Metropolitan Museum of Art, New York/Gift of Mr. and Mrs. J. J. Klejman, 1966. **pp.120–121** Gavin Hellier/robertharding/Getty Images. **p.123** New York Public Library. **p.124** Fine Art Images/Heritage Images/Getty Images. **p.125** Petar Milošević. **pp.126–127** MattGush/iStockphoto. **p.128** Gryffindor/robertharding/Alamy Stock Photo. **p.130** Wirestock Creators/Shutterstock. **p.133** agefotostock/Alamy Stock Photo. **pp.134–135** gvictoria/iStockphoto. **p.137** Metropolitan Museum of Art, New York/Rogers Fund, 1930. **pp.138–139** Metropolitan Museum of Art, New York/Rogers Fund, 1925. **p.142** Science Museum, London/CC BY 4.0/Wellcome Collection. **p.143** Granger Historical Picture Archive/Alamy Stock Photo. **p.147 t** Immanuel Giel/CC-PD/Wikicommons, **b** CC0 1.0 Daderot/Wikicommons. **p.148** CC0 1.0 British Library. **p.150** Chronicle/Alamy Stock Photo. **pp.152–153** Razvan Ciuca/Getty Images. **p.154** Sabena Jane Blackbird/Alamy Stock Photo. **p.156** Gordon Miller. **p.161** DEA Picture Library/De Agostini/Getty Images. **p.162** Zev Radovan/Alamy Stock Photo. **pp.164–165** Balage Balogh / Archaeology Illustrated. **p.167** Metropolitan Museum of Art, New York/William S. Lieberman, 2005. **p.169** Granger Historical Picture Archive/Alamy Stock Photo. **p.171** Gianni Muratore/Alamy Stock Photo. **pp.174–175** traumlichtfabrik/Getty Images. **p.177** zilber42/iStockphoto. **p.179** PjrArt/Alamy Stock Photo. **p.180** Grafissimo/iStockphoto. **p.183** Pedre/iStockphoto. **p.188** Metropolitan Museum of Art, New York/The Michael C. Rockefeller Memorial Collection, Bequest of Nelson A. Rockefeller, 1979. **p.189** boris_1983/iStockphoto. **p.191** Alfonsobouchot/Wikicommons. **p.192** Diego Delso, delso.photo/CC-BY-SA/Wikicommons. **p.197** Hung_Chung_Chih/iStockphoto. **pp.198–199** Artur Bogacki/Shutterstock. **p.203** ventdusud/iStockphoto. **p.204** classicpaintings/Alamy Stock Photo. **p.206** dinosmichail/iStockphoto. **p.210** The Stapleton Collection/Bridgeman Images. **p.216** Bibliotheque Nationale, Paris/Bridgeman Images. **p.217** De Agostini Picture Library/G. Dagli Orti/Bridgeman Images. **p.220** AndreaAstes/iStockphoto. **p.221** Attribution 4.0 International (CC BY 4.0)/Wellcome Collection. **p.223** SCStock/iStockphoto. **pp.224–225** Xinhua/Alamy Stock Photo. **p.226** Public Domain/International Dunhuang Project. **p.229** CPA Media Pte Ltd/Alamy Stock Photo. **p.231** De Agostini Picture Library/A. Dagli Orti/Bridgeman Images. **p.234** Werner Forman/Universal Images Group/Getty Images. **p.235** Canadian Museum of History. **pp.236–237** Musée de la Tapisserie,Bayeux,France/Bridgeman Images. **p.238** DavidCallan/iStockphoto. **p.240** Science History Images/Alamy Stock Photo. **p.242** The Picture Art Collection/Alamy Stock Photo. **pp.244–245** Timothy Allen/Getty Images. **p.246** rachel/iStockphoto. **pp.250–251** DEA/G. Dagli Orti/De Agostini/Getty Images. **p.252** Jekesai Njikizana/AFP/Getty Images. **p.254** Photo 12/Alamy Stock Photo. **p.255** World Digital Library Collection/Library of Congress. **p.256** Michael Hampshire. **p.258** Public domain/The British Library. **p.262** Pitt Rivers Museum. **p.265** Bibliotheque Nationale, Paris/Bridgeman Images. **pp.266–267** Sylvain Sonnet/Getty Images. **pp.268–269** Public Domain/Vienna Museum. **pp.270–271** ilyas Ayub/Alamy Stock Photo. **p.273** frans lemmens/Alamy Stock Photo. **p.274** Zoonar GmbH/Alamy Stock Photo. **p.275** Fritz Rudolf Künker GmbH & Co. KG, Osnabrück/Lübke + Wiedemann KG, Leonberg. **p.277** The Print Collector/Alamy Stock Photo. **pp.278–279** Public Domain/Naval Museum of Madrid. **p.282** Alamy Stock Photo. **p.283** Metropolitan Museum of Art, New York/Gift of H. L. Bache Foundation, 1969. **p.284** Biblioteca Nacional, Madrid/Bridgeman Images. **p.285** Prisma Archivo/Alamy Stock Photo. **p.286** Archives Charmet/Bridgeman Images. **p.288** Nicolas Gatti/EyeEm/Getty Images. **p.290** Science History Images/Alamy Stock Photo. **p.292** Prisma Archivo/Alamy Stock Photo. **pp.294–295** Alamy Stock Photo. **p.297** Kean Collection/Getty Images. **pp.298–299** Sternfahrer/Shutterstock. **p.303** NASA. **p.305** Library of Congress Washington, D.C. **p.306** Keith Lance/iStockphoto. **p.308** incamerastock/Alamy Stock Photo. **p.313** Public Domain/Wikicommons. **p.314** duncan1890/iStockphoto. **pp.316–317** Bettmann/Getty Images. **p.318** Chris Hellier/Getty Images. **p.321** Library of Congress Prints and Photographs Division Washington, D.C. **p.322** Hi-Story/Alamy Stock Photo. **p.323** Bettmann/Getty Images. **p.325** Granger Historical Picture Archive/Alamy Stock Photo. **pp.326–327** Public Domain/Wikicommons. **p.330** Culture Club/Getty Images. **p.332** Public Domain/Wikicommons. **p.334 t** pictore/Getty Images, **b** Granger Historical Picture Archive/Alamy Stock Photo. **p.336** Interfoto/Alamy Stock Photo. **p.339** Shawshots/Alamy Stock Photo. **p.341** Shawshots/Alamy Stock Photo. **p.343** Beata Zawrzel/NurPhoto/Getty Images. **p.345** coward_lion/Alamy Stock Photo. **pp.346–347** NASA. **p.350** aluxum/iStockphoto. **p.354** Attribution 4.0 International (CC BY 4.0)/Wikicommons. **p.355** Everett Collection Historical/Alamy Stock Photo. **p.357** Granger Historical Picture Archive/Alamy Stock Photo. **p.359** Geoffrey Robinson/Alamy Stock Photo. **p.363** Edward Neyburg/Getty Images. **pp.364–365** Bo Li/Dreamstime. **p.367** Wirestock, Inc./Alamy Stock Photo. **pp.368–369** Jdpoccia/Dreamstime.com. **p.371** GRANGER - Historical Picture Archive / Alamy Stock Photo. **p.375** Naked Prosthetics **p.376** David Gray/Getty Images. **p.378** DOUGLAS MAGNO/AFP/Getty Images. **p.380** WENN Rights Ltd / Alamy Stock Photo. **p.381** Peter Zay/Anadolu Agency/Getty Images. **p.382** SlavkoSereda/Dreamstime.com. **pp.386–387** Rafiq Maqbool/AP/Shutterstock. **p.388** Chen Chao/China News Service/Getty Images. **p.389** Science History Images / Alamy Stock Photo. **p.390** Sarah Holmlund/Shutterstock. **p.391** WikimediaCommons. Attribution 4.0 International (CC BY 4.0). **p.392** Robert Holmes/Getty Images. **p.394** NASA.

From the Author

On my research

I began my working life as a journalist, and that background—plus the research I did for my previous history books for adults and children—gave me a good start for researching the first edition of this book.

But as I started reviewing what on earth had happened since I wrote my earlier books, I saw how much the world—even its history—had been shifting and changing around me. There were exciting discoveries in physics, biology, paleontology, and archaeology, and of course current events, that changed the stories I wanted to tell.

But it wasn't just about finding new things to add. Our perspectives on the past, present, and future have shifted too, and in some really interesting ways. Some of the material I had highlighted in 2008 just wasn't quite right for 2018. I've found that the same was once again true when it was time to research this new edition of the book—so much has changed even in the five years between 2018 and 2023.

So, with the help of my editors, I dived back in. I read recent books, scientific papers, and articles in newspapers and magazines, selecting new stories and adding new perspectives to old ones. And I wrestled with the best way to talk about the uncertainty that attends all of our efforts to understand the world.

My goal has always been to tell this story in a way that is accessible, interesting, accurate, and balanced for young readers—and adults, too. In the end, this revision was more extensive than I expected. That's how research works. You might start down one path, but what you find leads you off in new directions you couldn't have anticipated. And that's why it's so much fun. The one thing in life that I find more exciting than anything else, is seeing what's around the next corner. Thank goodness for corners.

The full list of sources for this book is too long to include here, though for a taste, please take a look at the quote sources that come next.

Quote sources

p.14 Parsons, Aaron. October 11, 2016. "After our universe's cosmic dawn, what happened to all its original hydrogen?" *The Conversation* (theconversation.com); **p.24** Walcott, Charles D. 1916. "Evidences of Primitive Life" *Annual Report of the Board of Regents of the Smithsonian Institution 1915*: 246 (Government Printing Office, Washington, DC); **p.29** "UNESCO mission reveals rare footage of coral reef near Tahiti" *UNESCO* (www.unesco.org); **p.40** Simard, Suzanne, 2016. "Note from a Forest Scientist" In Wohlleben, Peter. *The Hidden Life of Trees.* (Greystone Books, Vancouver, BC, Canada); **p.44** Tudge, Colin. 2006. *The Variety of Life*: 571 (Oxford University Press, Oxford, UK); **p.45** Preston, Richard. December 3, 2012. "Flight of the Dragonflies" *New Yorker* (newyorker.com); **p.48** Sander, P. Martin. August 17, 2012. "Reproduction in Early Amniotes" *Science* Vol. 337, Issue 6096: 806 (AAAS, Washington, DC); **p.67** Rohrseitz, Kristin and Tautz, Jürgen. 1999. "Honey bee dance communication: waggle run direction coded in antennal contact?" *Journal of Comparative Physiology A* 184: 463 (Springer-Verlag, Berlin and Heidelberg, Germany); **p.70**; Sohn E. "The eyes of mammals reveal a dark past" *Nature*. April 2019; **p.73** Smith et al. November 26, 2010. "The Evolution of Maximum Body Size of Terrestrial Mammals" *Science* Vol. 330, Issue 6008: 1218 (AAAS, Washington, D.C.); **p.83** Wilford, John N. August 11, 2010. "Lucy's Kin Carved Up a Meaty Meal, Scientists Say" *New York Times* (nytimes.com); **p.86** Cam, Deniz. December 30, 2017. "How Cooking Made Us Smarter: A Q&A With Suzana Herculano-Houzel" *BrainWorld* (brainworldmagazine.com); **p.100** Huxley, Thomas H. 1894. "Biogenesis and Abiogenesis" *Collected Essays Vol. VIII*: 244 (Macmillan, London); **p.123** Layard, Austen. 1853. *Discoveries among the ruins of Nineveh and Babylon: with travels in Armenia, Kurdistan, and the desert*: 204 (G. P Putnam & Co., New York); **p.123** Mackay, Ernest. 1935 *The Indus Civilization* (Lovat Dickson and Thompson, Ltd., London); **p.143** Carter, Howard. *Howard Carter's Diary and Journal 1922*: November 5, 1922. Transcript retrieved from Griffith Institute (griffith.ox.ac.uk); **p.144** Hughes, Bettany. January 26, 2014. "How women's wisdom was lost" *The Guardian* (theguardian.com); **p.158** Muller, F.M. (trans.). 1990. *Hymns of the Atharva-Veda* VI 142: 141. (Atlantic Publishers & Distributors, New Delhi, India); **p.172** Buddharakkhita, Acharya. 1985. *The Dhammapada: The Buddha's Path of Wisdom* (Buddhist Publication Society, Sri Lanka); **p.182** Herodotus. 1920. *The Histories* 1.74.2. Trans. Godley, A. D. (Harvard University Press, Cambridge, MA); **p.185** Aristotle. *Nicomachean Ethics:* 116. Trans Irwin, Terence (Hackett Publishing Company, Indianapolis, IN, 1999); **p.188** Recinos, Adrián. 1950. *Popol Vuh: The Sacred Book of the Ancient Quiché Maya*: 83. Trans. Goetz, D and Sylvanus, G. M (University of Oklahoma Press, Norman, OK); **p.195** Foss, Clive, 2006. *The Tyrants: 2500 Years of Absolute Power and Corruption*: 10 (Quercus, London); **p.202** Vergano, Dan. February 25, 2014. "Gladiator School Discovery Reveals Hard Lives of Ancient Warriors" *National Geographic* (nationalgeographic.com); **p.204** New Testament. John 13:34, King James version; **p.227** Fitzgerald, C. P. 1954. *China: A Short Cultural History*: 382 (The Cresset Library, London); **p.243** Walsh, Bryan. March 10, 2014. "How Climate Change Drove the Rise of Genghis Khan" *Time* (time.com); **p.249** Davies, G. R. C. July 28, 2014. "English Translation of Magna Carta" *British Library* (bl.uk); **p.257** Bey, Lee. August 17, 2016. "Lost cities #8: mystery of Cahokia—why did North America's largest city vanish?" *The Guardian* (theguardian.com); **p.263** Cross, Robin. June 7, 2012. *50 Events You Really Need to Know: History of War*: 60 (Quercus, London); **p.278** Zamora, Margarita. 1993. *Reading Columbus:* 192. (Berkeley: University of California Press (ark.cdlib.org); **p.290** "AD 1513: El Requierimento: Spain demands subservience" (timeline entry). *Native Voices: Native Peoples' Concepts of Health and Illness* (website). (National Institutes of Health/ National Library of Medicine, www.nlm.nih.gov/nativevoices, Bethesda, MD,); **p.307** Jefferson, Thomas et al. 4 July 1776. "Declaration of Independence: A Transcription" Transcript retrieved from National Archives (archives.gov); **p.319** Backhouse, E. and Bland, J. O. P. 1914. *Annals & Memoirs of the Court of Peking*: 326 (Houghton Mifflin Company, Boston and New York); **p.321** Bell, Alexander Graham. "March 10th 1876" from Lab Notebook: 40. Transcript retrieved from Library of Congress (lcweb2.loc.gov); **p.331** Angier, Natalie,

August 22, 2000. "Do Races Differ? Not Really, Genes Show" *The New York Times* (nytimes.com); **p.301** Lincoln, Abraham. November 19, 1863. "The Gettysburg Address" Transcript retrieved from Cornell University Library (library.cornell.edu); **p.337** Erlanger, Steven, January 14, 2014. "Now Online, Diaries of British Soldiers Detail Horrors of World War I": *The New York Times* (nytimes.com); **p.351** Castro, Fidel, October 26, 1962. "Fidel Castro's Letter" Transcript retreived from John F. Kennedy Presidential Library and Museum (jfklibrary.org); **p.352** Armstrong, Neil. July 21, 1969. Transcript ed. Jones, E. M. and Glover, K. Retrieved from NASA (hq.nasa.gov); **p.355** Gandhi, Mahatma. 1969. *All Men Are Brothers*: 171 (United Nations Educational, Scientific and Cultural Organization, Paris); **p.356** Branch, Madeline, November 6, 2016. "10 Inspiring Eleanor Roosevelt Quotes" *United Nations Foundation* (unfoundation.org); **p.358** King, Martin Luther, Jr. August 28, 1963. Transcript retrieved from the Avalon Project, Yale Law School (avalon.law.edu); **p.361** Menchú Tum, Rigoberta, 10 December 1992. "Acceptance and Nobel Lecture" Transcript retreived from The Nobel Prize (nobelprize.org); **p.377** Subramaniam, Baba (editorial), 2020, 8. "Earth Day Reflections: Hope Amid the Pandemic" *ACS Sustainable Chemistry & Engineering*: 5817–5818 (https://pubs.acs.org/journal/ascecg); **p.390** Hassabis, Demis April 21, 2017. "The Mind in the Machine: Demis Hassabis on Artificial Intelligence" *Financial Times Magazine* (ft.com); **p.393** Mui, Chunka. April 4, 2017. "7 Steps for Inventing the Future" *Forbes* (forbes.com).

A message of thanks

This first edition of this book could not have happened without the super-human efforts of a great many people. I am especially grateful for the advice and support of Richard Atkinson, Natalie Bellos, John Gordon-Reid, Steve Carpenter, and Mark Skipworth.

I'm also incredibly grateful to the entire editorial and design team at What on Earth Books.

Ali Glossop, Project Manager, lived and breathed *Absolutely Everything!* for months. Assunção Sampayo, Designer, threw herself into every detail of this book, making sure its pages pulsated with energy.

Andy Forshaw, Art Director, has been my wing-man, illustrator and greatest friend for over ten years. None of this would have happened without you.

Nancy Feresten, Publisher, has edited, mentored, and chaperoned this story all the way from the Big Bang to the present day, transforming it from a pedestrian caterpillar into a soaring butterfly.

I am also hugely thankful to Patrick Skipworth, Catherine Brereton, Brenda Stones, Michelle Harris, Felicity Page, Emily Krieger, Cynthia Wolf, Justine Taylor, and Vicki Robinson for photo editing, fact-checking, indexing, glossary writing, copyediting, and proofreading. Without all of this support, the book would have been a terrible mess.

Thanks to the ever-dependable Helen Jones who made everything run smoothly. I am so grateful!

For the revised edition of this book, I am hugely grateful to everyone listed above but also to the tireless efforts of Senior Editor Katy Lennon and Designer Nell Wood. As ever, Nancy and Andy have driven this revised edition forward, rethinking it editorially and visually to give it a whole new lease on life through renewed relevance. Thank you both!

Thanks to Satu Fox, for rigorous fact-checking and suggested amendments and additions. And how lucky we are to have had the wonderfully talented Andy Smith design and illustrate this new cover. Thanks to Angela Modany Jones for turning my English into American for the U.S. edition, Helen Peters for creating the index, Priyanka Lamichhane and Sophie Macintyre for proofreading, and Marta Bescos and Paul Langan for finding the new photographs.

Helen Thewlis, Olivia Galyer, and Gracia Lukombo, from the What on Earth Marketing team, are hard at work right now making sure—with incredible creativity—that this revised and expanded edition reaches its audience. And without an audience, there is no point to any book. So, thanks to you, too.

Sincere thanks also to Ellen Myrick and her team at Publisher Spotlight in the U.S., the sales and marketing teams at Ingram Publisher Services and Publishers Group West, also in the U.S. In the UK, thanks to Robert Snuggs and the team at Bounce Sales and Marketing, as well as the indefatigable Laura Smythe for her work on publicity. And I can't forget Rachel Pidcock, Aby Mann, and Gwen Bennett of The Rights Solution for getting my books—including this one—into children's hands globally. All of these people do the most fabulous job.

I'd also like to thank all the journalists, teachers, librarians, parents, and children who reviewed the first edition or contacted me directly to say how much *Absolutely Everything!* has meant to them. Their many suggestions and thoughts have helped hugely in the framing of this revised edition.

And without Bob Worcester's inspirational enthusiasm and support, this book (and many more) would not, and could not, have happened. Thank you, Bob.

I am hugely indebted to my parents, Angus and Wanda Lloyd, who have given me constant support and shown unrelenting interest in all my endeavours over the years.

I dedicate this book to my three fabulous girls. Were it not for Matilda getting bored at school all those years ago, she, her sister Verity, their lovely mother, Virginia, and I would never have spent five wonderful months together in an RV traveling around Europe. And I would never have washed all those dishes out in the open, which ultimately led to the idea for this book!

And for our home-schooling adventure, Virginia gets the credit. Not only has she been the most fabulous mother, but she is also the most supportive, loving wife anyone could wish for. Gins, I can't thank you enough.

GOLD